THE TRAGIC VISION

A mammoth variation-piece of lamentation . . . broadens out in circles, each of which draws the other resistlessly after it: movements, large-scale variations, which correspond to the textual units of chapters of a book and in themselves are nothing else than series of variations. But all of them go back for the theme to a highly plastic fundamental figure of notes, which is inspired by a certain passage of the text.

THOMAS MANN, *Doctor Faustus*

MURRAY KRIEGER

The Tragic Vision

VARIATIONS ON A THEME
IN LITERARY INTERPRETATION

Phoenix Books

THE UNIVERSITY OF CHICAGO PRESS
CHICAGO AND LONDON

The University of Chicago Press, Chicago & London
The University of Toronto Press, Toronto 5, Canada

Originally published 1960 by Holt, Rinehart and Winston, Inc.
First Phoenix Edition 1966
Printed in the United States of America

For Joan

PREFACE

I believe it was in early 1949, while I was teaching at Kenyon College, that I first took hold of the body of ideas that moved me to do this volume. It happened, quite suddenly it seemed, while I was listening to a paper being delivered by my colleague, the late Philip Blair Rice, and by way of reaction against it. The paper, later printed in *The Kenyon Review* (Spring, 1949), was entitled "The Merging Parallels: Mann's *Doctor Faustus*." During his discussion of the novel, he spoke in general terms and somewhat condescendingly about the "equilibrists on the non-Euclidean parallels"—those "amphibious men of the galaxies and the sea-depths . . . obsessed with the angelic and demonic, in various mixtures." And while conceding the debt we owe such equilibrists as Kierkegaard, Dostoevsky, Kafka, he rather spoke for the healthier claims he found in Mann's complex humanism; a humanism that is broadened and somewhat spiritualized, it is true, but still one that Rice saw as traditionally liberal, democratic, naturalistic, classically positive. As for the Kierkegaards, Dostoevskys, and Kafkas, they had taught us their lesson and—thanks also to Mann—they had unsuperficialized humanism. But now, having said their piece, they were to get off the stage. And we, seeing their obsolescence but remembering them gratefully, were to "give the equilibrists something less than total homage for a while, in order to cultivate a better-proportioned doctrine."

Of course, I felt that Rice's Mann was not my Mann, that mine had begun by assuming the bankruptcy of this kind of humanism. But far more important, I remember perceiving in this moving plea a perhaps unconscious but forceful onslaught on our sense for the tragic that threatened to destroy it utterly. For I could not see how the tragic is conceivable without the dual vision that lies at its very center. While I conceded that high tragedy does not finally come to rest in the sickness and the vision that Rice thought of as equilibrism, I would not for a moment believe that the pleasant optimism of contemporary naturalism could, within its shallows, provide for the resolution of the tragic vision; a resolution that an older culture had found in the profundity of a cosmic order at once based in religious belief and sanctioning community and its values. And with these reflections about the values as well as the dangers of equilibrism and about its relations to a social morality that can permit life to be managed, I was launched on what was to grow into this book.

Although Existentialism and Personalism in general and Kierkegaard in particular will be seen to have considerable importance in this study, most of my acquaintance with them came after rather than before my entry upon my subject. Thus they lent their support to the notions that underlie my work here, although they did not give me initial access to them: they opened up new avenues within a general direction I had begun to explore on my own before calling upon their aid. For example, just about all my work on Conrad was done, substantially in the form in which it appears in this book, prior to my acquaintance with them.

I would, then, answer in an obvious way the obvious charge that I have trimmed the novels I have treated to my own terms by converting their authors into unconscious Existentialists. I would turn the logical priority around and suggest, rather, that it is works like these and the vision that informs them that created the dramatic categories out of which emerged Existentialism and the receptive cultural psychology that could make Existentialism fashionable. As usual, formal philosophy followed upon the discoveries of the literary imagination, systematizing the vision literature made available. And as usual, in recent European Existentialism the fullness of vision has been thinned in its philosophical reductions—always the price of discursive accessibility.

I must therefore claim that, rather than Existentialism, it was the direction of my pursuits in literary theory—however unrelated this field may seem to be to the sort of thematic analysis of novels I engage in here—that initially oriented my approach. In *The New Apologists for Poetry* I tried to work toward an aesthetics of poetry that I later felt found its thematic counterpart in the explorations of this volume. In the final chapter of what follows I specifically examine the analogies and the relations between my view of the complexities of poetic discourse and my view of the existential immediacy of moral experience. What I tried in *The New Apologists* to show as a necessity of literary form will there come to be seen as merely an aesthetic reflection of what many writers have taken as the immediate given-ness of moral existence. Thus, as I show in that chapter, this aesthetic, for all its seeming purity, can, through thematic analysis, be pushed back—perhaps where it belongs—into a metaphysic. And the new study of "thematics," as it is defined in my final chapter, reveals it to be a branch—and a telling branch—of pure aesthetics. This projection of my aesthetic onto thematics finds in the tragic vision its natural subject, for it is the tragic vision that this metaphysic must be designed to accommodate. In some ways, then, despite what may seem to be profound differences between them in subject, method, and objective, I look upon this volume as being a related structure—if not a sequel—to my *New Apologists* rather than an independent work indicating for me a radically new direction.

It will be clear to the reader that my primary interest is in the detailed consideration of specific novels rather than in the literary or intellectual careers of their authors, and that my interest in the novels is dictated by the extent to which they serve my theoretical scheme—although I hope that in the interest of empirical honesty I have permitted this scheme to be sufficiently flexible to accommodate their unique complexities rather than indifferently to swallow them whole. The scheme dictates that the chapters proceed from the more obvious to the less obvious; that is, from novels which are from my point of view rather easy to account for to those which are more crucial to my case even as they are more difficult. I move from clearly vicious protagonists, though even these demonstrate the values of tragic visionaries in general, to those whose motives are more nearly pure, though they end by retaining the "tragic" qualification as well. Put another way, I move from the self-conscious demon who is at war with the moral idea to the man of persistent good will whose identification with the moral idea causes him to pervert it: it is a movement from Faustus to the pseudo Jesus who yet remains Faustus within. By the time I complete the circuit, the argument should have been made pretty exhaustive, concluding with the example a fortiori that is to demonstrate that all moral action authentically undertaken—from the worst to the best intended, undertaken in pride and in humility alike—is for these authors doomed not only to destroy the agent but to damn him as well, even if we must cherish him as our indispensable deputy, sacrificed to our visionary need for vicarious daring.

Each chapter from the second through the seventh, then, is meant to be another step in that apparent progression from the most to the least demoniacal, except that each is meant finally to prove deceptive as we see the reduction and—almost—the identification of all, however significant the differences appear with which I begin. But within each of these chapters too there are the contrast and the similarity that befit my intention of thematic variation. For, after treating in the first part of each chapter the example of the tragic vision, in the second part I try to add a second voice in counterpoint. These constitute what I might call nontragic or sometimes even anti-tragic analogues to the novels with which these chapters begin—in all but the last of these chapters of analysis, Chapter Seven, where what seems to be an answer to the tragic finally returns even more forcefully to it.

There are several reasons for my giving voice to these nontragic works that seem committed to dismantling my framework. The most obvious is that an increasing awareness of what the tragic is *not* may help us to sharpen our notion of what it is. And on the other side, I would expect my notion of the tragic to demonstrate its usefulness by illuminating in a special way materials to which it cannot apply but which are close to it if clearly distinct from it. It may be that the tragic not only will illuminate some alternative visions but will expose some aesthetically (and psychologically?) *ersatz* visions. Perhaps most importantly, these contrapuntal responses to the dominant movement allow me to enter the realm of dialogue by allowing a hearing to voices alien to the one I sound most prominently—at times, especially with Camus in Chapter Five, so hostile to it as to wish to obliterate it altogether. I have preferred to sound these alternatives myself in order not to be limited by the thematic commitments of the works that helped me to frame my principal claims about the tragic. For this volume is meant to be critique of lamentation as well as apology for lamentation, reply as well as expostulation.

Although individual portions were completed earlier, the bulk of the work which created this book as a unit was done on free time that was made possible by a grant awarded me by The John Simon Guggenheim Memorial Foundation, by a research appointment given me by the University of Minnesota, and by the special generosity of Rinehart & Company. Consequently, I wish here to thank Mr. Henry Allen Moe and Mr. James F. Mathias and their staff, Dean Theodore G. Blegen, and Mr. Ranald P. Hobbs, for their kindness in my behalf. I am grateful also to Mr. John Crowe Ransom, editor of *The Kenyon Review*, and to Mr. Herbert Weisinger, editor of *The Centennial Review*, for allowing portions of this book to make their first appearance in these quarterlies.

My dearest friends and teachers, Professors Eliseo Vivas and Milton O. Percival, have been especially profound influences on this work. Professor Vivas, with the discriminations of a literary man, early led me through many of the philosophical intricacies of the modern novel considered internationally, and

Professor Percival initiated me ever so gently and persuasively into the mysteries of Kierkegaard and the Existentialist-Personalist tradition. What they gave me as teachers, however, was greatly enhanced by what they lent me as authors. In Professor Vivas' work on Dostoevsky and Kafka (in *Creation and Discovery*, New York, 1955) and in Professor Percival's incomparable *A Reading of Moby Dick* (Chicago, 1951) I was furnished luminous examples of the sort of thematic analyses I might try to undertake in this volume. I am grateful also to Professor Leonard Unger, who in those crucial embryonic stages helped me to think through the relation of aesthetic and thematic aspects of recent literary theory; and to Professor Jay Vogelbaum, whose healthy antipathy to the tragic vision continually kept my own sympathies within the bounds of the objectivity my role demanded.

In dedicating this volume to my wife, Joan, as her book, I am committing no routine act of marital piety. From the outset the ideas seemed to be about as much hers as mine. And she remained their ever alert guardian as she doggedly watched over me struggling to transcribe them onto these pages. Only after great patience would she finally relent and accept my partial failures as being the best I could do. Thus whatever weaknesses there are here demand my apologies to her as well as to the reader.

M.K.

Urbana, Illinois

TABLE OF CONTENTS

Preface *vii*

ONE Tragedy and the Tragic Vision *1*

TWO Rebellion and the "State of Dialogue" *22*

1. The Huguenot Anti-Ethic of André Gide, *22*
2. The State of Monologue in D. H. Lawrence, *37*

THREE Satanism, Sainthood, and the Revolution *50*

1. André Malraux: Rebellion and the Realization of Self, *50*
2. Ignazio Silone: The Failure of the Secular Christ, *72*

FOUR Disease and Health: The Tragic and the Human Realms of Thomas Mann *86*

1. The End of Faustus: Death and Transfiguration, *87*
2. *The Magic Mountain:* The Failure of "*Spirituel*" Mediation, *102*

FIVE The World of Law as Pasteboard Mask *114*

1. Franz Kafka: Nonentity and the Tragic, *114*
2. Albert Camus: Beyond Nonentity and the Rejection of the Tragic, *144*

SIX Joseph Conrad: Action, Inaction, and Extremity *154*

1. The Varieties of Extremity, *154*
   Heart of Darkness, *154*
   Lord Jim, *165*
2. *Victory:* Pseudo Tragedy and the Failure of Vision, *179*

SEVEN The Perils of "Enthusiast" Virtue *195*

1. Melville's "Enthusiast": The Perversion of Innocence, *195*
2. Dostoevsky's "Idiot": The Curse of Saintliness, *209*

EIGHT Recent Criticism, "Thematics," and the Existential Dilemma *228*

1. Recent Criticism: Formalism and Beyond, *229*
2. "Thematics": A Manichaean Consequence, *241*
3. A Pseudo-Christian Consequence and the Retreat from Extremity, *257*

Index *269*

THE TRAGIC VISION

CHAPTER ONE

Tragedy and The Tragic Vision

> If there were no eternal consciousness in a man, if at the foundation of all there lay only a wildly seething power which writhing with obscure passions produced everything that is great and everything that is insignificant, if a bottomless void never satiated lay hidden beneath all—what then would life be but despair?
>
> Soren Kierkegaard, *Fear and Trembling*

Now of course the tragic is not the only vision projected by our serious literature and philosophy, nor is it necessarily the profoundest vision. But it is surely the most spectacular, and the most expressive of the crisis-mentality of our time. Consequently, it has won for those works obsessed with it the excited attention of our most stimulating critical minds. Perhaps in their excitement over the individual work they have neglected to define in general terms what this vision is—which is probably as it ought to be with the practicing critic. In any case there does not seem to be a systematic effort to say what is meant by the phrase and what, given this meaning, it has meant to recent writing.

It must be granted that, as with all terms of this kind, any meaning imposed upon it must be an arbitrary one that may or may not command agreement. But, agreed upon or not, it is valuable critically as it throws a consistently clear albeit diffuse light upon a broad enough and deep enough area in our literature. I propose here to create for the term a tentative definition that

I have found most illuminating of modern literature and the modern mind, and in the balance of this volume to use it to conduct exploratory operations on a certain few novels of the last hundred or so years in order to demonstrate its incisive powers. Since I have some idea about where I shall come out, I must admit that my explorations will have all too much direction to them and that consequently they will somewhat mislead us about the total reality of the works in the interest of showing the widespread relevance of my definition. By way of defense I can plead only that the definition was empirical in its origin and that it followed my probings into the individual novels rather than the other way round; in other words, that the meaning I am trying to create for the term is one that in my reading of these novels I feel that I have discovered.

It is surely needless to add that the act of enclosing a number of literary works within the limits of a given definition hardly passes any judgment upon works on either side of the boundary. For a work not to qualify as an example of the tragic vision is hardly a mark against it. Indeed, in the eyes of many, it may be quite the contrary. Of course, the meaning I want to establish for the tragic vision—indeed, any that would be worth very much—will be far more restrictive than the general lay usage of "tragedy" or "the tragic," which somehow broadens out to synonymity with catastrophe, the sorrowful, that which stems from or leads to "pessimism." But how, if we limit ourselves to technical literary definition, can we find for the tragic any meaning beyond that of Aristotle? The answer is, by moving from formalistic aesthetics to what I would term "thematics." [1]

Thus it becomes necessary first to determine the extent to which we want the meaning of "the tragic vision" entangled with that of "tragedy," surely a term well enough defined in our critical tradition. The most obvious difference I would mark between the two is also a crucial one: "tragedy" refers to an object's literary form, "the tragic vision" to a subject's psy-

[1] This is a term to which considerable discussion is devoted in my final chapter.

chology, his view and version of reality. It is more than a difference between two extant approaches to the tragic. Rather, the second has usurped the very possibility of the first after having been born side by side with it. Perhaps it would be more accurate to say that the tragic vision was born *in*side tragedy, as a part of it: as a possession of the tragic hero, the vision was a reflection in the realm of thematics of the fully fashioned aesthetic totality which was tragedy. But fearful and even demoniac in its revelations, the vision needed the ultimate soothing power of the aesthetic form which contained it—of tragedy itself—in order to preserve for the world a sanity which the vision itself denied.

It is for these reasons that the reader who as a modern is obsessed with notions of the tragic ought in a way to find himself disappointed on turning for the first time to Aristotle's celebrated definition in the *Poetics*. We have been so accustomed to doing this treatise deference—and rightfully so from a formalistic point of view—that we can no longer approach it freshly and feel the letdown that should be ours as we glance over its superficial formal prescriptions that are to pass as a description of so sacred and reverenced a literary genre. All this about magnitude and completeness and catharsis—are these to do justice to the profound complex of metaphysical and psychological forces which the tragic unleashes? Or so, at least, we ought as moderns to say superciliously. But probably we should have expected no more than this from the *Poetics*. Perhaps it was not for the Greek theoretical consciousness—even in as late a representative as Aristotle—to be as self-consciously aware of the disturbing implications of the tragic mentality as it was of the formal requirements which transcended, or rather absorbed, this mentality and restored order to the universe threatened by it.

The cathartic principle itself, in maintaining that pity and fear are not merely to be aroused but to be purged, is evidence of the need in tragedy to have dissonance exploded, leaving only the serenity of harmony behind. As has often been noted, the peace of cosmic reconciliation is most explicitly insisted upon in the concluding portion of the *Oresteia*—the sublime *Eumenides*—

or in the magnificent end of Oedipus' story at *Colonus*. Here is the restorative spirit of superhuman purgation at its most refined. Even in the less exceptional tragedies which do not conclude in such thorough and profound tranquillity—in those, that is, which end more "tragically" in the lay sense—there is often the touch of transcendent grace which saves the cosmos for us in the midst of the irrevocable devastation of human resources. It may, on rare and splendid occasions, be the pure shining thing of *Lear*; it may more often be little more than the matter-of-fact re-establishment of political order—an order, however, that reflects and is sanctioned by the cosmic order—which may be one of the reasons that it is so helpful to have tragedy concern itself with the fortunes of ruling princes.

But even if there were none of these, so long as tragedy remained a defined literary form, the fearsome chaotic necessities of the tragic vision would have to surrender finally to the higher unity which contained them. It is perhaps in this sense that we can speak of the formally sustained literary work ultimately coming to terms with itself. And from the standpoint of the audience—or at least the trained and sophisticated audience—even if there were no thematic elements of release for the passions aroused by the tragic performers, the disciplining and restricting demands upon aesthetic contemplation made by the rounded aesthetic whole would effect the catharsis demanded by Aristotle. The purging of dangerously aroused emotions, following as it does upon the satisfaction, the soothing grace, bestowed upon wayward materials by aesthetic completeness, uses form to overcome the threat of these materials and, consequently, these emotions. This roundedness, this completeness, carrying "aesthetic distance" with it as it brings us the assurances of form, presents us its formal order as a token, a security—something given in hand—to guarantee the cosmic order beyond the turbulence it has conquered. Thus it is that the cathartic principle *is* ultimately a purely formalistic one, even as tragedy, despite its foreboding rumblings, can remain a force for affirmation through its formal powers alone. Thus it is too that in the

Poetics Aristotle rightly limits himself to formal considerations, leaving to later and less solvent generations the thematic implications of the vision which, so long as it is aesthetically framed in tragedy, is denied in its very assertion.

It is finally Hegel who, after many centuries during which no radically new approaches are made to tragedy—or at least none that are relevant to my interests here—takes up the task of explaining tragedy and catharsis in the thematic terms that Aristotle could afford to take for granted. Although it must be conceded that Hegel's analysis is clearly indebted to his metaphysic and his general philosophic method and although he does not concern himself with purely formal considerations, it is just this notion of reconciliation, of a final uniting or reuniting, that he emphasizes as the conclusive power of tragedy.[2] His insistence on the absoluteness, the wholeness, the indivisibility of what A. C. Bradley translates as "the ethical substance" is clue to Hegel's attempt to create a metaphysical equivalent for the unity of the Greek world—the unity which, translated into form, allowed tragedy to overcome the heretical defiance of its hero.

For Hegel the *hamartia* that defines the tragic hero always arises from his exclusive identification with a single moral claim, a claim which, however just within its own sphere, is, from the view of a total morality—that is, the ethical substance—merely partial, a too-assertive particular. Thus the hero's vision is necessarily destructive of the unity of the moral world, threatening with its monomaniac tendencies to produce an anarchy of unsupported metonymic leaps. And in defense of its absolute claims, the ethical substance must justly assert its oneness by ensuring the defeat of the hero whose nature it is, "at once his greatness and his doom, that he knows no shrinking or half-heartedness, but identifies himself wholly with the power

[2] For Hegel on tragedy, see his *The Philosophy of Fine Art*, trans. F. P. B. Osmaston (London, 1920), I, 272–313; II, 213–215; IV, 295–303, 308–326, 330–342. A. C. Bradley's is of course a brilliantly succinct and, by now, a classical summary of the Hegelian view ("Hegel's Theory of Tragedy," *Oxford Lectures on Poetry* [London, 1909], pp. 69–95).

that moves him, and will admit the justification of no other power."[3]

But this assertion of the ultimate unity of the moral order is what for Hegel leaves Greek tragedy with a final affirmation that transcends the carnage, "an aspect of reconciliation" that authoritatively seals the moral universe for even the most harshly devastated of its sacrificial victims, the bearers of the tragic vision. Here is a significant attempt to account thematically for the cathartic principle, to bring tragedy—for all its deadly turbulence—to the very threshold of a Wordsworthian "tranquil restoration." And who is to say that this restoration is not part of what may seem to be implied by the Aristotelian concept of *dénouement*—a falling action which does not usually stop with the hero's final destruction but leads to a quiet beyond the grave: to a resettling of things in acceptance of this destruction?

Of course it is this final inhibition of the tragic vision, this imposition of formal and moral order upon that which threatens it, that allows these dramas to be properly called classical in the best sense. And when the embracing frame is lost, the romantic tragic vision bursts forth unencumbered—often in merely melodramatic splendor—in no longer reconcilable defiance of traditional aesthetic as well as ethical order. Thus it may seem that Hegel, in assuming the virtues of the Greek world to be those of his own philosophic construct, is hardly representative of the self-conscious modernism that has dominated the last century and a half of our psychological history; the modernism that is characterized by fragmentation rather than by the ever-uniting synthesis which Hegel tried valiantly, if vainly, to impose upon it as its salvation. Can his or can any all-resolving "ethical substance" have validity for us as an absolute and claim our allegiance accordingly? Can it now claim the all-commanding universality that justly, though ruthlessly, imposes itself on the subversive tragic hero in its midst? Or is the tragic hero, as modern, fulfilling a proper human function and even a proper human obligation in standing with his integrity as an individual

[3] Bradley, p. 72.

outside the universal? Which is another way of suggesting that whatever universals we may be left with do not deserve the obedience of the most daring of us. Hegel created a system whose universals, like those of the Greek world or even of the Elizabethan world as we find it reflected in Shakespeare, have a metaphysical sanction; whose social and political institutions have a cosmic sanction. How accurate an account is this of the shabby, Babbitt-like arbitrary things that must—if anything does—pass with our world as universals, given our secularized, hand-to-mouth versions of the claims of religion, of politics, of social morality? Surely the absolute is not to be found immanently within such as these. Justice, then, has passed from the universal to the rebellious individual; accordingly, our appropriate spokesman on matters relating the individual to the universal and the absolute is not the anachronistic system builder, Hegel, but that heterodox and unprofessional wrecker of the Hegelian universe, Soren Kierkegaard.

> Faith is precisely this paradox, that the individual as the particular is higher than the universal, is justified over against it, is not subordinate but superior—yet in such a way, be it observed, that it is the particular individual who, after he has been subordinated as the particular to the universal, now through the universal becomes the individual who as the particular is superior to the universal, for the fact that the individual as the particular stands in an absolute relation to the absolute.[4]

At what is for Kierkegaard the most crucial moment of man's existence—the moment of the leap to faith—the absolute is attainable only through the individual, the particular, the purely personal. It is denied to the universal. Here, unhappily enough perhaps, is the answer of modernism's "isolato" to the Hegelian attempt to restore the union of men within a congenial universe that sanctioned, indeed commanded, and fixed its divine blessing

[4] *Fear and Trembling*, by Soren Kierkegaard, trans. Walter Lowrie (Princeton, N.J.: Princeton University Press, 1941), p. 82.

upon, this union. For Kierkegaard, the ultimate act—the act of faith—cannot be mediated, since only universals can mediate. Consequently, the paradox of faith is "inaccessible to thought" and cannot be verbally communicated, both thought and language—like reason, on which they largely depend—necessarily expressing universals. Further, it is the inaccessibility of faith to mediation that makes the Abraham who intended to sacrifice Isaac either a murderer or a "true knight of faith"—in my terminology, either a tragic visionary [5] or a religious visionary —but *not* the sacrificer of his individual self to the universal expressed in moral law. The latter individual would be the highest form of ethical man but, for Kierkegaard, something less than either visionary. And Kierkegaard's Abraham, whichever visionary he may be, repudiates the universal. Thus the "immediacy" of either the tragic or the religious vision eliminates the universal as a possible resting place for the errant, as a possible justification of what he has so privately dared to will. And we can never be sure which of the two visions he carries. Indeed, now beyond reason, how can he himself claim certainty? For the religious vision would be too easy for Kierkegaard if one could *know* its authenticity.

The categories which Kierkegaard can help us impose provide our insecure world with alternatives to the way of Greek tragedy as it is interpreted by Nietzsche as well as by Hegel. While Nietzsche is, like Kierkegaard, an unhappy epitome of modern man, an alienated creature who is close to being himself a tragic visionary, he is like Hegel in wistfully finding and admiring in early tragedy the elements of reconciliation that give order to elements of chaotic conflict. Nietzsche sees united in tragedy the Apollonian and Dionysian motives, appropriately named by him for their respective gods: the one the dreamlike, sublime, and gracefully measured order of the light principle, in

[5] In light of the shriveling of the tragic concept in the modern world and the reduction of a total view to the psychology of the protagonist, I believe that this protagonist is now more appropriately designated "tragic visionary" than he is "tragic hero."

the highest sense the civilizing principle; the other the primordial, orgiastic release of the natural principle—the "underground" reality probably related to Jung's "racial unconscious" or to Freud's "id"—the barbarizing principle.[6] Nietzsche sees these motives as akin to the forces represented by the creative and yet restrained Olympians and by the chaos-producing Titans, except, of course, that instead of the unreconcilable warfare between Olympians and Titans there is in Greek culture a perfect blending of the Apollonian and the Dionysian.

> The Greek knew and felt the terror and horror of existence. That he might endure this terror at all, he had to interpose between himself and life the radiant dream-birth of the Olympians. . . . out of the original Titan thearchy of terror the Olympian thearchy of joy gradually evolved through the Apollonian impulse towards beauty . . . How else could this people, so sensitive, so vehement in its desires, so singularly constituted for *suffering*, how could they have endured existence, if it had not been revealed to them in their gods, surrounded with a higher glory?

Thus the Apollonian can so transform Dionysian terror "that lamentation itself becomes a song of praise."

Here is another thematic rendering of the principle of catharsis. But in order to make the formula work properly, both motives have to be maintained and maintained in equal strength. The Dionysian must be there for the Apollonian to transform, so that Apollonian radiance can retain its brilliance only by continually illuminating the Dionysian abyss. But it is an abyss which must not be denied, indeed must be acknowledged for what it is. Without the Dionysian, the Apollonian would seem to reflect a shallow, unearned optimism, a misreading of life that leaves the inescapable terror out of it. Thus Nietzsche can scorn the bland interpretations of "the serious and

[6] For this entire discussion, see "The Birth of Tragedy," trans. C. P. Fadiman, *The Philosophy of Nietzsche* (New York: Modern Library, n.d.), especially pp. 951–969, 992–1017.

significant idea of Greek cheerfulness": "no matter where we turn at the present time we encounter the false notion that this cheerfulness results from a state of unendangered comfort." For the Apollonian cannot sustain itself in isolation; it can exist only in counterposition to the Dionysian. Otherwise it becomes perverted—as Nietzsche tells us it was perverted through Euripides—into the merely "Socratic," that moralistic denier of the Dionysian and consequently the destroyer of tragedy.

But what if we should find the Dionysian without the Apollonian? Here we would have life unalleviated, endlessly and unendurably dangerous, finally destructive and self-destructive —in short, the demoniacal. In effect it would be like tragedy without that moment in which the play comes round and the cosmos is saved and returned to us intact. It would be, in other words, the tragic vision wandering free of its capacious home in tragedy. The therapy produced by catharsis, which allowed the subversive elements to be healthily exposed and aesthetically overcome, would no longer be available. And the alienated members, now unchallenged, would be free to turn inward upon themselves to nourish their indignation in the dark underground. Nietzsche himself has told us:

> The tradition is undisputed that Greek tragedy in its earliest form had for its sole theme the sufferings of Dionysus, and that for a long time the only stage-hero was simply Dionysus himself. . . . until Euripides, Dionysus never once ceased to be the tragic hero . . . in fact all the celebrated figures of the Greek Stage—Prometheus, Oedipus, etc.—are but masks of this original hero, Dionysus.

But picture a world into which Dionysus cannot be reabsorbed by way of the Apollonian with its final assertion of Greek "cheerfulness" and aesthetic form, a world in which the Apollonian and Dionysian—long since torn asunder—must live in a lasting separation that causes each to pervert its nature, the Apollonian becoming the superficial worship of happiness and the Dionysian the abandoned worship of demonism. Our modern tragic vision is the Dionysian vision still, except that the visionary is now utterly lost, since there is no cosmic order to allow a return to the world for him who has dared stray beyond.

The Kierkegaardian spirit would rather characterize the tragic vision as "despair," perhaps finally much the same thing. It is despair which for Kierkegaard is both the most wretched and the most hopeful stage of man's sub-Christian existence. With some interpolation and considerable simplification on my part, the phenomenological pattern one may draw from Kierkegaard for the tragic visionary may be seen as something like the following sketch.[7] A man lives his day-to-day existence below the religious level, either "aesthetically," as an amoral or submoral hedonist, or "ethically," by easily subscribing, consciously or unconsciously, but for the most part automatically, to that hierarchy of moral values which enables him comfortably to function. If he is a self-conscious moralist, he is concerned with the discovery of order in apparent disorder; concerned, that is, with universal principles, but principles that are discoverable in and referable to the world of human relations.

While the ethical level is certainly an advance over the mindless complacency in the midst of an unperceived chaos found on Kierkegaard's "aesthetic" [8] level, nevertheless this

[7] In the interest of accuracy it must be acknowledged that Kierkegaard himself explicitly defines what he calls the tragic hero very differently from the way I am attributing to his view here. In *Fear and Trembling* he specifically claims that "the tragic hero still remains within the ethical." He sees the tragic hero as allowing himself to be embraced by the universal, his most cherished interests to be sacrificed to it. Perhaps here, as in so many other instances, Kierkegaard finds himself borrowing from the very Hegelianism he is bent on destroying. I believe that, as part of his dissatisfaction with the aesthetic in general, he never took this matter of the tragic as seriously as he might have taken it, that he never realized the revolutionary treatment of it that is promised by his other philosophic claims. It is thus, I hope, in the Kierkegaardian spirit, that I use Kierkegaard to support my own claims about the tragic though they run counter to his own occasional declarations.

[8] Whenever I use this term in the very special way of Kierkegaard I shall set it in quotation marks. Where it appears without them, it is being

ethical level, because it sees values—and the order constructed in terms of values—as immanent rather than as transcendent, must itself remain pragmatic in its dictates for action. The orderly and abstract principles, bounded by the uses of this world and resting on rationality, much resist the paradox or absurdity which for Kierkegaard characterizes the immediacy and subjectivity of Christian consciousness. Thus finally common-sense pragmatism must inhere in the ethical level.[9] And our ethical man, assuming the validity of his abstract and universal principles inasmuch as they are conducive to order, can make decisions cleanly, can act in accordance with these principles—as if they were the absolute—since they blink the possible existence of a true moral dilemma characterized by endless ambiguity. This is the farthest reach of Hegelian man.

But our man can undergo a cosmic "shock": he can one day, to use Kafka's metaphor, wake up and find himself irrevocably arrested "without having done anything wrong." Or an Ahab,

---

used in its common sense that pertains primarily to works of art and to our proper and limited responses to them as art.

[9] It is here, in his insistence that religion has dimensions beyond morality, that Kierkegaard strikes at the roots of that naturalistic humanism which would identify the two. Of course one may claim that Kierkegaard rather overdoes their separation since for him, it seems, the one (religion) can begin only where the other (morality) leaves off. I must, however, make it clear that, whenever speaking here of Kierkegaard's concept of religion, I mean only his version of Christianity. It must be conceded that in many places he refers to a pre-Christian, almost naturalistic religion, one in which the absolute is still immanent in the universal and which, consequently, still falls within the ethical. But if this stoical kind of religion can produce "the knight of infinite resignation," in its security it of course cannot begin to reach toward "the true knight of faith," who is rather a product of the loneliness and daring, the absurdity and subjectivity of Christian consciousness. It is only his notion of Christianity—defiant as it is of the ethical—to which Kierkegaard attributes absolute value, so that, to simplify matters, I have felt justified in speaking of it informally as his notion of religion in general, to the neglect of his other, inferior kind of religion.

living until then by the proper laws of seamanship, can one day lose his leg to the leviathan; a Lord Jim, living until then by a schoolboy's code of honor, can one day be paralyzed into inaction and be made to play the coward's role. Melville's Pierre, having dedicated himself at all costs to absolute righteousness, can discover in his righteousness a lust that has led to incest; Conrad's Kurtz, having dedicated himself through altruism to a missionary zeal, can discover in his zeal a worship of self and of gold that has led to blood sacrifice. Perhaps this shattering seizure is precisely what ethical man has had coming for assuming, as fallible individual, his identification with an ethical absolute. For the ethical is, by definition, the universal. And, however well meaning, the individual may very well be doomed to pervert the absolute he claims to represent, since he comes to it as individual and particular, and thus as unsanctioned.

In any case, with the shock our man is jarred loose. For "aesthetic" man the oblivious evasions of hedonic existence will of course no longer do. And ethical man, confronted by a moral contradiction which resists the elimination of either pole as well as the synthesis of both, finds suddenly that the neatly ordered and easily enacted worldly rights and wrongs of his ethical assumptions are utterly inadequate to the data of his moral experience. Unless he yields to "infinite resignation" by blindly, if courageously, sacrificing himself to the implacable demands of ethical absoluteness—thus at all costs still remaining Hegelian man [10]—he must deny its authority forever. And then, hopelessly adrift from his or any other moorings, he can float into willlessness and thus abdicate from tragic heroism, or he can surge toward the demoniac. If his rebellion has rendered him unfit for society and its necessary universals—its laws—it is because, at whatever price, he has seen beyond them. If his end, as tragic, must be condemned even as it is pitied by the trim categories of

[10] This is in effect Kierkegaard's own definition of the tragic hero. He allows him to go no further; and this admission on my part indicates how far beyond him I have without authorization moved using his tools.

worldly morality, he may, prideful as he is, take further pride in the fact that he has defiantly looked upon those insoluble cosmic antinomies which have dictated his fall.

Someone like Conrad's Marlow, however—the sensible even if sensitive man—must, at whatever cost to his pride and his vision, finally rest in the ethical level, however sympathetic he may be to those who have renounced it to move into the realm of the tragic. Who is to say whether it is out of a "failure of nerve" or out of a special strength flowing from a profoundly tranquil vision, hardly known to us since the Greeks, that he has resisted the unmitigated tragic? It depends, very likely, on whether our view is Kierkegaard's or that of a less austere, less Protestant authority; on whether ours is the tragic vision or the classic vision.

On the other hand, our excommunicated ethical man, realizing the complete futility of human existence, cannot find a relationship with anything beyond it. His permanent forsaking of the universal seems to forbid it. This, the essence of the tragic vision, is "the sickness unto death," despair. It is the stage induced by the shock; the stage which, beyond the "aesthetic" and the ethical, yet falls short of Kierkegaard's version of the Christian. An advance over the first two, it is yet much more treacherous and, if one remains in it continually, far more miserable. If one can attain a break-through—a bravely irrational one unmediated by universals—he can reach the glories of transcendence; if he fails, he must live in the contemplation of nothingness. Or, to put it more specifically, at best he can become a Kierkegaard, if we grant that Kierkegaard ever, or for very long, accomplished the leap of faith; if not, he must remain in the torments of the Zarathustrian Nietzsche or of a more consistent Heidegger who constantly and unblinkingly dares encounter the nothingness that has capriciously hurled him into momentary existence. But he can never again rest in the self-deceptions of our John Deweys: those of our insistent naturalists who, for all the hardheadedness of their religious disbelief, are yet naively optimistic believers in a structured social morality and in social progress. These are, from the Kierkegaardian standpoint, the men of little heart; those who, evading the atheist's existential obligation to confront nothingness and its frighteningly empty consequences, construct elaborate rational structures based on nothing else: who whistle in the dark as if all were light.

One may prefer to say that it represents a supreme act of human courage to create meaningful communal structures of value on a substructure of acknowledged nothingness. Perhaps, as humanists say, man's creating God *is* a more sublime act than God's creating man. Perhaps. But the honest existentialist—anxious to confront his ontological status—would see the naturalist's structure in the void as an evasive act of bravado, not a closing act of bravery.

In the Kierkegaardian universe, then, there are two authentic visions—those I have termed the tragic and the religious—that can be earned through crisis by being forged in what Dostoevsky spoke of as the "great furnace of doubt." The other I have referred to is in this sense an illusory one. For the cheerfully naturalistic vision, which, pampering its security, denies itself nothing despite the fearsome implications of its own metaphysical denials, which existentially shirks the void it must rationally insist upon, is a pre-crisis vision, an illusion of ethical man demanded by his comfort, but one the stricken man can no longer afford. Like Kurtz, the tragic visionary may at the critical moment search within and find himself "hollow at the core," but only because he has suddenly been seized from without by the hollowness of his moral universe, whose structure and meaning have until then sustained him. What the shock reveals to its victim—the existential absurdity of the moral life—explodes the meaning of the moral life, its immanent god and ground. And there can be no post-crisis meaning and god except in defiance of reason, in acknowledgment of the impossibly paradoxical nature of moral existence. But this is to go beyond the despair that defines the tragic visionary and to make the leap to the transcendent subjectivity of the only kind of religious vision that the Kierkegaardian Protestant world leaves to the stricken.[11]

On the other hand, the tragic visionary, in taking the alternative of defiance and seizing upon nothingness, is alone bold enough to take the existential consequences of his godlessness; and he takes them with pride, the very *hybris* that, in its sinfulness, moved him to godlessness rather than to transcendence. But he does not, like the naturalist, try to play both sides of the street to earn the prize of an ungrounded something: a world philosophically negated which is somehow made to yield the existential ease that would come if there were a meaning and purpose to be grasped. Sick of his pre-crisis delusion, the tragic visionary is God's angry man who will take only the real thing. He will refuse any longer to fool himself with the comfortable communal halfway houses of good works as a substitute for

[11] Although this issue may not seem germane to a discussion of the tragic vision, it is worth adding—in order to expose another favorite illusion of our naturalistic and anti-existential tradition—that the religious vision described here cannot in fairness be reduced to any so-called "failure of nerve." This phrase the Kierkegaardian would reserve for the ethical man who flees the impact of the shock, for the naturalist himself. The shock may indeed cause our nerves to quake, but they fail only with the failure of our inner strength to manage, from the depths of despair, the awesome leap that makes "the true knight of faith"—no easy accomplishment and hardly a soothing one. The earned religious vision must not be cheapened. It is a vision that runs quite counter to that implied by the Philistine claim that there were "no atheists on Bataan." No matter how devout the final protestations of these doomed souls, these protestations were all simply too comforting in their urgency, from the Kierkegaardian point of view, to have a claim to religious authenticity. Thus Kierkegaard comments on people who want to make an easy, escapist thing of faith:

> . . . these caricatures of faith are part and parcel of life's wretchedness, and the infinite resignation has already consigned them to infinite contempt. . . . They would suck worldly wisdom out of the paradox. Perhaps one or another may succeed in that, for our age is not willing to stop with faith, with its miracle of turning water into wine, it goes further, it turns wine into water. (*Fear and Trembling*, p. 50)

the absolute dedication of a religious faith which his inherited skepticism, issuing its curse, has denied him.

Of course, from a less severely Protestant point of view, other "authentic" visions would be sanctioned. One that concerned me earlier is what I called the classic vision, a vision that is of the world without being crass, that is universal and conducive to order without optimistically thinning moral reality as the superficially ethical man would. This vision is the all-embracing one of an older world and an older order. It is what I have tried to talk about in discussing the formal and thematic triumph of tragedy over the errant tragic vision it contained within it. It is as if the security of the older order wanted to test the profundity of its assurances, its capacity to account for the whole of human experience, and thus bred within itself the tragic vision as its *agent provocateur*. And by having the rebellion incarnate in the tragic visionary finally succumb to a higher order which absorbs but never denies the "destructive element," by purifying itself through the cathartic principle, tragedy is asserting the argument a fortiori for the affirmation of its humanistic and yet superhumanistic values. Consequently, it can witness all that befalls its hero without sharing in his disavowal of the meaning of our moral life; without denying, with him, the sensibleness of the universe and of life despite the explosive terrors they can hold in store.

But human possibilities, reduced as they are by disintegrations within the world that produced a Kierkegaard as its spokesman, no longer can reach to so inclusive a vision. If the only appeal to universals, to order, is pre-religious as well as pre-tragic, then the path of the religious visionary is as solitary as the tragic visionary's. And the ethical once shattered, there is no higher return to community—although, of course, for the less daring there may always be a retreat. The tragic vision remains what it was, but it can no longer be made through tragedy to yield to an order and a shared religious vision. The ultimately absorbent power of tragedy, symbolic of the earned affirmation of universals, is gone, with the result that the solitary visionary is left unchallenged, except by the threats of uncomprehending and unsympathizing destruction at the hands of aroused ethical righteousness, the arm of social practicality. This is hardly the all-deserving antagonist the tragic vision once had, nor is it one that can command a satisfying aesthetic completeness any more than it can a moral-religious unity. Instead, in the Kierkegaardian universe, we now find for the aware and authentic existent an unresolvable disjunctive: either the way of nothingness or the way of transcendence, but both equally the way of utter solitude. The universals which must damn him have been left behind.

It is perhaps for these reasons that recent literature expressing an earned religious vision is hard to come by. For this kind of religious vision is primarily characterized by the fact that it cannot be shared. Equally subjective, the tragic as the demoniac vision can at least be dramatized by being contrasted to the ethical with which it is at war and which, in defense of society, must seek to punish it—for good reasons and for bad. We can be shown the ambiguous nature of the values at stake in this struggle: the need for the insights provided by the tragic to advance our understanding beyond the unaccommodating caution of social necessity as institutionalized in the ethical; and yet the need to strike out at the visionary, to cling to the props society provides, at whatever cost to insight, since, man being a social animal, his struggle through daily drudgeries is a crucial and ordering activity that must not be threatened.

To sustain a balance and, consequently, an aesthetic tension between these antagonists, the author must resist identifying himself too thoroughly either with the tragic visionary or with the representative of the ethical. If he becomes one with his ethical man, he must dismiss the tragic realm too summarily, without granting its power—however costly—of revealing the full density of moral experience and the shallowness of the reasonable order it has been forced to cast off. And he must sell the vision short as vision, however quick he is to see it as tragic, or anyway as doomed, if not as at worst merely execrable or at best pathetic. Or if, on the other hand, the author becomes one with his tragic visionary, he so cuts himself off from man's communal need that, in surrendering to moral chaos, he surrenders also the only possibility left him to impose aesthetic form. Further, he shows himself to be too sure of the vision to acknowledge it as really tragic, however quick he is—in contrast to our too ethical author—to grant its value as a vision. Only within the balance, and the mutual qualifications it provides, can the vision be maintained both as tragic and as a vision worthy of our concern and our wonder. Thus, at the one extreme, in *Heart of Darkness*, for example, Conrad, through his alter ego Marlow, rejects Kurtz—indeed is utterly offended by the man—only in continual acknowledgment that his rebellion against decency, however odious, renders him in some way superior even to Marlow. And, at the other extreme, close as Gide comes to embracing the reckless passions of his hero in *The Immoralist*, the classical artist in him maintains enough distance to reveal to us honestly, and even with some condemnation, their destructive and self-destructive consequences.

Even with the ethical and the tragic held in such balance, however, the ethical may seem finally to be treated superciliously and even as at least half blind to what really is going on. And since the tragic is from the ethical standpoint so dangerously evil, there would seem to be a need for some level beyond the ethical from which the tragic visionary would be judged absolutely—a level which would include his insight and with it soar beyond a parochial pragmatism, but one which would have passed beyond the rage of rebellion to a final, perhaps otherworldly affirmation. But this is to call once again for what we no longer have—for the transformations that only tragedy can perform. For how are we now to distinguish outwardly between the religious and the tragic, between the angelic and the demoniac, when both equally transgress the ethical and the universal? As Kierkegaard in such brilliant detail asks, how shall we tell the Abraham among us from the self-deceived, maddened infanticide? To stop short of the religious insight is of course to rest in demonism; yet to leap to the religious vision, itself a perilous undertaking, is not to deny the temporal and, of course, the dramatic validity of the tragic. In neither instance is a retreat to the ethical possible. And the balance of necessities between the tragic and the ethical must continue as the primary mode of dramatic conflict, with the inherent weaknesses of each—the moral failing of the one and the visionary failing of the other—poised against each other to create the unresolvable tension that must now replace tragedy's more sublime catharsis as the principle of aesthetic control.

By now I hope I have clarified the sense in which I have been speaking of the unrelieved tragic vision as a modern vision, which is to claim also that it is a Protestant vision and, in an obvious sense, a romantic vision. Further, in its seizing upon the particular and its denial of any totality it is an heretical vision; and in its defiance of all rational moral order it is a demoniac vision. Finally, in a very special sense it is a casuistic vision; and it is this characteristic, perhaps, that makes it especially accessible to literary portrayal. The tragic vision, a product of crisis and of shock, is an expression of man only in an extreme situation, never in a normal or routine one. Literature dealing with it frequently dwells on the exceptional man; and when it does choose a normal man it does so only to convert him, by way of the extremity he lives through, into the exceptional man. The tragic vision is, by my definition, a vision of extreme cases, a distillate of the rebellion, the godlessness which, once induced by crisis, purifies itself by rejecting all palliatives. And the tragic visionary, by the stark austerity of his ontological position and of his dramatic position in the fable, is the extremist who—despite his rich intermingling with the stuff of experience—finds himself transformed from character to parable.

The literary obsession with extremity, with the exceptional, may represent an attempt at realism ultimately more sincere and more authentic than the cultivation of the norm, of what Lionel Trilling celebrates as "the common routine." If one wishes to assume the Kierkegaardian version of the human predicament, he will insist that it does and that at all times it has represented the only authentic attempt at realism. Even without Kierkegaardian psychoanalysis, however, we must admit that, at least in our time, driven as it is by crises and "arrests" and blind as it is to the healing power and saving grace of tragedy, the tragic has come, however unfortunately, to loom as a necessary vision and—or so it seems to the sadder of us—as one that can be neither reduced nor absorbed. Or is it, perhaps, that the Kierkegaardian version is right and that our world has itself become the tragic visionary, in its unbelief using self-destructive crises to force itself finally to confront the absurdities of earthly reality—those which have always been there lurking beneath for the visionary who would dare give up all to read them? Which is to ask, fearfully and even unwillingly, whether we have not been beguiled by aesthetic satisfactions and whether the utterly stripped tragic vision may not after all be less illusory than the fullness which shines through tragedy.

CHAPTER TWO

Rebellion and the "State of Dialogue"

> I have never been able to renounce anything: and protecting in me both the best and the worst, I have lived as a man torn asunder. . . . The most opposite tendencies never succeeded in making me a tormented person; but made me, rather, perplexed—for torment accompanies a state one longs to get away from, and I did not long to escape what brought into operation all the potentialities of my being. That *state of dialogue* which, for so many others, is almost intolerable became necessary to me. This is also because, for those others, it can only be injurious to action, whereas for me, far from leading to sterility, it invited me to the work of art and immediately preceded creation, led to equilibrium and harmony.
>
> Gide's *Journals*

1. The Huguenot Anti-Ethic of André Gide

The work of André Gide, and *The Immoralist* in particular, would seem to afford a strategic entry upon our subject. Indeed, this novel fits my categories almost too readily—so readily as to impugn its aesthetic quality as a uniquely constituted work of fictional art. We must remember, of course, that this is an early production whose many thematic overstatements and aesthetic weaknesses—its too great reliance on symbols rather than on action—all but override its values. But, frankly, it is too handy an opening wedge for me to overlook, although I should hope that it has more serious advantages as well that will emerge as I proceed.

In its austerity of spirit and its alienating force, Gide's rebellion, for all its sensuality, is as fiercely Protestant as are the values against which it is directed. In embracing the flesh Gide must embrace also the dualism between flesh and spirit which underlies the tradition he tries to spurn even as it creates the only categories in terms of which he can spurn it. To have been born a Protestant in a devout home is an earnest beginning, and if the home is intruded into a Catholic country like France one is dead earnest in his movement toward isolation and alienation; further, to reply in scorn—directed later at his wife too as another representative of the pristine life—through an exaggerated sensuality is only to enforce the psychology of Protestantism even if the terms are but inverted; and if the sensuality itself becomes an object of rebellion by being forced, self-consciously and pridefully, to take a purely homosexual form, the retreat to the self is complete.

For Gide is enough of an artist to see both sides of the coin and to see that he could never keep it turned face down. He sees that he did not abandon but only more urgently proclaimed what Arnold termed "the dissidence of dissent" when he tried to abandon puritanism for the sensual life, indeed—from the standpoint of the world—for a perversion of (and thus, unconsciously, a revolution against?) the sensual life. He sees too that, held fast by its psychological forms, neither can he finally shake the hold of the substance of puritanism. Hence the devoutness that remains to mar—or must we not say to redeem?—the ecstasy of his most impious moments.

All this Gide sees, as Michel, his Immoralist, very largely does not. To this extent the novelist exceeds his protagonist even though, as he feared, his life and his journals clearly invite us to identify the two and to limit Gide as he has limited Michel.[1]

[1] This identification ("I seemed indeed within an ace of being confounded with him") is precisely what Gide warned against in his preface:

If I had held my hero up as an example, it must be admitted that my

After all, we must remember that Michel's tale is not quite the whole of the novel, that the brief letter from the friend to his brother that encloses it creates for it an aesthetic frame, however frail and unsubstantial. The letter need not be more. It must in its attitude represent a man on the one hand normal, sensible, worldly, and thus properly shocked by the disclosures, and on the other hand suffering a sympathetic involvement with Michel so acute as to lead almost to spiritual identification with him, and yet necessarily falling crucially short of it. Beyond this general disposition there is a world of details that is largely unimportant. What is important is that, as fictional device, this frame sets Michel's first-person narration at a further remove, gives it a dramatic validity so that, though it comes to us directly, without being refracted through a sensibility, yet the few words at the opening and the close give us throughout the novel the sense of his having an intimate audience whose presence provides an echo for his every word. In short, the epistolary frame converts Michel's story into monologue. Is it too much to say that, thanks to the values this frame allows us to project upon Michel's devoted "comforters," it in effect converts the novel itself into dialogue?

Surely this is enough to separate novelist from protagonist and, despite the temptations of biography, to force us to concede that Gide sees beyond Michel, is outside as well as inside his creature—indeed may even share some of our objections to some of his tasteless effusions—even if he sees no equally "authentic" alternative to him or his way. And this is merely to acknowledge what Gide has told us about his need, as man and artist, for the "state of dialogue," a phrase that effectively sums up my earlier claim that the ethical and the tragic be delicately balanced by the author who would maintain the tragic vision both as demoniac and yet, however fearfully so, as authentic. It is Michel's

---

success would have been small. . . . If I had intended this book to be an indictment of Michel, I should have succeeded as little . . . But I intended to make this book as little an indictment as an apology and took care to pass no judgment.

inability to move beyond monologue, to confront the self with the anti-self, that makes it necessary for a Gide to create him within a dialogistic context in order to place him for us. That Michel is a part of Gide is only proof that Gide's being is not, like Michel's, exhausted in the creation of a supposedly free, if surely wayward, self. And what is left can conduct the searching critique which, through the drama of dialogue, emerges as art.

The elements of critique arise to challenge the blatant anti-ethic in many ways. Perhaps the most admirable appears in the portions of the novel which approach *Symboliste* poetry, in places evoking quite literal *Fleurs du Mal*. The shock which shatters the "dry," complacent, duty-bound pedantry of our hero comes in the form of blood, the blood of sickness that betrays his deadness within. The hemorrhage is the lifeless man's futile answer to the healthy spurt of blood from the violent native boy. This blood is the turbulent sap of natural man: it wills life in contrast to the deadness of the scholar's history—"like plants in a herbarium, permanently dried, so that it was easy to forget they had once upon a time been juicy with sap and alive in the sun." [2] The metaphor is an extended one, running the length of the novel. And as we see the pungent lushness of Michel's garden so indulge itself as finally to turn swamplike, almost fetid, we know that some counterstatement has been made.

Michel insists throughout that the moment of his tubercular seizure was critical for him. It is what made it impossible for him to "rise again the same as before and be able . . . to reknit [his] present to [his] past" (62). "After that touch from the wing of Death, what seemed important is so no longer" (64). "Inasmuch as I was a specialist, I appeared to myself senseless; inasmuch as I was a man, did I know myself at all? I had only just been born

[2] From *The Immoralist*, by André Gide, trans. Dorothy Bussy (New York: Alfred A. Knopf, Inc., 1930), p. 62. Copyright 1930, Alfred A. Knopf, Inc. Hereafter references to the novel will be to this edition, with the page numbers appearing in parentheses in the text after the quotation. Excerpts are reprinted with the permission of Alfred A. Knopf, Inc.

and could not as yet know *what* I had been born" (63–64). Thus, out of the ashes of a sickness well nigh unto death, "the authentic creature" is free to emerge. And his difference, his utter separateness from other people, is sanctioned by "the secret . . . of one who has known death," who "moved a stranger among ordinary people, like a man who has risen from the grave" (118). Only in his brush with death does the scholar feel "along the blood," as Wordsworth says, that he has never lived. It is surely the specific occasion of the hemorrhage that prompts and fosters the revelation. That night on the diligence it was as if the blood broke from him in its sickliness to remind him that as his life it has been contained within him all along, has been repressed and has turned foul. Now he must give way to it completely, must worship the life in it in order to keep himself from the death he has for so long been willing upon himself. The second hemorrhage, following as it does Bachir's slight knife wound, allows Michel to compare blood with blood and to pledge himself utterly to the "beautiful, brilliant" blood of life.

The ethical, then, represented by the archaeologist's disciplined and single-minded dedication to history's remnants—"the terrifying fixity . . . the immobility of death"—has had to bury and keep buried the authentic which can alone answer what is demanded once the shock has struck. And so, in a distorted echo of the biblical—if not the Gidean—"If it die," death must die that life may live, death in the ethical for life in the aesthetic. Man, if he is not naturally primitive, must make himself over, must make himself into a physical work of art and, like art, must follow nature. At least Michel does, quite readily, even if he does not quite read all that nature sets before him as symbol. Nor, it must be added in passing, does he pause to distinguish between the aesthetic, pre-ethical life—that which he imitates in imitating the natural principle as it exists for the primitive—and the post-ethical, demoniac form it must take in his sophisticated perversion of it.

Michel is sometimes less aware than we of the extent to which the nature about him echoes his condition at crucial moments, or rather the extent to which he finds and cherishes that in nature which reflects his condition. Perhaps for this reason he does not fully see its excesses as his own. There are some idyllic scenes movingly described, scenes of classic balance between freedom and restraint, without austerity as without extravagance, neither static nor violent, and—to return to his metaphor—compromising between dryness and wetness, between thirst and satiety. At the start of Michel's recovery, he discovers an Eden that answers his first, still pure awakening of sense. It is a fresh and yet subdued Apollonian vision that he comes upon in his first visit to Lassif's orchard. All is languor and yet there is movement; there is ease and spontaneity and yet there is form and guidance.

> [The path] meanders indolently between two fairly high mud walls; the shape of the gardens they enclose directs its leisurely course; sometimes it winds; sometimes it is broken; a sudden turning as you enter it and you lose your bearings; you cease to know where you came from or where you are going. The water of the river follows the path faithfully and runs alongside one of the walls; the walls are made of the same earth as the path—the same as that of the whole oasis—a pinkish or soft gray clay, which is turned a little darker by the water, which the burning sun crackles, which hardens in the heat and softens with the first shower, so that it becomes a plastic soil that keeps the imprint of every naked foot. (49–50)

To complete the idyll there is even the "almost naked" goatherd playing his flute, who may remind us of the beautiful dreamy-eyed boy Thomas Mann's Hans Castorp so convincingly dreamed of in the snow. Lassif humanizes the natural enchantment his orchard holds for Michel.

> I walked on in a sort of ecstasy, of silent joy, of elation of the senses and the flesh. At that moment there came a gentle breath of wind; all the palms waved and we saw the tallest of the trees bending; then the whole air grew calm again, and I distinctly

heard, coming from behind the wall, the song of a flute. A breach in the wall; we went in.

> It was a place full of light and shade; tranquil; it seemed beyond the touch of time; full of silence; full of rustlings—the soft noise of running water that feeds the palms and slips from tree to tree, the quiet call of the pigeons, the song of the flute the boy was playing. (50–51)

Michel learns from Lassif about the irrigation of the garden:

> . . . [the canals] do not all run every day, he explained; the water, wisely and parsimoniously distributed, satisfies the thirst of the plants, and is then at once withdrawn. At the foot of each palm the ground is hollowed out into a small cup which holds water enough for the tree's needs; an ingenious system of sluices, which the boy worked for me to see, controls the water, conducts it wherever the ground is thirstiest. (52)

In the weeks that follow, Michel moves toward the merely licentious and even the lawless. The key incident, in which he secretly sanctions Moktir's theft of his scissors, occurs here. Outside, during the same interval, the rains have come, and after they conclude, Michel returns to Lassif's garden to a very different scene:

> . . . the stems of the plants looked heavy, sodden and swollen with water. This African land, whose thirsty season of waiting was not then known to me, had lain submerged for many long days and was now awaking from its winter sleep, drunken with water, bursting with the fresh rise of sap; throughout it rang the wild laughter of an exultant spring which found an echo, a double, as it were, in my own heart. (57–58)

Other aphrodisiac and watered lands wait upon his whetted appetites. And, perhaps surprisingly in Gide, he has ascribed to some of them the sexual properties of feminine receptivity. Michel says of Ravello, where he gave his body over to sun worship, "There, a keener air, the charm of the rocks, their recesses, their surprises, the unexplored depths of the valleys, all contributed to my strength and enjoyment and gave impetus to my enthusiasm" (66–67). A bit later he adds:

> In a hollow of the rocks I have mentioned, there flowed a spring of transparent water. At this very place it fell in a little cascade —not a very abundant one to be sure, but the fall had hollowed out a deeper basin at its foot in which the water lingered, exquisitely pure and clear. Three times already I had been there, leant over it, stretched myself along its bank, thirsty and longing . . . (70)

There too, as if in proof of the land's sexuality, a secret, orgasmic moment comes upon him:

> I turned my steps towards some mossy, grass-grown rocks, in a place far from any habitation, far from any road, where I knew no-one could see me. When I got there, I undressed slowly. The air was almost sharp, but the sun was burning. I exposed my whole body to its flame. I sat down, lay down, turned myself about. I felt the ground hard beneath me; the waving grass brushed me. Though I was sheltered from the wind, I shivered and thrilled at every breath. Soon a delicious burning enveloped me; my whole being surged up into my skin. (69–70)

But still Michel, as if heeding the lesson of Lassif's orchard, resists the recklessness beyond all reason of utter indulgence. The arrival at his estate, La Morinière, seems for a while likely to maintain the balance of the powers at war in him. It is a land rich and luxuriant, but still mild. In this Norman country the coolness of shadows, in contrast to the African or Italian sun, offsets the symbolic significance of its incomparable wetness.

> La Morinière is situated . . . in the shadiest, wettest country I know. . . . There is no horizon; some few copse-woods, filled with mysterious shade, some few fields of corn, but chiefly meadow land—softly sloping pastures, where the lush

grass is mown twice a year, where the apple-trees, when the sun is low, join shadow to shadow, where flocks and herds graze untended; in every hollow there is water—pond or pool or river . . . (89)

Appropriately, Michel reports that his will "seemed softened, as though by hearkening to the counsels of that temperate land" (91). They are like the counsels given by Lassif's canals:

> From this ordered abundance, this joyous acceptance of service imposed, this smiling cultivation, had arisen a harmony that was the result not of chance but of intention, a rhythm, a beauty, at once human and natural, in which the teeming fecundity of nature and the wise effort of man to regulate it, were combined in such perfect agreement, that one no longer knew which was most admirable. What would man's effort be worth, thought I, without the savagery of the power it controls? What would the wild rush of these upwelling forces become without the intelligent effort that banks it, curbs it, leads it by such pleasant ways to its outcome of luxury? (92) [3]

Michel, now largely under the domination of La Morinière and of its efficient representative—Charles—as well as of his love for Marceline, can well wonder, "Where had my rebelliousness vanished to?"

Of course, his rebelliousness betrays its continued presence in many underground ways. It shows itself especially in his attraction to the crude Gothic barbarism, so destructive of civilization, in defense of which he formulates his new historical thesis.

> With a boldness, for which I was afterwards blamed, I took the line throughout my lectures of making the apology and

[3] When we turn later to the work of Thomas Mann, we may sense echoes of this fine Goethean humanistic sentiment. There, as here, its promise is delusive, as what is hoped to be a sublimely balanced human end degenerates into a momentary meeting place for extremes that are moving apart to poles of mutual destruction.

> eulogy of non-culture; but, at the same time, in my private life, I was laboriously doing all I could to control, if not to suppress, everything about me and within me that in any way suggested it. How far did I not push this wisdom—or this folly? (106)

In his life he has merely replaced his dependence on the dead past with a dependence on the alive future. He is positively and hopefully dedicated to the sap of life, celebrating fertility with a "hatred of fallow land" (98). But rebelliousness is to achieve full sway once more, and this time in a more degenerate form. His apprenticeship to Ménalque's self-conscious demonism prepares the way. And his second major shock—the failure of his sap, the death of the fertility rite when his child dies while being born—delivers him to Ménalque's doctrine for good. After this crisis nothing, either of past or of future, can be allowed to rob him of an authenticity always to be won anew, moment by moment.

But his reckless dedication this time—in this land of water and shadow—is perverse rather than healthy, filled with the stealth of night rather than the openness of the sun-baked day, drugged with "fumes of the abyss."

> . . . I went back across the fields, through the dew-drenched grass, my head reeling with darkness, with lawlessness, with anarchy; dripping, muddy, covered with leaves. In the distance there shone from the sleeping house, guiding me like a peaceful beacon, the lamp I had left alight in my study, where Marceline thought I was working, or the lamp of Marceline's own bedroom. (167)

The beckoning lamp, with all its promise of tranquillity, is the symbol of all that Michel is now shutting himself off from irrevocably, of the now totally rejected light of Marceline—and in its relation to her is appropriately religious in its connotation. It may remind us of Justin O'Brien's enlightening suggestion that Gide's Emmanuèle, who of course is in many ways Marceline too, may very well have borne her name because the Bible interprets it as meaning "God with us." [4] Hence it is clear that Marceline's light must be extinguished for Michel's complete freedom to be achieved, for the fearsome burden of his godless and thus "objectless liberty" to be assumed. Accordingly, the symbolism directs the action to its end just as it has in its development cast a crucial judgment upon the whole of that action.

There are other than metaphorical evidences of Gide's unrelaxed ambivalence, his sustaining of the state of dialogue. The most obvious, perhaps, is the often warmly sympathetic portrait of Marceline that comes through despite Michel's tormented distortions. But, lest we are misled by a conventional tenderheartedness, we must locate other less impressionistic clues. We find persuasive ones when we see how Michel's attitudes and actions toward Marceline are related to his championing of "authenticity."

The shock, in precipitating the creation of a thoroughly alive person, must precipitate the search for "the authentic creature," "the old Adam" that lies hidden beneath all the counterfeit trappings of convention. The newly endowed scholar, Michel, turns, in revulsion against death, from the history of culture to the history of anti-culture as epitomized for him by his new idol, the debauched Athalaric. But he must finally reject even this portion of history since it too has already happened. Instead, he must search for what can be made to happen to himself alone:

> But now the youthful Athalaric himself might have risen from the grave to speak to me, I should not have listened to him. How could the ancient past have answered my present question?— What can man do more? . . . Is there nothing in himself he has overlooked? Can he do nothing but repeat himself? (184–185)

[4] Introduction, by Justin O'Brien, to *Madeleine*, his translation of André Gide's *Et nunc manet in te* (New York: Alfred A. Knopf, Inc., 1952), p. xiv.

The uniquely real, the sincere Michel must—to assert his Michelness—reject whatever he has in common with other people, and of course this means he must arbitrarily reject the universals of the ethical sphere, if only on principle. No price seems too great for Michel to pay for utter honesty, not even the price—at once so strangely austere and licentious—paid by his bizarre master, Ménalque.

And yet the inverted puritanism, the overrefinement of Ménalque's demands upon him must lead us to ask how complete Michel's liberation from the counterfeit has been or could be. For in the subversive ideal toward which Michel tries to move, the precious and the primitive are absurdly confused; and from this confusion must spring our doubts. We have seen that his embracing of the instinctual, the barbaric, and with these the lawless, is signaled by the crucial incident in which Moktir steals his scissors while Michel, thinking himself unobserved, condones the act, takes a profound joy in it. Indeed, this is the incident which later first binds him to Ménalque. And yet even at this outset of his new career, supposedly dedicated only to authenticity, there is a bewildering network of deceptions and counterdeceptions. His favorite from this time forward, Moktir is engaging in that most primitive deception, theft; Michel, in attempting to appear unaware of it, is trying to cheat the thief by not letting him know that the victim is a willing, even an anxious one; and, as we later learn from Ménalque, Moktir has given this perverse situation an even further turn by witnessing Michel's complicity and yet concealing his awareness of it. These interrelations are echoed in the even more intricate pattern of deceptions—leading to the end of the episode at La Morinière and of all experiments with an orderly life—among Michel, Bute, Alcide, and old Bocage. This is the situation in which Michel gleefully if secretly succeeds in cheating himself several ways at once, in which, as the priggish Charles puts it, the master makes a fool of his well-intended, faithful servant. Finally, and significantly, it is the same Moktir who leads Michel out from

Marceline's side to a final night of lawlessness as she lies dying.

From the earliest discovery of his new self, deception pervades his relations with Marceline also. Michel tells us that, as he enjoyed being unclothed in order, symbolically, to strip away his conventional self, so he had to shave off his beard as he would remove a mask, since he felt it to be utterly "false": ". . . my mind had been stripped of all disguise . . ." (73) Yet in the passage which immediately follows, he dwells at length and repetitiously on his need to "dissemble" to Marceline, to hide his new self so that every day he may become "falser and falser." And seeing in this deception another aspect of lawlessness, he ends "by taking pleasure in [his] dissimulation itself, by protracting it, as if it afforded opportunity for the play of [his] undiscovered faculties" (75). It does not seem to occur to Michel—although the juxtaposition of his removal of one kind of falsehood with his assumption of another indicates that it does occur and seems significant to Gide—that there is manifest in his actions a continual irony arising from his counterfeiting his ethical relations in order to protect the development of a self whose only justification lies in its claim to validity, to sincerity.

Or is it, perhaps, that Michel has not been freed from the counterfeit at all? that he has merely substituted one form of counterfeiting for another? that immoralism demands sacrifices of authenticity as severe as those demanded by moralism? If in the earlier pages Michel speaks continually—as does Ménalque later—of the hidden wells of personality that moral man disguises, suppresses, with what sense of irony do we hear him, at the very end, after relating the death of Marceline, say, "Sometimes I am afraid that what I have suppressed will take vengeance on me" (213)? For here what he admits to suppressing is the sense of decency, the very sense that he earlier accused of suppressing the authentic creature, the creature that has now exercised its freedom as ruthlessly, and as austerely, in denying *its* antagonist. All of which is to suggest Gide's awareness of the obvious fact that, while it is difficult to prove one's utter freedom except by breaking the law, this need to break the law—and the word *need* is perhaps indication enough—simply introduces another form of bondage. His asserted liberty is far too self-conscious and insistent, and of course consistent, to merit the name of caprice—of purely "gratuitous" action—which is after all what is ultimately being aimed at. But, as centuries of arguments about freedom of the will have evidenced, caprice is a pretty hard affair to establish; and an attempt to establish it will surely destroy any slightest remnant of it. Has not Michel acknowledged as much when, having asserted an unbridled freedom, he can cry, "No longer do I know what dark mysterious God I serve" (204)?

We would not, however, do justice to Gide's state of dialogue either if we merely reversed the coin; that is, if we failed to note continually that, in seeing the futilities of diabolism, he still sees, for him who would consecrate his person, no alternative to the nay-saying, to the violent upheavals diabolism requires. Yet occasionally even Michel is afforded some slight glimpse of the self-defeating, though perilous, nature of his venture, even if, to be sure, it is never a glimpse that is persuasive enough to veer him from his course. Perhaps nowhere does Michel come closer to recognizing not only the tragic but even the ineffectual nature of his choice than in the two identical moonlit scenes which just precede the two departures from Biskra. Separated by two years and, marking as they do the reversal in Michel's and Marceline's relation as invalid and nurse, these scenes help provide a structure for Michel's narrative. They return us to the very marked and even, perhaps, overaccentuated pattern of natural symbols which Gide imposes on his tale. We have seen that the enemy of sense has always been death, death in life—another term for asceticism—as well as literal death. In these scenes the new Michel almost traumatically, if rather unoriginally, realizes the limitations of his new self: that even he finally cannot deny death but can only postpone it—". . . a day will come when I shall not even be strong enough to lift to my lips the very water I most thirst for" (60). This metaphor by now must be the one we would expect to represent desire and satisfaction. And, appropriately for Gide, the diabolist turns to the New Testament, read in the moonlight, for the words of warning that confirm the ultimate inefficacy of physical, of sensual, reality.

Indeed, it is the moon—through the kind of light and shadow it creates—that is the bringer as it is the harbinger of death. It creates the two scenes that so profoundly shake Michel's assurance. It is under its spell that ". . . nothing seemed asleep; everything seemed dead" (59). In recollection of the first scene he can speak of "the terrifying fixity of the nocturnal shadows in the little courtyard of Biskra—the immobility of death" (62). In the second of the scenes, with Marceline so close to death, the fatality of the moon is considerably heightened:

> The moon has been up some time and is flooding the terrace. The brightness is almost terrifying. There is no hiding from it. The floor of my room is tiled with white, and there the light is brightest. It streams through the wide open window. (203–204)

And, recalling the night two years earlier, once again he echoes Christ's words. Is it too fanciful to see the relentless moonlight as somehow akin to the "powerful beacon," the projection of Marceline, which Michel, newly awakened to darkness, earlier rejected? After all, the austere spirituality of Marceline equally represented death to him. I have claimed that, once she is symbolized by the beckoning lamp, her extinction is thematically required, is indeed foreshadowed. And is it not to be this death, occurring very few days and very few pages after the second scene in the moonlight, that transfixes Michel in his waywardness, though it of course cannot return him from it—in effect killing his so carefully, if not cautiously, nurtured new self?

Surely, then, the inescapable moonlight does not so much forecast Marceline's death as it does Michel's envelopment by what is to him the deadness, the deadliness, of Marceline's spirituality through the burden of guilt her death throws upon him. The insistent moon will follow the sun he has worshiped and end the day. From the moonlight, as from the "powerful beacon," "there *is* no hiding": instead of extinguishing the "beacon," he has come to be bathed in it. Accordingly, having with her death achieved "objectless liberty," he can only claim, "I cannot move of myself. Something in my will is broken" (212–213). No wonder the moonlight twice summoned up before the infidel the words of Christ. And when he beckons his three friends to hear his tale—the three who are bitterly and unjustly compared to Job's comforters by one of them, the too scrupulous letter writer who is our narrator—Michel is doing more than allowing Gide to create a narrative frame for his novel. He is, perhaps unknowingly, carrying out the injunction implied in that utterance of Christ to Peter which the moonlight led him to read and enabled him to read:

> When thou wast young, thou girdedst thyself and walkedst whither thou wouldest: but when thou shalt be old, thou shalt stretch forth thy hands . . .

For the summons to the friends acknowledges that he is old and tired of willfulness. There is no hope in him and, surely, no real desire to return to the ethical community. He has come too far to re-enter the common stream of history. But, as has been foretold, he must make some gesture, in his desolation, toward human acceptance: with desperate trust in human loyalty and in a human sympathy that surpasses understanding, to friends whose receptiveness is indicated by our letter writer's tone, Michel has indeed stretched forth his hands.

2. The State of Monologue in D. H. Lawrence

Those telling scenes in the moonlight may remind us of a far more brilliant and an even more obviously symbolic moon that would not be denied: the moon, mirrored in the water, which is stoned futilely by Rupert Birkin in D. H. Lawrence's *Women in Love*. And at the very end of the novel, as Gerald Crich wanders to his death in the endless waste of snow, the moon—it is surely the same moon once again—makes another brief, if devastating, appearance:

> To add to his difficulty, a small bright moon shone brilliantly just ahead, on the right, a painful brilliant thing that was always there, unremitting, from which there was no escape. He wanted so to come to the end—he had had enough. (527) [5]

But we should be well acquainted with the moon by the time it comes to preside over Gerald's death march. In the earlier scene, even before Rupert's stoning begins, Ursula Brangwen finds much the same meaning in the moon—and it is just about the meaning that Gide's Michel found in it:

> It was like a great presence, watching her, dodging her. She started violently. It was only the moon, risen through the thin trees. But it seemed so mysterious, with its white and deathly smile. And there was no avoiding it. Night or day, one could not escape the sinister face, triumphant and radiant like this moon, with a high smile. She hurried on, cowering from the white planet. . . . The moon was transcendent over the bare, open space, she suffered from being exposed to it. (272)

When she comes upon the moon reflected in the water she comes upon Rupert also, and the moon obviously has affected him the same way. In about two pages of breathtaking writing, Lawrence describes Birkin's repeated attempts to stone the moon's reflection off the pond. At first he merely disfigures it, forcing it to radiate fiery arms of light; but its center remains intact. Finally he seems for the moment to have destroyed "the heart of the moon," to have fragmented it utterly. But of course the transformation of the coldly integral wholeness into a chaos of darting flames is momentary only. Inevitably the moon re-

[5] From *Women in Love*, by D. H. Lawrence, privately printed, 1920. Copyright 1920 by D. H. Lawrence, 1948 by Frieda Lawrence. All page references are to the 1920 edition. Excerpts are reprinted with the permission of The Viking Press.

gathers itself: "it was re-asserting itself, the inviolable moon" (274). And inevitably it is to the unbroken calm, to what Gide called "the terrifying fixity . . . the immobility of death" that the moon returns:

> . . . a distorted, frayed moon was shaking upon the waters again, re-asserted, renewed, trying to recover from its convulsion, to get over the disfigurement and the agitation, to be whole and composed, at peace. (276)

The source of the deathliness of the moon—properly a feminine symbol—is revealed to us by Birkin early in the scene when he prefaces his attack upon the moon's reflection with a curse upon the goddess Cybele. For he has spoken before of the cult of the Magna Mater as being all-destructive of life as it is the perverter of human sexual relations:

> She wanted to have, to own, to control, to be dominant. Everything must be referred back to her, to Woman, the Great Mother of everything, out of whom proceeded everything and to whom everything must finally be rendered up. . . . Man was hers because she had borne him. . . . she now claimed him again, soul and body, sex, meaning, and all. He had a horror of the Magna Mater, she was detestable. . . . Hermione . . . in her subservience, claiming with horrible, insidious arrogance and female tyranny, her own again, claiming back the man she had borne in suffering. By her very suffering and humility she bound her son with chains, she held him her everlasting prisoner. (220)

This is even more devastatingly true of the willfully sensual Gudrun than it is of the willfully and perversely intellectual Hermione. And it is the Magna Mater in Gudrun that the panicky Gerald, stunned by his involvement with death and emptiness, needs: "And she, she was the great bath of life, he worshipped her. Mother and substance of all life she was. And he, child and man, received of her and was made whole" (384). Here is the fatality of their conjunction. How strikingly the consummation attained by that more fortunate couple, Rupert and Ursula, contrasts with this: "It was the *daughters* of *men* coming back to the *sons* of *God*, the strange inhuman sons of God who are in the beginning" (348, my italics). Nothing here of Woman as deity, as the source and receptacle of all. Or, to state the contrast less metaphorically, Rupert-Ursula: "She had her desire fulfilled, he had his desire fulfilled. For she was to him what he was to her, the immemorial magnificence of mystic, palpable, real otherness" (356). And, on the other side, Gerald-Gudrun: "The terrible frictional violence of death filled her, and she received it in an ecstasy of subjection . . ." (383). "His passion was awful to her, tense and ghastly, and impersonal, like a destruction, ultimate. She felt it would kill her. She was being killed" (495). "They would never be together. Ah, this awful, inhuman distance which would always be interposed between her and the other being!" (385)

But from the beginning Gerald and Gudrun have been characterized—again in Gide-like metaphors—as "marsh-flowers," "pure flowers of dark corruption," as part of "the flowering mystery of the death-process," of "dissolution" (189). Gerald, for all the power of manly life within him, is, like the Criches in general, associated with death throughout. He is discovered in the novel with the mark of Cain upon him, his sister also dies in a way that allows him to claim responsibility, and the only other death in the tale to occur before his own is his father's. It is surely significant, incidentally, that in dying his sister strangles the young man, her would-be savior, thus in effect acting out the role of the Magna Mater. Gerald himself is driven continually—but especially as he senses death as the familial companion—by fear of "the void," "the abyss . . . the same bottomless void, in which his heart swung perishing" (361, 375). It is this desperation which has led to the violent excesses of willfulness that characterize him. Hollow within, he has had to appropriate everything about him. Hence his role as all-dominant "industrial magnate." When, with a surfeit of success, his keen sensibility can no longer be roused by so dull and conventional a stimulant, nothingness challenges him and his mechanical sense of control: "He was suspended motionless, in an agony of inertia, like a machine that is without power" (296). When the brush of death nearby hastens him to panic, his will as an ultimate act seizes upon Gudrun—just the proper object—as both the enemy it must subdue and the Magna Mater in whom it must smother itself. Nor can he relinquish her and revert to the void: he dare not "stand by himself, in sheer nothingness" (496).

Gudrun has her own desperation. It also results from a mechanical acting out of her days that leaves her outside life, that allows her to think of herself as "a little, twelve-hour clock" (518). ". . . she lay with dark, wide eyes looking into the darkness. She could see so far, as far as eternity—yet she saw nothing" (385). So she also is an "infernal machine." And her failure to create herself, to overcome her mechanical passivity, leads her too into defiance and to the violent exercise of willfulness. She is ready to do sexual combat to the death with Gerald, accepting him on his terms as both her master and her child. For this is the way to destroy him, to revenge herself upon him for transforming her person into instrument as they struggle on in their Sartrean way through the ruthless sexual use and abuse of each other. She succeeds, as Hermione barely fails with Rupert. Gudrun throws the gauntlet at Gerald in the wild early scene when with her unrestrained movements she maddens his bullocks, while she feels an avid sensual enjoyment of her peril and their physical nearness. She mocks Gerald's warning that the bullocks can be deadly when they "turn" against her: "You think I'm afraid of you and your cattle, don't you?" (186) And the identification between the bullocks and their master is furthered when she strikes him, completing the aggression she was practicing on his beasts. But it is not until the end that she maddens him to final violence, forces him to "turn" on her: "She was afraid, but confident. She knew her life trembled on the edge of an abyss. But she was curiously sure of her footing. She knew her cunning could outwit him" (515). As Magna Mater she has transformed Gerald, the would-be male principle incarnate, into one of his mutilated cattle—those bullocks before whose impotence she so daringly flaunted her femaleness. His death in the snow is only the official, if necessary, tribute to her victory.

It is fitting that Gerald die in the snow. He has much earlier been described for us by Birkin as "one of these strange white wonderful demons from the north, fulfilled in the destructive frost mystery," as possibly "an omen of the universal dissolution into whiteness and snow" (282). When we see his "race," with its "ice-destructive knowledge, snow-abstract annihilation" contrasted to the "sun-destruction" of the West Africans (282), we recall that this passage follows by very few pages that crucial scene in the moonlight by the pond and we understand that Gerald's "dissolution into whiteness and snow" could also be termed moon destruction. That the moon, as we have seen, supervises his death in the snow at the end satisfies our expectation that these symbols must join. Just before, during their snow-filled holiday, Gerald describes Gudrun in a way that unmistakably implicates her too in the snow imagery and its awesome meaning. In the midst of the eternity of snow, he tells the departing Birkin of his affair with Gudrun: "It blasts your soul's eye . . . and leaves you sightless. Yet you *want* to be sightless, you *want* to be blasted, you don't want it any different" (489). This is indeed "the blind valley, the great cul-de-sac of snow and mountain peaks" from which "there was no way out" (446). No wonder the saved—if still imperfect—couple, Ursula and Rupert, feel the need to leave "the frozen eternality" (454) about which Rupert complains and which Ursula feels "slowly strangling her soul" (482).

> Now suddenly, as by a miracle she remembered that away beyond, below her, lay the dark fruitful earth, that towards the south there were stretches of land dark with orange trees and cypress, grey with olives, that ilex trees lifted wonderful plumy tufts in shadow against a blue sky. (483)

But here it is worth remembering that Gide also introduces this contrast between the mountains and the south to serve a similar symbolic purpose.[6] Marceline's tuberculosis requires an Alpine cure while Michel's, which originally was the cause of her infection, vanished in the south. Even as Marceline begins to thrive in Switzerland, Michel, at whatever cost to her, feels the need to leave: ". . . my boredom became a kind of frenzy and my one thought was to fly . . . so utterly sick was I of those mountain heights" (186–187). And after he persuades her and himself of the wisdom of leaving:

> That descent into Italy gave me all the dizzy sensations of a fall. . . . As we dropped into a warmer and denser air, the rigid trees of the highlands—the larches and symmetrical fir-trees—gave way to the softness, the grace and ease of a luxuriant vegetation. I felt I was leaving abstraction for life . . . My abstemiousness had gone to my head and I was drunk with thirst as others are with wine . . . all my appetites broke out with sudden vehemence. (187–188)

In Italy Marceline deteriorates rapidly. Her lunar qualities, far more admirable in Gide than in Lawrence, cannot flourish in Michel's country. The very perfumes which the sense-worshiping Michel craved are too strong for her as, in her illness, her simple asceticism materializes in her being, or rather dematerializes—spiritualizes—her vanishing being. But Michel persists until her death.

> By what aberration, what obstinate blindness, what deliberate folly did I persuade myself, did I above all try and persuade her that what she wanted was still more light and warmth? Why did I remind her of my convalescence at Biskra? (195)

In both novels the moon and the frost of a northern mountain appear to symbolize the major threat to life, except that Gide

[6] This is apparently a favorite symbolic complex for modern novelists. It serves even more centrally for Thomas Mann, as, for example, in the "Snow" chapter of *The Magic Mountain* or in *Death in Venice*. And of course there is Melville's great chapter on "The Whiteness of the Whale" in his *Moby Dick*, whose title character has a "hump like a snow-hill."

is not unqualifiedly certain that the threatened vitality ought to be preserved. Michel fears possessions as Rupert fears possessiveness and as Gerald seeks both. Michel and Rupert shun the lunar and its feminine claims, fear absorption by it, and, were it only possible, would extinguish its cool, unchanging rays. But there is in it for Michel an acknowledged moral quality, however much it seeks to restrain his acknowledged licentiousness, while Rupert rather finds there only a ruthlessness of blind aggrandizement that profoundly intimidates his justly treasured freedom.

Lawrence, then, does not appear, like Gide, to have more than a single constellation of values in *Women in Love*. In the sense in which I have been speaking of Gide's state of dialogue, Lawrence seems not to have gone beyond monologue. And, lacking the self-distrust that Gide so continually evidences, Lawrence does not here embody anything like a tragic vision. Not, I suppose, that he ever meant to or that the novel necessarily suffers for not having it. But to see, for all its similarities to Gide's work, that it comes not to have this vision should for our purposes be instructive, though it may be irrelevant to the novel or to any judgment of it that ought to proceed from even so incomplete an analysis.

The grasp of nothingness lurks, ready for the final seizure, about all the characters in *Women in Love*, Rupert and Ursula as well as Gerald and Gudrun. Apart from occasions when, as undiscriminating "Salvator Mundi," he is preaching his doctrine to bolster his hopes, Rupert is pretty well reconciled to universal dissolution. Before his union with Ursula there is only a single, naked, literally orgasmic moment in nature (115)—very much like Michel's—in which he finds any meaning; and even this, we are told, demands his resignation from the race of man. Ursula herself, just before meeting Birkin in the moonlight, is deeply sunk in crisis: "One was a tiny little rock with the tide of nothingness rising higher and higher" (271). Yet Birkin, asked by Ursula whether they, like Gerald and Gudrun, are "flowers of dissolution—fleurs du mal," replies with a forecast of their imperfect but not quite destructive union: "I don't feel as if we were, *altogether*" (189). Through the somewhat free and unappropriating nature of their relation, Rupert and Ursula learn how, at least partially and momentarily, to keep free of the fearsome grasp. Gerald and Gudrun succumb.

It would seem, then, that despite all the ways in which Birkin's beliefs and role in the novel are similar to Michel's, it is rather Gerald who is the demoniac figure. And yet, oddly, it is Gerald who is the more conventional figure, who represents "solid" values, too much so for him to attain the spiritual dignity needed to render him a tragic figure. It is the Michel-like Birkin who speaks of a "life which belongs to death" and a "life which isn't death," of a need to be "born again" into "new air . . . that has never been breathed before" (204); who wants exceptional men, unlike Gerald, "to like the purely individual thing in themselves, which makes them act in singleness" (32). Yet Birkin's more rigorously pursued way of rebellion is rather—despite his personal foolishness on occasion and Lawrence's fun at his expense—in the direction of salvation. Lawrence refuses to attribute any ultimately demoniacal character to this way since it is the assumed source of values for the novel. Refusing Birkin's rebelliousness, Gerald rather decides "he would accept the established order, in which he did not livingly believe, and then he would retreat to the underworld for his life" (393). Only one who like Gerald cannot, through organic self-creation, attain a kind of Schopenhauerian suspension of will and self-consciousness need enter the human community and then only, as an "underworld" device, to use it willfully—which is to say brutally—to control it as a mechanical sublimation for his failure. Thus Gerald and Gudrun are demoniacal because they are not rebellious enough—honestly and "livingly" rebellious—because they have not said "nay" single-mindedly enough to the way of the world. There is no aspect of life in community that can have any validity for Lawrence here: it is but the conventional mask for the sickness of willful self-assertion—also a "sickness unto death"—while there is validity, and life, only in the assertion of a mystically selfless self. Although Gide also scorns all communal values, he does so only in constant awareness of the perils of defiance, the horrors it carves upon the defier. Lawrence is surer of himself. His rebel can succeed in the quest of his mysterious freedom to the extent that he rebels purely, "livingly," as he rejects all shared values. There is not even a slight moral aftertaste to bother him. . . .

"A land free from works of art; I despise those who cannot recognize beauty until it has been transcribed and interpreted" (*The Immoralist*, 199). Michel's statement is consistent with his hatred of culture. We might expect it to reflect Gide's feelings as well, in view of his own reaction against traditional values. But in that we would be mistaken. We would have forgotten one side of Gide's unyielding dualism and the austerity within him which, at whatever cost to personal consistency, forced his self-conscious devotion not only to art but to a rigidly classical ideal of art. Lawrence, on the other hand, decries art as we would expect—and in his work is true to his beliefs.

This difference between them may account for the differences between these novels. I began with a quotation from Gide in which he cites the contradictory quality of his state of dialogue as a necessary condition for his art. He is holding out for ideological self-distrust in the artist, for the doubling of his voice. However it may mar the dramatic honesty of his report, Lawrence is overconcerned with his one voice, trusts it too far to allow it to share the stage with any other he would have us hear sympathetically. If the state of dialogue is a requisite only of the tragic vision, we can hardly insist upon it from Lawrence; but if—through the double critique it furnishes—it is indeed a requisite of fictional art in general, we dare be more demanding. For is it not this state that allows *The Immoralist*, for all its weaknesses, to qualify as both? . . .

But we must not push our contrast so far that we underestimate the imperfection of Ursula's relation to Birkin. Birkin the talker was worthy of Hermione as Gerald is worthy of

Gudrun. And in the struggle for mastery between their wills, Birkin barely escapes Hermione with his life. His theories are better than he is, although they reveal that a part of him may be open for an alternative to dissolution. Instinctively he flees from Hermione to the soothing, orgasmic union with nature, a union that becomes a symbolic forecast of his union with Ursula, "one of the first most luminous daughters of men" (348). For Ursula, frequently spoken of as a "bud" awaiting the force that will allow her to flower, is also a daughter of nature—and of the future. Having (in *The Rainbow*) tasted the dissatisfactions of oppressively willful love and now finished with them, she is once more the youth that, in the spirit of Birkin's theories, rejuvenates him and keeps him safe from the dissolute attractions of Hermione. But as a fall from the idealized union we have seen celebrated in their first sexual act, Lawrence allows us a more honest glimpse of her later reticence:

> She knew he loved her; she was sure of him. Yet she could not let go a certain hold over herself, she could not bear him to question her. She gave herself up in delight to being loved by him. She knew that, in spite of his joy when she abandoned herself, he was a little bit saddened too. She could give herself up to his activity. But she could not be herself, she *dared* not come forth quite nakedly to his nakedness, abandoning all adjustment, lapsing in pure faith with him. She abandoned herself to *him*, or she took hold of him and gathered her joy of him. And she enjoyed him fully. But they were never *quite* together, at the same moment, one was always a little left out. Nevertheless she was glad in hope, glorious and free, full of life and liberty. And he was still and soft and patient, for the time. (484)

Still, in "the quest of Rupert's Blessed Isles" (488) theirs remains, essentially, a way of hope and of life rather than a way of nothingness and of destruction. By contrast, just before his march into "snow-abstract annihilation," Gerald recognizes that in coming to the end of the line with Gudrun he must again face the desperation out of which he originally seized upon her demonism, clutching it to his own. So he accepts as a reflection of himself the Gudrun-like frigidity, the nothingness of the snow; and thus accepts death as well. Meanwhile Gudrun, turning mechanically to "the rock-bottom of all life" (474), to "little, ultimate *creatures* like Loerke," to "the final craftsman" (503–504), has given up her life to the nothingness of snow also.

> Anything might come to pass on the morrow. And to-day was the white, snowy iridescent threshold of all possibility. All possibility—that was the charm to her, the lovely, iridescent, indefinite charm,—pure illusion. All possibility—because death was inevitable, and *nothing* was possible but death. (521)

Gerald's death recalls Rupert and Ursula from the warm south to the snow that they tried to escape. And it reminds Birkin of the dissolution theme that, thanks to Ursula, he has almost shaken. Consequently, the novel ends in partial retreat. Birkin muses about Gerald's death and his own life:

> Gerald might have found this rope. He might have hauled himself up to the crest. He might have heard the dogs in the Marienhütte, and found shelter. He might have gone on, down the steep, steep fall of the south-side, down into the dark valley with its pines, on to the great Imperial road leading south to Italy.
>
> He might! And what then? The Imperial road! The south? Italy? What then? Was it a way out?— It was only a way in again. Birkin stood high in the painful air, looking at the peaks, and the way south. Was it any good going south, to Italy? Down the old, old Imperial road? (532–533)

It is as if Birkin remembers that, as an alternative to the way of snow destruction, the way of the sun finally produces destruction also (282). We leave Rupert and Ursula arguing because Rupert is unhappy over his failure to establish a complete mystic brotherhood with Gerald. Here, perhaps, despite the dominantly hopeful note, we almost approach dialogue and, with it, something like the tragic. As we witness Ursula's desire to monopolize Rupert, we are meant to wonder if one is ever totally free from the clutches of the Magna Mater. After all, at the crucial symbolic moment, Birkin, for all the fury of his stoning, could not keep the face of the moon from inevitably reasserting itself on the still surface of the pond.

CHAPTER THREE

Satanism, Sainthood, and the Revolution [1]

> It is worthy of note that the slavery of a man may be the result alike of his being exclusively engulfed by his own ego and concentrated upon his own condition without taking note of the world and other people; and of his being ejected exclusively into the external, into the objectivity of the world and losing the consciousness of his own ego. Both the one and the other are the result of a breach between the subjective and the objective. The "objective" either entirely engulfs and enslaves human subjectivity or it arouses repulsion and disgust and so isolates human subjectivity and shuts it up in itself. But such estrangement and exteriorization of the object in relation to the subject is again what I call objectivization. Engulfed entirely by his own ego the subject is a slave, just as a subject which is wholly ejected into an object is a slave. Both in the one case and in the other personality is disintegrated or else it has not yet taken shape.
>
> Nicolas Berdyaev, *Slavery and Freedom*

1. André Malraux: Rebellion and the Realization of Self

Every man is a madman . . . but what is a human destiny if not a life of effort to unite this madman and the universe. . . . (357) [2]

[1] Perhaps partly in answer to Irving Howe. He has tried to make politics out of the apparently nonpolitical novel, while I claim one must rather make metapolitical ethics out of the apparently political novel.

[2] From *Man's Fate*, by André Malraux, trans. Haakon M. Chevalier

There may be something surprising about my including *Man's Fate* within the framework I have been using—and especially about my including it so early, when I am still dealing with protagonists whose demonism is self-evident. For this novel, as much as any other in our century, seems to support the popular notion—with its continuing belief in heroism—that the tragic can find its justification in social solidarity; that the self-effacing ideal of brotherhood can still allow us the affirmation of tragedy. In view of my earlier claims that the rational and sharable objectives of social meliorism can hardly allow for the tragic vision—to say nothing of providing the all-appeasing restoration needed for tragedy—I could hardly be expected to introduce a novel whose protagonist is usually seen as having achieved such heights of heroism and of tragedy. There ought then to be little need for this warning that my reading of the novel—in which I must grant the primary role to the subjective force of alienation—can occur only in constant disagreement with the more apparent one.

The most obvious thematic scheme in the novel—and I will not question that this was as Malraux intended—finds Kyo as the heroic synthesis between the inhuman discipline of the Party apparatus, most purely symbolized by Vologin, and the all-too-human private fanaticism of the terrorist Ch'en; between the depersonalized institutional instrument, the person reduced to his public function on the one hand, and the utterly subjectivized self that never need look beyond self for sanction on the other. As Malraux's hero, Kyo must succeed in somehow being at once neither and both. For, in the words of Old Gisors which I have quoted, he must unite the "madman" and the "universe." Or the heroic Kyo may be seen, once again with the author's sanction, as the synthesis between the ecstasy of action for action's sake—again best represented by Ch'en—and the paral-

(New York: Random House, Inc., 1934). Copyright 1934 by Harrison Smith and Robert Haas. Page references appear in the text after the quotation. Excerpts are reprinted with the permission of Random House, Inc.

ysis of pure thought—represented by Kyo's father, Old Gisors, and symbolized by his addiction to opium. Old Gisors himself tells us of Kyo's "conviction that ideas were not to be thought, but lived"; of his "having chosen action, in a grave and premeditated way, as others choose a military career, or the sea" (69). Yet Old Gisors would not say of him, as he does of Ch'en, that "he hated contemplation" and bothered with ideology only because it could "immediately become transformed into action" (69).

Kyo, then, would appear to be the ideal Marxist hero embodying the dialectically sanctioned interactions between individual and society and between thought and action. And so, I suppose, Malraux planned it. But his plans may have suffered from the fact that he was writing a novel and that he was an immensely talented and acutely perceptive dramatist of experience. Of course the mere fact that he was writing a novel rather than a treatise need not have been troublesome to his plans, as ideological novels, unhappily, are continually demonstrating to us. But the integrity that forced him to be true to his poetic vision was a more serious matter, and it led him, perhaps unconsciously, to subvert the subversive movement he hoped to serve.

It is surely in the relation of Kyo and Ch'en to each other and to the reader that the struggle between Malraux the ideologue and Malraux the artist can be most profitably traced. We have seen that the book's ideological structure demands that Ch'en, as terrorism incarnate, be damned not only as demoniac but—to shift to the "great world" of power politics—as dangerous. He is perhaps the last stand, the ultimate version, of that anarchic self-willfulness which cannot serve the very revolution its fury helped create. Rather it must destroy that revolution to preserve its own integrity. Malraux, like Kyo, cannot afford to tolerate this temperament, attractive as it must be to the revolutionary in its unrestrained celebration of his drive to heroic, and thus individual, action. We even find Malraux explicitly condemning the rather tame artistic equivalent of this temperament in the simple call to arms that constitutes the preface to his more consistently Marxist novel, the tour de force *Days of Wrath* (1936). Ch'en is surely a far cry from Flaubert, whom Malraux cites among others; but their common egocentricity and their isolation, their detachment from their kind, may permit us to read Ch'en for Flaubert when making the transference to politics from aesthetics which Malraux in those days made with such facility.

> The history of artistic sensibility in France for the past fifty years might be called the death-agony of the brotherhood of man. Its real enemy is an unformulated individualism which existed sporadically throughout the nineteenth century and which sprang less from the will to create a man whole than from a fanatical desire to be different.[3]

A bit later in this preface, we can find a reflection of Kyo in Malraux's statement of the alternative to "the great contempt"[4] of our maddened individualist tradition in his claim that the revolution "restores to the individual all the creative potentialities of his nature." He goes on, developing his properly Marxian opposition between the Kyo-type and the Ch'en-type:

> If he happens to be a subject of the Roman Empire, an early Christian, a soldier of the French revolution, a Soviet worker, a man is an integral part of the society in which he lives; if, on the other hand, he is an Alexandrian or an eighteenth century French writer, he is separate from it, and, unless he identifies himself with the social order which is struggling to be born, his essential expression cannot be heroic. . . . It is difficult to be a man. But it is not more difficult to become one by enrich-

[3] From *Days of Wrath*, by André Malraux, trans. Haakon M. Chevalier (New York: Random House, Inc., 1936), p. 5.

[4] The Nietzschean echo is intended. And, in view of the fact that elements of Nietzsche are frequently found elsewhere in Malraux, my attributing this phrase to those he rejects should point up the extent to which I doubt Malraux's ability to down the Ch'en within himself even in the Marxist stage of his career.

ing one's fellowship with other men than by cultivating one's individual peculiarities. The former nourishes with at least as much force as the latter that which makes man human, which enables him to surpass himself, to create, invent, or realize himself. (pp. 7–8)

Clearly, the Marxian Malraux, himself an intellectual in the tradition of rebellious individualism, seems to have been deeply disturbed by the attractions of a Ch'en and to have been continually anxious to persuade us and himself against him. Malraux can afford to be less fearful of the other extreme—the unyielding inhumanity of Party discipline—even though he may be more revolted by it. Through his hero Kyo, Malraux can reject it out of hand as a way of life. Kyo may finally retain unbroken his tie to the Party that at times so profoundly offends him, but he does so only because he can use the tie as a stay against the beckoning madness of Ch'en. And, unattractive as the Party is to him, he can use it without endangering the sanctity of his essential self. He need not fear that this self can be smothered by the dead hand of Hankow. But, with whatever ideological persistence Malraux creates a hero who directs the subjective satisfactions of willful rebellion by way of the mediating rationality of an external political dogma, we may still sense an ambivalence that suggests his inability to shake himself free of the reckless grasp of Ch'en. If, then, Kyo should be no more than "synthetic," if he should be only ideologically "postulated" insofar as he represents the Marxian dialectical compromise with romanticism, then we may doubt that he represents in the unraveling of the drama of experience the place Malraux would assign him. We may, in other words, doubt that the intention of Malraux's novel—the *telos* in accordance with which his characters and his fable seem to move—truly reflects his explicit ideological intention. It is, then, Kyo's consistency, his dramatic validity, and the justness of his place in the novel's hierarchical structure, that we must investigate.

Yet it is from the position of Ch'en that Kyo can be best approached, since it is primarily Ch'en that he has been designed to answer. Ch'en earns his role as the unmitigated demon through his dedication to murder and suicide. And this role is not mitigated by the fact that he is engaged in moral sacrifice—that through his action he dedicates himself also to his notion of human betterment. The drive to self-destruction is apparent in Ch'en early, as early as the magnificent opening scene in which we see also his drive to kill others. Before this initial murder he "convulsively" stabs his arm with the very knife with which he is to kill his sleeping victim. And before his final attempt to assassinate Chiang Kai-shek—having arranged it so that he cannot escape with his life—Ch'en gashes his thigh with a piece of the lamp he has stumbled across in his confused frenzy: " 'One always does the same thing,' he said to himself, disturbed, thinking of the knife he had driven into his arm" (198). Following his first political murder, Ch'en's talk with Old Gisors reveals his ambivalence toward violence and death. As he acknowledges feeling "not *only* horror" at the sight of his victim's blood, Gisors recognizes that "terrorism was beginning to fascinate him," that his willed destiny now is "to die on the highest possible plane" (64–65).

His projected assassination of Chiang gives his demonism full play. He speaks of this ultimate act of terrorism to his friend Kyo in Hankow, where the two have heard the objections of the "neanderthal" Vologin to their respective plans, Ch'en's far wilder than Kyo's but both of them too willful for the Central Committee—perhaps representative of the unbending ethical. Ch'en for the first time gives Kyo a full sense of the fascination death can hold for those who, like Kyo as well as Ch'en, have lived so intimately with it. He describes his reaction to the idea of his own death.

> I'm looking for a word stronger than joy. There is no word. Even in Chinese. A . . . complete peace. A kind of . . . how do you say it? of . . . I don't know. There is only one thing that is even deeper. Farther from man, nearer . . . Do you know opium? . . . Nearer what you call . . . ecstasy. Yes. But

thick. Deep. Not light. An ecstasy towards . . . downward. (158)

The comparison with opium reminds us, of course, of Gisors and my earlier suggestion that Malraux means Ch'en and Gisors to represent equally untenable extremes that meet happily in Kyo. The notion of monomania and its symbolic relation to opium is echoed later for us by Gisors, with Kyo once again uniquely exempt:

> "There is always a need for intoxication: this country has opium, Islam has hashish, the West has women." . . . Under his words flowed an obscure and hidden counter-current of figures: Ch'en and murder, Clappique and his madness, Katov and the Revolution, May and love, himself and opium. . . . Kyo alone, in his eyes, resisted these categories. (241)

Kyo can conclude from Ch'en's report of *his* intoxication, "Perhaps he would kill Chiang only to kill himself" (159). This is about the conclusion his fellow terrorists, Pei and Suan, come to later when Ch'en defends his plan for them to throw themselves under Chiang's car with their bomb. He expects his cohorts, like him, to feel a "need" to do it, to exalt terrorism into "the meaning of life . . . the complete possession of oneself. Total. Absolute" (196). Suan, whose terrorism is less fanatic, having suggested the greater wisdom of not wagering all in the single attempt, resists joining Ch'en, saying, "If I agreed, you see, it would seem to me that I was not dying for all the others, but . . . for you" (197). Abandoned by the others, "Never had Ch'en thought one could be so alone" (198). Most rebellious of the rebels, in his extremity of sacrificial dedication he is alienated even from those who have with him alienated themselves from the social fabric; and he thus fulfills the individualist type that we have seen so concerned Malraux.

But there is one who envies him and who, finally, is given the chance to emulate him. Hemmelrich longs for the revolution to bring him release also through the violence of killing and the hope of death. And, again, as with Ch'en, although he knows against whom to direct this violence, his drive to rebellion is propelled by more than ideological hatred. But all his gory hopes are frustrated by his wretched family's dependence on him. He cannot even give sanctuary to the bomb-carrying Ch'en and his accomplices. "You don't know, Ch'en, you can't know how lucky you are to be free! . . ." And, to himself, "Won't I ever be in his place?" (189)

> But all the things he wanted were things he could not have. He wanted to give shelter to Ch'en and go with him. Go. Offset by violence—any kind of violence—by bombs, this atrocious life that had poisoned him since he was born . . . Go out with Ch'en, take one of the bombs hidden in the brief-cases, throw it. That was good sense. In fact the only thing that had a sense, in his present life. . . . Bombs, for God's sake, bombs! . . . He kept his wife, his kid, from dying. That was nothing. Less than nothing. If he had had money, if he could have left it to them, he would have been free to go and get killed. As if the universe had not treated him all his life with kicks in the belly, it now despoiled him of the only dignity he could ever possess—his death. The smell of corpses was blown in upon the motionless sunbeams by every gust of wind. He saturated himself in it with a sense of gratified horror, obsessed by Ch'en as by a friend in the throes of death, and seeking—as though it were of any consequence—whether the feeling uppermost in him was shame, fraternity or an atrocious craving. (190–192)

Here surely is another modulation of the Ch'en type, one who feels the "need" Ch'en ultimately found missing in Pei and Suan, his fellow terrorists. Hemmelrich is at last given the chance to respond to this need when he finds his wife and child needlessly and mercilessly killed. Tortured as he is by the catastrophe, surely he feels release too. His first thought on seeing them—"if only they are dead!"—of course refers to his hope that they need not undergo prolonged and hopeless suffering; but from what we have seen and what we are shortly to see we may very well suspect him of having a hope that he has been liberated for violence. Indeed, we are soon told that the grief that has enveloped him is yet surrounded by "a halo of indifference."

> This time, however, destiny had played badly: by tearing from him everything he still possessed, it freed him. . . . he could not banish from his mind the atrocious, weighty, profound joy of liberation. With horror and satisfaction he felt it rumble within him like a subterranean river, grow nearer . . . an intense exaltation was overwhelming him, the most powerful that he had ever known; he abandoned himself to this frightful intoxication with entire consent. "One can kill with love. With love, by God!" (270–271)

While all this goes on within him, the blood of his wife and child, splattered everywhere, has been bewitching him, by smell and touch, under his feet on the floor, under his fist as it madly pounds the counter. And as we read of his "frightful intoxication" and of the mixture in him of "horror and satisfaction," we must recall Ch'en's description of his own opiumlike ecstasy and his confession to Gisors that at the sight of his victim's blood he felt "not *only* horror." The later description of Hemmelrich engaged in combat leaves no doubt that he has not restrained the violent impulses that have now been freed to act.

I have had to treat Hemmelrich at this length in order to establish how completely we can use the terms of Ch'en to explain him. Considered this way, Hemmelrich can be shown to point to the split in Malraux between artist and ideologue. The aesthetic imperfections this split leads him into in *Man's Fate* allow the novel its continuing interest because it develops a metapolitical interest. The Ch'en-like temperament, which I hope will by now be conceded to include Hemmelrich, can of course not be contained by Marxist doctrine, cannot be satisfied or even appeased by the Communist version of revolution. The "need" that characterizes it is not one that social-political conditions alone create or that a change in these conditions can dissipate, all of which suggests we are dealing with an ontological affair rather than a political one. A Ch'en may "use" the revolution even as the revolutionary Party may "use" him. But the revolution is never more than his instrument, which is about all the movement deserves since it has refused to see him as anything more. At the final moment, after Ch'en has thrown himself with his bomb upon the car and lies dying, even the death of Chiang himself is not of primary significance: "Ch'en wanted to ask if Chiang Kai-shek was dead, but he wanted to know this in another world; in this world, that death itself was unimportant to him" (249). Kyo himself is aware of Ch'en's relative indifference to the Party program. He recognizes that "none of the present orders of the International satisfied the profound passion which had made him a revolutionary; if he accepted them, through discipline, he would not longer be able to act" (134). (We shall later wonder whether these words are not in part applicable to Kyo himself.) And at the close of the book May gives us what would appear to be Malraux's final word on Ch'en: ". . . I don't think he would have lived out of the Revolution even a year" (356).

Yet in this same epilogue we learn that Hemmelrich is now a soothed and blissful Soviet citizen in Moscow, "a mounter in the electric plant" (352), who testifies to Kyo's properly doctrinaire claim, made earlier, that socialized labor guarantees the dignity of everyman. Not Hemmelrich any more than Ch'en! Both are too far gone into demonism to return to this shabby, prefabricated, superficial modern version of the ethical. How absurd a picture of a docility and an integration newly ordered—by which word I mean commanded as well as formed—in accordance with the Stakhanovite "heroism" that realizes the "five-year plans." The novel, with all it has taught us of Ch'en and, by justifiable transference, of Hemmelrich, gives this picture the lie. Malraux the ideologue has foisted it upon us, perhaps out of a final and desperate distrust for the less conclusive profundity that the almost fully licensed artist has revealed. But we must now be on our guard also against other unearned ideological intrusions that may deny the very depths of Malraux's dramatic perception. And since it is Kyo who, in his character and his claims, constantly provides intimations of this final beatific vision, it is on him and his place atop the hierarchy of characters that our suspicion must come to rest.

In *Man's Fate* there is the revolution, there is Marxism, and there is the Party. Somehow Kyo is to mediate among all three. The revolution is to satisfy man's profound need to give meaning to his life, a meaning achieved by the exertion of his willfulness in order to justify his fate by founding it in dignity. Man's fate, then, must be transformed to man's will. And the revolution is justified by the subjective satisfactions it provides. Marxism is the supposedly ethical doctrine that is to direct the revolution in order to achieve this dignity for as many as possible through the reordering of the society the revolution is to destroy. And the Party is the immediate instrument to determine method; it is to adapt Marxist doctrine to the immediate demands of the revolutionary situation so as to ensure the success of the revolution. But this success is to be measured, *not* in terms of the drives that constitute the revolutionary psychology but in terms of specified objectives dictated from the outside, absolutely, by Marxism. To these objectives all may be sacrificed, individuals and their subjective drives, their drive to dignity most easily of all. In other words, as Kyo all too explicitly fears in Hankow, "will" cannot help being transformed by the external pressures of Marxism and Party into "fatality," thereby subverting the very motive that makes revolution humanly—by which I mean personally and subjectively, existentially—justifiable. But Kyo must remain true to all, however critical he may be of the Party's tendency to yield to fatality. He is never to lose the subjective purity of his drive to the revolution, but is to manage to put it at the service of Marxist doctrine—and without openly breaking with Party discipline, however its austere, inhuman detachment may oppress his willfulness. Where he quarrels with the Party over methods, he can fall back upon Marxism and find support there for his quarrel. Since he has a stay this side of uninhibited subjectivity, he is still safe for the Party as well.

The antagonistic, indeed at times contradictory, quality of

these supposedly complementary forces is obvious enough. Very likely it is Malraux's Nietzscheanism that causes much of the trouble. As I have stated it, what is involved in revolutionary psychology, with its emphasis on irrepressible will over an externally imposed, intractable destiny, is not a political response but an existential one. What we are dealing with is not local revolution—insurrection—capable of victory and thus termination; rather it is the state of rebellion as we have seen it—pridefully sinful or pridefully triumphant—in Satan, in Ivan Karamazov, in Zarathustra. How is this state, post-ethical rather than pre-ethical, to submit to the ravages of doctrine and of Party? And if Kyo is true to the subjective justification of the rebel, can he with consistency yield? How can there be any final resting place for the rebel even if Moscow were all that Moscow is not?

Ultimately, then, the novel may be anti-Marxist as well as anti-Communist. The externally imposed absolute cannot do justice to the revolutionary's subjective demands. It can only enslave the revolutionary as it uses his revolution. The absolute cannot be the appropriate object, the adequate objective, for his sacrifices. Its unspiritual qualities do not allow it to respond to his gesture. The optimistic quality of its ultimate naturalism runs superficially counter to his demoniac vision. If all this should be what Malraux's novel reveals at those moments of its most convincing insights, we may—out of respect for Malraux's devotion to his own dramatic conception—expect that at crucial points even the synthetic Kyo may be made to give way to a more alive, a more authentic and brilliant Kyo, whose self-delusion may be a reflection of Malraux's. For Kyo must either acknowledge the final rightness of Party authority or acknowledge the rightness of Ch'en's rebelling on his own. Yet at all costs he must never give way completely to the Ch'en within himself, perhaps because he is Malraux's device to stave off the Ch'en who lurks within *him*. But, on the other hand, Malraux has too much fidelity to his fiction to allow Kyo completely to escape the Ch'en he harbors.

But how much of Ch'en is in Kyo, with or without Kyo's

(or even Malraux's) consciousness of his presence? After his early and painful interview with the Ch'en who has just murdered for the first time, Old Gisors seems to be confident of his distinctness from Kyo. Or does Gisors nourish a doubt that may be a clue to our own?

> For the first time he found himself face to face, not with fighting, but with blood. And as always, he thought of Kyo. Kyo would have found the universe in which Ch'en moved unbreathable. . . . Was he really sure of this? Ch'en also detested hunting. Ch'en also had a horror of blood—before. How well did he know his son at this depth? (66)

We have seen Kyo and Ch'en in Hankow, together resisting the impersonal coldness of Party calculation, although we must grant that Kyo can attempt to justify his waywardness by appealing to a different reading of Marxism while Ch'en—trying to get approval for his attempt on Chiang—can finally appeal only to his unique, individual "need." Kyo sees this at once as he witnesses Ch'en's dispute with Vologin: "Kyo knew the argument had no essential validity for Ch'en, even though he had come here. Destruction alone could put him in accord with himself" (150). But behind Kyo's appeal to rational principle is there not concealed the need for him to resist having his will paralyzed by the inflexibility of doctrine? In brief, the issue between Vologin and him concerns whether the Communist groups yield peacefully to Chiang's demands until a riper time, since they are still the weaker group within the Kuomintang, or whether they hold onto their arms and fight him openly for supremacy, however unlikely their chances. As we would expect, Kyo insists on the latter course even though Vologin's impassive arguments give him considerable trouble. For Kyo's stubbornness may have other than dialectical sources. His major argument, he acknowledges to Vologin, is at bottom a personal one: ". . . in Marxism there is the sense of a fatality, and also the exaltation of a will. Every time fatality comes before will I'm suspicious" (147). Here surely is the subjective voice of Nietzschean rebellion we hear talking of the sovereignty of the will within and of the treason to the willing self if one submits to an objective will imposed from the outside—by the forces of history or by a political party that claims to move with the forces of history. This may seem more a rationale for Ch'en than for the moderation we have come to expect from Kyo. After all, Nietzsche goes neither with Marx nor with Hegel. And it may be that Ch'en is speaking for Kyo as well as himself when he answers Vologin's demand—made, curiously enough, to Kyo rather than to Ch'en—for obedience to the Party line: "It's not through obedience that men go out of their way to get killed—nor through obedience that they kill. . . . Except cowards" (154).

Of course Kyo also objects to what he feels is an excessive reliance on fatality in Ch'en as well. He feels that Ch'en's very insistence on the violent expression of his will is but a self-deception concealing his passive submission to implacable powers whose pawn he is. As Ch'en speaks of his determination to act his own way, "Kyo felt that Ch'en's will in the matter played a very small role. If destiny lived somewhere, it was there tonight, by his side" (159). But we have noted, despite the obvious differences between them, how parallel are the positions of Kyo and Ch'en in the face of Party inflexibility at Hankow. And just before leaving, at a most rare moment of complete self-knowledge, Kyo seems anxious to give us the very evidence we need to uncover his Ch'en-filled, fully humanized self:

> It was easy to explain [Ch'en's] departure; but the explanation was not sufficient. Ch'en's unexpected arrival, Vologin's reticences, the list, Kyo understood all that; but each of Ch'en's gestures brought him nearer again to murder, and things themselves seemed to be pulled along by his destiny. Moths fluttered about the little lamp. "Perhaps Ch'en is a moth who secretes his own light—in which he will destroy himself. . . . Perhaps man himself . . ." Is it only the fatality of others that one sees, never one's own? Was it not like a moth that he himself now wanted to leave for Shanghai as soon as possible, to maintain the sections at any price? (166–167)

Thus Kyo can explain how what seems to Ch'en like the free play of his pure willfulness is seen from the outside as his submission to fatality. Note how Kyo's mind works here: He moves from the moths to the mothlike quality of Ch'en; then suggests this may characterize all men, each of whom sees it in all but himself; and finally makes the awesome extension of his discovery to himself. But in recognizing that the comparison to the moth is as well applied to himself as to Ch'en, Kyo in effect acknowledges that, despite his insistent distrust of fatality, he may be no more exempt from it—no surer of the spontaneity of his will—than is the equally determined Ch'en. Further, in suggesting that, unlike a moth—indeed rather like the Phoenix—Ch'en secretes "his own light . . . in which he will destroy himself," Kyo is after all conceding a significant role to Ch'en's will as well.

It ought to be pointed out that Kyo's suspicions about Ch'en's willfulness arise from his own more deliberate voluntarism that cannot escape its reliance on intelligence. And Marxist dogma furnishes the ground for the operation of Kyo's reason. Thus what to Ch'en is the spontaneous expression of self is to Kyo the passive enslavement to powers which lead him to evade the rational responsibility that alone can for Kyo ensure true willfulness. But Ch'en is responsible to the spirit of the revolution rather than to the dialectic of Marxism. In a sense, then, he is indeed the pure passion of willfulness even as he is the reflection of a fatality. On the one hand, Ch'en's self has become so dominant in his actions that it is no longer bound up with its fellow forces in the revolution that has brought it to full realization. On the other hand, his self has been so sacrificed to the passionate tide of revolution, so submerged in it, as to strive only for its own loss of identity. Ch'en was initially propelled toward the revolution by a moral imperative—perhaps the remnants of his discarded Christian training—as well as by a mystic and demoniac force. But once Ch'en was in it, this mystic force, seeing in the revolution its perfect embodiment, seized upon Ch'en as its own and so completely identified him with the blind violence of rebellion that he has become both all Ch'en and no Ch'en, all Ch'en and all revolutionary fury. And in the concession we have seen Kyo finally make to Ch'en's will and in his questioning of his own, we may prefer to read Kyo's growing awareness that he has been deluding himself in calling upon Marxism as the rational mediator he saw as required for any truly willful decision. Perhaps his disputes with Vologin and Possoz, in which he must have observed that variant interpretations of doctrines were wholly conditioned by the needs of the interpreting self, have taught him to see his reasoned arguments as tools of his personal needs rather than as their master. Thus his defiant return to Shanghai and his desperate desire "to maintain the sections" which the Party as well as the Kuomintang wants dissolved—and to maintain them "*at any price*," be it noted—are acknowledged to involve Kyo in the same mothlike deception in which Ch'en's less rationalized decision involve him, and for the same reasons.

During the entire interlude in Hankow, as Kyo witnesses his impotence before the Party and sees it as a reflection of the revolution's impotence before the impersonal forces that resist willfulness, he senses a new kinship with the reckless Ch'en:

> At the same time that the fellowship of the night brought Ch'en closer to him, Kyo was seized by a feeling of dependence, the anguish of being nothing more than a man, than himself; there came back to him the memory of Chinese Mohammedans he had seen, on nights just like this, prostrate on the plains covered with sun-scorched lavender, howling those songs that for thousands of years have torn the man who suffers and who knows he is to die. . . . What he had heard, much more distinctly than the arguments of Vologin, was the silence of the factories, the distress of the dying city, bedecked with revolutionary glory, but dying none the less. They might as well bequeath this cadaver to the next insurrectional wave, instead of letting it dissolve in crafty schemes. No doubt they were all condemned: the essential was that it should not be in vain. It was certain that Ch'en also felt bound to him by a prisoner's friendship. (156)

And while Ch'en is speaking the wild thoughts we have read about his own prospective death, Kyo hears him

> as if his words were brought forth by the same nocturnal power as his own anguish, by the all-powerful intimacy of anxiety, silence and fatigue. . . . he felt in himself the shudder of the primordial anguish, the same as that which threw Ch'en into the arms of the octopuses of sleep [those of Ch'en's nightmares] and into those of death. (158–159)

But suddenly the momentary sense of identity becomes painful. When Kyo asks why Ch'en feels he must be the one to attempt the assassination, Ch'en answers, "Because I don't like the woman I love to be kissed by others" (160). Unknown to Ch'en, this is as painful a reply as he could make: "The words opened the flood-gates to all the suffering Kyo had forgotten." For Kyo's personal crisis in the novel arises because he cannot live up to the Marxist sexual freedom he claimed to allow May: because he cannot "like the woman [he loves] to be kissed by others." And he is crushed both because she is kissed and because he cannot like it. It is another instance of Kyo's refusal to yield up the emotional demands of the self to coldly rational doctrine. And in Ch'en's simple reply we understand how much this is his refusal too.

It is Kyo's relation with May that helps us see the all-important breach between the private and the public Kyo. After all, if Ch'en is a tragic visionary, then however he suffers from his sense of a solitude never to be broken—and we see him continually suffering from it—he must accept it as part of the price for his vision. But Kyo, as the ideal Marxist who has completely merged with those for whose dignity he struggles, ought to have escaped Ch'en's aloneness into an ever-widening fellowship. If the revolution has not broken the shell of his isolation, we must ask whether he, any more than Ch'en, has really passed beyond the private state of rebellion into the human community toward which the Marxist direction (or misdirection) of the revolution was supposed to point. And the anguished private Kyo shows us how untouched the revolutionary camaraderie has left his inmost self.

The problem is symbolized by Kyo's single experience to which his troubled mind constantly reverts: he hears recordings made of his voice and cannot recognize it as his own even though he is assured it is accurately reproduced. He learns that no one normally hears his own voice as he hears the voices of others, that one's own voice is to himself as it is to no one else. Gisors explains to him that one's own is the single voice one does not need ears to hear. One hears it with his throat. Gisors adds significantly, "Opium is also a world we do not hear with our ears" (48). Precisely. For this world one hears alone, in his own way. And we must remember also that in this novel opium symbolizes the unrestrained subjectivity of monomaniac ecstasy. What one seems to be to the rest of the world is something else altogether, an object, a thing to be sensed from the outside only. The subjective person remains cut off, abandoned, invulnerable to the perceptions of others. It is no wonder that Kyo, who lives only to have his self open outward to his fellows, is haunted by his memory of the phonograph records.

And the revolution, as Ch'en has shown, furnishes no cure for the solitude since it only feeds the recklessness of subjectivity. Nor can there, for Kyo any more than for Ch'en, be found a home in Marxism or its haven, the Party. For the person, the source of the drive that creates the revolution and gives it its demoniac value, is a sanctuary beyond the reach of its dogmatic representative. To political action the person remains irrelevant. If Kyo does achieve some break-through beyond aloneness, as Ch'en does not, it is through the I-Thou relation he has with May, not through their political relation or through any political relation. We are told explicitly how nonpolitical their relation is:

> First of all there was solitude, the inescapable aloneness behind the living multitude like the great primitive night behind the dense, low night under which this city of deserted streets was expectantly waiting, full of hope and hatred. "But I, to myself,

to my throat, what am I? A kind of absolute, the affirmation of an idiot: an intensity greater than that of all the rest. To others, I am what I have done." To May alone, he was not what he had done; to him alone, she was something altogether different from her biography. The embrace by which love holds beings together against solitude did not bring its relief to man; it brought relief only to the madman, to the incomparable monster, dear above all things, that every being is to himself and that he cherishes in his heart. . . . "Men are not my kind, they are those who look at me and judge me; my kind are those who love me and do not look at me, who love me in spite of everything, degradation, baseness, treason—*me* and not what I have done or shall do . . . (59)

A Communist granting to love the power to ignore even political treason! Perhaps now we can understand why Kyo could not from the depths of him grant to May the license dictated by their impersonal creed. And Kyo's final advantage over Ch'en —his partial victory over solitude—is won, not through his more faithful allegiance to doctrine and Party, but through his capacity to cherish a single, carefully discriminated other person in whom the sense of otherness is dissolved. Yet this love is of value "only to the madman" of whom we have seen Gisors also speak; it does not unite him to "the universe." That is, in its inwardness it does not serve Marxism so much as it serves the Ch'en-like spirit of revolution. Thus, returning to take May with him on his most dangerous mission, Kyo "understood now that the willingness to lead the being one loves to death itself is perhaps the complete expression of love, that which cannot be surpassed" (216).

Kyo's love for May contrasts extremely with Ferral's abusive attempt to possess Valérie, even more extremely than it contrasts with Kyo's own isolation from his cohorts and his doctrine. But perhaps things opposed to the same thing may in this case be somewhat alike, so that Ferral's world and Kyo's Party may be surprisingly related. Obviously, Ferral, like Gerald Crich in *Women in Love*, represents the acquisitive magnate who must dominate his world by converting all who come within his orbit into things subject to his manipulation. Obviously, too, it is in this way that Ferral is meant by the Marxist Malraux to portray the sick octopus of capitalism which our heroes vainly struggle to dismember. But is Ferral, after all, so different from the anti-capitalist world, that world politically sympathetic to Kyo that yet can do no more than use him? Ferral's judgment of men, as he defines it for Gisors, is precisely what we have just seen Kyo unhappily expecting from his comrades, from all but May: "A man is the sum of his actions, of what he has *done*, of what he can do. Nothing else. I am not what such and such an encounter with a man or woman may have done to shape my life; I am my roads . . ." (242). So while Ferral, who defines intelligence as "the means of coercing things or men" (239), is surely intended as Kyo's opposite number and as representative of the alternative to the revolution, he may also be seen—only in part despite Malraux—as reflecting a psychology hardly opposed to that of the Party. And yet, ironically, even Ferral is defeated at the end by the petty, unimaginative, circumspect bankers of Paris. He is, even in his own misdirections, too willful, too subjectively driven for this dull machine of a world. Thus he is as obsolete as are Ch'en and Kyo, like them finally unsuited to the coldly formulated objective his will has been serving (even while it has also been serving the cravings of his violent self). But, unless I have done my job well, what may be shocking, as it is certainly counter to Malraux's conscious intention, is that the two objectives, so antithetical from the Marxist point of view, are so similar and so similarly intolerant and intolerable from the existential point of view Malraux the artist seems, perhaps unwittingly, to foist upon us.

Needless to say, the existential sense that gives the novel its deepest life frequently has the Marxist sense intruded upon it, if nowhere so painfully and blatantly as in the picture of Hemmelrich as the pacified, even docile, Soviet worker. Thus Kyo faces his death not only with the exaltation his revolutionary sense of violence and dignity and the "meaning of life" should lead us to expect, but also with a gratified awareness that he is as one with his comrades and that together their deaths shall serve the future of their cause.

> It is easy to die when one does not die alone. A death saturated with this brotherly quavering, an assembly of the vanquished in which multitudes would recognize their martyrs, a bloody legend of which the golden legends are made! (323)

Oddly, this passage occurs only very shortly after Kyo is found lamenting that through death he must desert May. "For more than a year May had freed him from all solitude, if not from all bitterness" (322). Surely without May this Kyo does die alone. His fellow prisoners cannot replace her, cannot break through to the private, subjective Kyo. It is only the public Kyo who can share with them; the Kyo who—a creature of Ferral's universe —is no more than the sum of his actions, "what he has *done*"; the Kyo of the phonograph records, heard with the ears and not the throat. Is this perhaps why, just before he thinks of May as he lies there contemplating his own immediate death, "He remembered—his heart stopped beating—the phonograph records" (321)? For, Malraux to the contrary, the private Kyo is doomed to die alone, beyond the touch of political associates and their common cause.

Even Ch'en, before his death, is seen justifying it by placing his terroristic act in the context of the revolutionary future. The comfort he gives himself sounds not very different from Kyo's:

> Give an immediate meaning to the individual without hope and multiply the attempts, not by an organization, but by an idea: revive the martyrs. Pei, writing, would be listened to because he, Ch'en, was going to die; he knew how much weight an idea acquires through the blood that is shed in its name. (247)

But Ch'en is even more out of character seeking this sort of comfort than is Kyo seeking his. Nor is Ch'en a character we might expect to find deluding himself. It is once again the doctrinaire Malraux deluding either himself or us, in either case doing less than justice to his deeper penetrations into the nature of revolutionary fervor. And these penetrations have convinced us, too much so for us to be convinced now.

I said at the outset that Malraux, like many other moderns, has passed through several conflicting phases. By now, however, we may see that it would be more accurate to have said that he was poised upon several of them at the same time. His sense of the complexity of contemporary experience was too keen for all of him to rest satisfied with a single formulation that was to contain it, especially with so superficial a formulation as Marxism. And although it runs counter to his Marxism, Malraux in *Man's Fate* seems in spite of himself to feel his way through to a vision of the nature of revolution as demoniac. It may be that as the years passed, despite the orthodox defense of the Communist in *Days of Wrath* (1936), Malraux, wisely adjusting ideology to experiential insight rather than the other way round, changed his ideology accordingly. Eventually he may himself have come to realize the full significance of his ambiguous, perhaps even confused, picture of the revolutionary in *Man's Fate*.

These inartistic but strikingly instructive ambiguities should not now be hard to follow. Beginning with a synthetic, ideologically postulated Kyo who is to serve as the Marxian corrective to the recklessly solipsistic Ch'en, Malraux rather provides Ch'en with the psychological authenticity that persuades us to accept him and his uninhibited subjectivity as properly representative of the revolutionary. But we may go further. We may claim that Malraux's dramatic sensibility forced him to undercut the synthetic Kyo by having him in many places unconsciously reflect facets of the purer, more extreme Ch'en. Kyo struggles against the dominance of these forces within himself by denying the claims of the Ch'en who is their absolute embodiment. Thus Kyo, or Malraux, deluded about the nature of faithfulness to the revolution, fails to see that Ch'en is the revolution incarnate, the satanic archetype of rebellion, and thus the logical consequent of Kyo's own subjective commitment, the consequent Kyo dare not consistently face. So Marxian hangovers and intrusions persist, and hence the ambiguities. But it is this extreme symbol of revolutionary force, acting as the norm against which other manifestations of revolution may be measured, that turns *Man's Fate* largely into an anti-Marxist, indeed an anti-political novel, and into a moving revelation of the tragic vision. It is the extremity as well as the demonism of Ch'en that is crucial here. For extremity—the exceptional as the purification of the more commonly acceptable—is a defining characteristic of the tragic. And Ch'en, who in his illogic is yet the logical extremity of his more muddled fellows, shows the function of the casuistic element in the tragic. As the avant-garde and the purist, he casts behind him a long image that bestows upon Kyo a brilliant and frightening clarity, in light of which he too, however reluctantly, must be seen by us as at last entering Ch'en's tragic circle. It must follow that Ch'en has also bestowed upon him the ontological status of fellow visionary.

2. Ignazio Silone: The Failure of the Secular Christ

> There are neurotics for whom revolution is a form of intoxication, a kind of lyrical exaltation. "Better a day as a lion than a hundred days as a sheep." (284) [5]

This statement, made in *Bread and Wine* by Silone's obvious spokesman, Pietro Spina, is to dispose of the Ch'en mentality for us clearly enough. The minor character, Uliva, is the one analogue to Ch'en in the novel. Some of the similarities are striking. We are introduced to Uliva immediately after the Party functionary, Romeo, has enunciated the truism, "Scratch an intellectual, and you always find an anarchist!" (173) Uliva insists on the bankruptcy of the Party apparatus and its tyrannical

[5] From *Bread and Wine*, by Ignazio Silone, trans. Gwenda David and Eric Mosbacher (New York: Harper & Brothers, 1937). Copyright 1937 by Harper & Brothers. All page references are to this edition. Excerpts are reprinted with the permission of Harper & Brothers.

nature, on the inevitability of a "Red inquisition [succeeding] the present inquisition" (175). And with the willful anti-fatality of Kyo, Spina answers:

> Destiny is an invention of the cowardly and the resigned. . . . Why should there be no way out? Are we hens shut up in a hen-coop? Why should we remain the victims of an inexorable fate, powerless to fight against it? (175–176).

Spina admits that if he were to accept this fate he could not reconcile himself to life but would have to fear it. Uliva can accept it and reconcile himself, but in a way similar to Ch'en's:

> I am not afraid of life, but I am still less afraid of death. Against a life which is dominated by pitiless laws the only weapon left to man's free will is non-life, the destruction of life, death, beautiful death. . . . Life can control man, but man can control death—his own death, and, with a little wariness, the death of tyrants. (177)

So the resort must again be to terrorism: to assassination and to suicide. And, like Ch'en, Uliva is killed by an explosion of his own making, one intended to destroy his enemies, those that make up the repressive government.

Spina, perhaps with more justifiable confidence than Kyo's, sees that he and Uliva "belonged to different worlds" (177). Of course there are important differences between Malraux and Silone. They are partly indicated by the fact that Uliva's disaffection from the Party and his dedication to reckless individual action stem more from his refusal to compromise his moral integrity than from his subjective need for self-assertion. Silone as a revolutionary is primarily a moralist, interested in the moral—if not the spiritual—aspect of Christianity; interested, that is, in the private person and through him the creation of a "different race of men" (250). While the revolution is of course aimed at reconstituting society, it is to be aimed even earlier at reconstituting people. As in Malraux, the very process of revolution has a value for the individual apart from its chances for victory. The struggle to be free, Spina tells us, is already a kind of freedom. Thus, our unusual revolutionary Socialist can say, "You can be a free man under a dictatorship" (32). But of course what the revolution can do for Silone's individual is something quite apart from the subjective satisfactions that obsessed Malraux's demoniac creatures. It is for Silone a question of moral "conversion" that he thinks of as bordering on the Christian.

It is the relation of the Christian to the revolutionary that is primary in Silone. And it is crucial because somehow Silone must resolve the inevitable difficulties that arise when the revolutionary need to convert society at large conflicts with the moral need to convert the private person. Of course Silone modifies the notion of the Christian in such a way that he excludes mystery and spirit since, as he shows us through Cristina, any divorce from materialism drives Christianity into the arms of political and economic reaction. But if revolutionary Marxian materialism denudes Christianity by reducing it to the brotherliness of socialist equality in things, so the introduction of the pure and absolute moralism of Christianity purges revolutionary activity of its pragmatic ruthlessness. Thus Spina the adolescent drawn to the Church and Spina the hardened professional revolutionary come to transform each other into a union at once sweet and effective. The cautious Dr. Sacca, in choosing a priestly disguise for his hunted friend, is sound in his assurance that Spina was not "capable of putting these garments to irreverent use" (36). It is rather the garments that do violence to Spina's doctrinaire notions:

> Gradually and imperceptibly he became more and more completely absorbed by his fictitious rôle, which he nurtured with the still living dreams of his youth. He became a prisoner of his own fantasy. (84)

He returns to his early fascination with devotional books and with the blessings of sainthood. Consequently, he must distrust the collective and Machiavellian tactics of his Party, even if his still remaining social idealism forces him still to distrust the Church. Political idealism and moral-religious idealism join, as ways of sanctifying the individual, in their abhorrence of institutions, religious or political: "Have I escaped from the opportunism of a decadent Church only to fall into bondage to the opportunism of a party?" (83). And Karl Marx is not needed to find one's way to this fusion. Spina's old teacher, Don Benedetto, comes to it solely through his religion, since he has purged that religion of everything except what seems to Silone essential primitive elements that lead it to become identified with modern socialism, also properly purged.

Thus it is that despite the Party's disdain for individual action, sainthood becomes for Spina the only effective weapon in the revolutionary struggle. In Don Benedetto's words,

> No word and no gesture can be more persuasive than the life, and, if necessary, the death, of a man who strives to be free, loyal, just, sincere, disinterested; a man who shows what a man can be. (250)

And Don Benedetto, Spina himself, and the newly converted Murica become by their examples elements of further conversion of the seemingly hopeless masses among whom "the news was spread" so that they can say of their saints, "If only everyone were like him" (240, 251).

It is of course all too obvious that in his anxiety to press the analogy between the New Testament and the trials of the modern purified Socialist, Silone has sprinkled his story liberally with familiar parabolic elements. Spina's clerical garb, the breviary he so frequently peruses, and the victims sacrificed in governmental atrocities give Silone ample opportunity, and he rarely passes it up. But there is one central way in which he uses the biblical model to fashion his modern parable. When in 1944 Silone returned to these characters, this plot, and this theme to modulate them in the direction in which he had moved, he accentuated the analogy to Christ by entitling his play *And He Hid Himself*. This title emphasizes what Silone may have recognized as his most expressive manipulation of the biblical motif in the earlier novel. From the start of the novel with its Manger scene, the role of Spina is created and given significance in response to his need to hide himself. Ironically, the atheist must hide himself in the priest's clothing. Yet, in Silone's eyes, what he has done is symbolically justified: surface reality has merely caught up with essential reality in that Spina has been doing the work of the true Christian while the Churchmen have not. Don Benedetto acknowledges as much by giving another turn to the metaphor of "hiding":

> . . . he who lives for justice and truth, without caring for the consequences, is not an atheist, but he is in the Lord and the Lord is in him. (21) In times of conspiratorial and secret struggle the Lord is obliged to hide Himself and assume pseudonyms. . . . Might not the ideal of social justice that animates the masses today be one of the pseudonyms the Lord is using to free Himself from the control of the churches and the banks? (241)

Thus true Christianity is hiding within the atheistic revolutionary movement even as Spina is hiding within the invented priest, Don Paolo Spada. While God is missing from the movement's belief, the moral idea of God is there and, paradoxically, only there where his nonexistence is professed. And once again, after almost two thousand years, God as revolutionary has gone "out of the temple."

In the play, where in the words of John the hiding man-God enters the title itself, the obvious elements of parable are multiplied and dwelled upon until the drama is pretty well transformed into passion play. A new character is introduced to make explicit also the going out of the temple: Brother Gioacchino, the friar who insists on the continuing Crucifixion of man by denying the Resurrection and by rejecting the Church that falsely tries to console man in his agony by affirming it. Spina and Brother Gioacchino are so juxtaposed that the one enters the priestly habit as the other discards his. The atheistic man of violence hides himself within the temple, thus purifying it, and the dedicated man of religion-without-mystery, in order to preserve his dedication, leaves it. For Silone both are equally proper versions of the sacrificial Son of Man in his sufferings. And they are accordingly joined together for future action at the play's close.

But what is the relation of this naturalized Christianity or this mild and sweetened Marxism to Malraux and to the tragic vision beyond the obvious fact that it rejects them both? That, very likely contrary to Silone's intention, there is such a relation becomes increasingly clear as we examine what I have spoken of as the inevitable conflict between the need for the revolution to strive for victory and the need for it to convert the individual. Like Malraux, Silone presents a contrasting trio, shading from the character who breaks too completely with the Party, leaving himself ineffectively and terroristically alone, to the character who through his critical faculty maintains an independent humanity while resisting a final break with the Party, to the character who accepts the Party so uncritically as to merge with it as apparatus. And in Malraux, we must remember, these shadings managed sometimes to touch and sometimes to produce reflections as well as contrasts. As we have seen the somewhat analogous roles played by Ch'en and Uliva and by Kyo and Spina, so Silone provides analogues for Vologin, Malraux's representative of unyielding Party authority. Romeo appears as the Party underground leader in both the novel and the play, although we have a more sharply critical, a more dehumanized version of him in the later work. Perhaps Silone has fused Bolla, the other and more hardened Party leader of the novel, with Romeo in order to create the Romeo of the play. This Romeo tells the sensitive Annina, who properly is Spina's "convert" to the Party, that the only useful revolutionaries

> are those who manage to put their nerves out of the game. . . . It's a sort of narcosis. . . . we must manage to put our normal sensibility to sleep, we must chloroform it. . . . never trust sentimental revolutionaries. . . . we must merge our normal feelings in our will to fight. We must draw them away from our epidermis and our nerves and hide them in our bones. (29–30) [6]

Romeo is ready to face the fact, insisted on by Annina, that this prescribed disposition constitutes a betrayal of the very moral sensibility that led him into the struggle. Annina maintains that Spina has resisted this narcosis while retaining his usefulness, and the play bears out her claims. When Annina breaks with the Party to follow Murica, the discredited and haunted informer, Romeo is "disappointed in her" while Spina "never dreamed she was so close to perfection" (74). He attributes to her "a spirit in which our fierce fanaticisms melt away" (75). But at this stage Spina himself is not up to this spirit and perhaps more properly attributes to himself the fanaticism of Romeo. Accordingly he insists that he alone must be the one to execute Murica "without hatred and without pity. Like a surgeon" (77). Even later, just before he is forced to hear Murica's confession, Spina admits that, unlike "confessors and psychiatrists," "a revolutionary movement, if it's not to betray its mission, in certain cases has got to be merciless to the point of cruelty" (93).

In the novel as in the play Spina changes after hearing this painful confession. He frees himself from the need to make a Party judgment and acknowledges the human difficulty in making any other judgment:

> If I were the head of a party or a political group . . . I should judge you according to the party statutes. Every party is based

[6] From *And He Hid Himself*, by Ignazio Silone, trans. Darina Tranquilli (New York: Harper & Brothers, 1945). Copyright 1945, 1946 by Harper & Brothers. All page references are to the 1945 edition. Excerpts are reprinted with the permission of Harper & Brothers.

on a definite ideology and is equipped with a corresponding morality, which is codified in objective rules. Often these rules are very like those with which every man is inspired by his own conscience, often they are the very reverse. But I am not, or am no longer, a political leader. I am just an ordinary mortal, and, if I am to judge another man, I can have nothing to guide me but my own conscience. Besides, it is only within the narrowest limits that one man has the right to judge another. (*Bread and Wine*, p. 264)

Murica has already opposed pure morality to Party necessity in describing his reactions to his sense of guilt as a renegade:

> The idea that everything was matter, that the idea of good was inseparable from the idea of utility (even if it were social utility) and was based on the idea of punishment, became insupportable to me. Punishment by whom? The state? The group? Public opinion? But what if the state, the group, public opinion were immoral? Besides, supposing there were a definite method, a definite technique, of doing evil with assured impunity: what would then be the basis of morality? Could a technique which eliminated all danger of retribution destroy the distinction between good and evil? That thought terrified me. I became filled with dread of chaos, of the void. . . . I did not believe in God, but I started wishing with my whole soul that God existed. I had need of Him to escape from my fear of the void. (262–263)

This awareness of utter despair, this confrontation of nothingness, leads to his need to suffer for his guilt by returning to an absolute morality, as he tells Spina in the play at the close of the analogous passage to the one just quoted from the novel:

> The most frightful punishment imaginable seemed to me infinitely preferable to placid acceptance of a world in which the problem of evil could be solved by a little cunning and dexterity of execution. If I finally decided to confess everything, taking no thought of the consequences, it was with the deliberate and clear-cut intent of setting up order once again

> between the world and myself, of restoring the ancient boundary between good and evil, without which I couldn't go on living any more. (100)

These are all echoes of the metapolitical definition of evil that Silone and his reformed revolutionaries arrive at. In the novel Don Benedetto puts it this way:

> The evil I see around me is deeper than politics. It is a canker. You cannot heal a putrefying corpse with warm poultices. There is the class struggle, the town and the country, but underlying all these things there is man, a poor, weak, terrified animal. The canker has penetrated to his marrow. . . . (249)

And Spina comes to see his own anguished, if unacknowledged, acceptance of this notion:

> He had always instinctively avoided penetrating man's individual troubles and secrets—perhaps because he feared that the rather simple idea he had formed of human sufferings and their solution might be destroyed in the process; perhaps, also, because he was afraid of being confronted with sufferings that had no solution. Uliva's trenchant judgment of him suddenly returned to his mind. "You are afraid of the truth. You force yourself to believe in progress, to be an optimist and a revolutionary, because you are terrified of the opposite." (271)

How, then, can the Spina who sees so deeply continue to act as revolutionary and as a revolutionary who, whatever his reservations, finally remains within the confines of the Party and its objectives? Should not Spina the activist find himself paralyzed by such nonpragmatic notions of a good and evil that transcend social-economic organization and rather relate directly to the fallen nature of man? If, as a properly humble individual person, he has sense enough of his own weakness to find judgment of others difficult, if not impossible; and if he recognizes that as individual he cannot surrender this private problem of judgment to a Party's collective and doctrinaire judgment; then how can he persist in inspiring himself and others to revolutionary violence as, with whatever reservations, he does to the end of both novel and play?

The difficulties in Silone's attempt to identify the Christian and the revolutionary emerge at this point. In novel and play there is, first, the corrupt law of the government and of its perverted Church. This is answered by the seemingly opposed law of revolutionary Party doctrine which, however, through Uliva and the humanized Spina, comes to be seen as equally corrupt. The answer, then, is not the substitution of one apparatus for another but the substitution of the individual as a unique value for the apparatus and its collective values. And no collective agent, not even a party supposedly dedicated to individuals, can serve without subverting its objective. If we see this far, what kind of individual can we have to provide the answer? Silone would want him to be at once the pure individual revolutionary and the all-loving individual Christian. But the former of these, what might be termed a naturalistic humanist, knows whom to hate as well as whom to love: he has his source in pride. He is proud of his own values and of his ability to discriminate the loved from the hated in terms of them. We can speak of *Agape* only in reference to the Christian, who has his source in humility. But its price is an inability to act that follows from an inability to hate and a refusal to judge. Here is the consequence of holding with consistency that the individual is a unique value. Spina cannot do completely without this notion of Christianity, since he must move beyond the Party's humanistic expediency. But of course Spina will not fully accept this Christianity since it would finally lead him to the position which in *Bread and Wine* he finds so intolerable in Cristina: to a morality that is "purely contemplative" (81). Instead of his converting Cristina to his revolutionary humanism, as he does, she would convert him to her unworldly, spiritual Christianity. He would be brought to see that the very moral integrity that led him to reject the Party's way would lead him to reject all action; that he cannot indulge in the pride and self-righteousness that permit action without courting the same moral bankruptcy. So he would have to cease being a revolutionary altogether.

While Spina resists recognizing these consequences, he manages only to jumble messily together his roles as revolutionary and as Christian, sometimes invoking the one and sometimes the other. Neither in the novel nor in the play can Silone show them as merging into the single glorified role of the new saint, although it was clearly his objective to do so. If he were content to dissociate himself from this failure by putting it off on Spina and to reveal it as an inevitable failure—if, that is, he were writing an existential rather than a political and ideological novel or play—Spina could have been developed into a moving version of the demoniac. There are some rather explicit suggestions in this direction, especially in the play, but Silone hardly seems aware of them. He is so anxious to unite the Christian and the revolutionary that he is less than fully alert to his own evidences of their opposition.

When in the play (39–43) the sympathetic landlady protests the jailing of an innocent man, one of the government representatives somewhat ironically states the Christian doctrine that "no man is wholly and entirely innocent." The landlady forces them to admit that this fallen state applies to everyone and then asks about the apparent exemption from it of "the powers that be." While they are men, she is told, as "exceptional men" "for themselves they have made a special law." She replies at once that Spina is also an exceptional man who "has made himself a special law," who "is a law unto himself." Through the rest of the play this notion of a special law for the Spinas—a "proud race," a "headstrong . . . truly unaccommodating race"—is insisted upon. As we would expect, it is applied also to Brother Gioacchino and Murica. Surely, however, the juxtaposition of Spina and "the powers that be" as being outside the law of common humanity carries its own irony. In the assertion of pridefulness, in the claim to be above human failings they are only too obviously alike, so that we must recognize that the rebel has fashioned his mentality as a reflection of the mentality he means to be struggling against. Can the individual be "a law unto himself" without assuming the infallibility which is as falsely assumed by the government he hates and the party he distrusts?

The theme of pride is even more explicitly dwelt upon in the Magdalene episode of the play (83–84). Spina becomes interested in the outcast "reprobate woman" when he learns she has reacted against society proudly. Dressed as a priest, he tells her he would like to "preach a sermon on pride." "On the vice of pride?" she asks. He answers, "No, on the virtue of pride." When she requests Spina's aid in having her bastard child admitted to catechism class, he rather asks about another kind of education: "Can he throw stones? . . . Can he use his fists?" Here he is willing to help. And he takes the boy off to teach him these prideful responses to society rather than the submissive ones. We next hear that the child, educated by Spina, has been stoning the "pious women." This is surely an inversion of the stone-casting motif found in the New Testament, and it makes Spina into a very different sort of Jesus, looking for a very different sort of disciple.

Near the close of the play, as people speak of Murica, who has undergone the modern equivalent of crucifixion, they speak of him as "one of those that have made themselves a special law, a new notion of right and wrong" (107). This claim is immediately followed by a description of his tortures by the state police that all too clearly parallel Christ's, complete with crown and purple robe. This sequence surely seems meant firmly to establish those who create special laws for themselves as Christ figures—as those who are continually crucified during mankind's unending Good Friday, according to Brother Gioacchino. And we may be tempted to forget that all this about exceptional men and special laws beyond "the ancient one" (64) began by being applied, however ironically, to the viciously illegal rulers, "the powers that be." It is the old problem: which is the saint and how do we know? And if the would-be saint is man rather than Jesus, does not his messianic complex—what Spina himself has termed "fierce fanaticism"—lead straight to the anti-Christ, to demonism? Uliva is allowed an additional speech in the play which Silone puts in at his peril, since he has Spina neither heed it nor become less Christ-like for ignoring it.

> You spoke to me once about a secret dream of yours. You expressed it in homemade terms: you would make a Soviet out of the Fucino Plain and nominate Jesus Christ President of the Soviet. The idea perhaps mightn't be a bad one if the son of the Nazareth carpenter were really on this earth still and could exercise that function in person; but, when the nomination was made and note duly taken of his absence, you would have to find a substitute for him. And we in this country know how the representatives of Jesus begin and how they end; eh, and don't we know it! The poor newly converted Negroes and Indians of the missions don't know it, but we know it only too well. (60)

Uliva points to the literal fact that reveals Brother Gioacchino's claim about permanent crucifixion and his denial of the Resurrection to be in the end only symbolic. Agonized modern man must face the literal fact that he is, after all, only man and not Jesus: parable is thus reduced to parody. No wonder that Uliva speaks patronizingly of Spina as engaged in "the struggle of the creature to break down his limitations" (59). He is aware that Spina is better than his party but is even more aware that he must end up as its victim and the revolution's. For he is but "creature" so that only the blindness of pride can lead him to deny his "limitations." The fully Christian individual, with his humble spirituality, is the only alternative that avoids compromise; but Uliva cannot consider this alternative any more than Spina can. The assertion of a private ethical from outside all ethical structures ("a special law" for oneself "different from the ancient one" as well as from society's laws) is already a demoniacal assertion. In foregoing all laws it foregoes all that can be shared, and thus by definition foregoes the ethical. Law that is created only for oneself is hardly law, of course. Beyond the ethical and thus cut off from the claim to a universal sanction, the individual, in acting under the sanction of his unique law, lays claim to being himself an absolute. Nor does he claim, as absolute, an extra-ethical relationship. He is indeed "a law unto himself."

Here once more, then, we may find—in spite of Silone, as before we found in spite of Malraux—the essence of metaphysical rebellion, of prideful defiance, of the tragic. As Eliot discovered in *Murder in the Cathedral*, it is almost impossible to explore the problem of sainthood, if one deals with man instead of God-man, without hearkening to these fearful, underground stirrings toward the diabolical. Of course we must not rewrite Silone, and our critical common sense must warn us that his work will hardly allow these insinuations. He seems scarcely ready to acknowledge any faintest movement in these directions. It is not, as in Malraux, that he is at war with himself, the artist giving ground to motions that the ideologue would prefer to have stilled. Rather with Silone the ideologue is so securely in control that the artist never has a chance. If occasionally, through his ideological shabbiness, a subversive notion creeps in and threatens to reveal all about the glaring self-deception that lurks barely hidden beneath, he seems not to be wholly aware of it. So he neither removes it nor gives it its head. And it remains, undeveloped, more to belie his claims than to rival them. I cannot say that the tragic is a very alive vision in either the novel or the play, as I would claim it is in *Man's Fate*. But it may be seen undercutting the shallow ideology which the too-committed Silone tried to mask dramatically, and pointing to the real drama he might have seen if, following his own clues as Malraux did, he had opened himself to the tragic vision and to art.

CHAPTER FOUR

Disease and Health: The Tragic and the Human Realms of Thomas Mann

> Life is not prudish, and it is probably safe to say that life prefers creative, genius-bestowing disease a thousand times over to prosaic health; prefers disease, surmounting obstacles proudly on horseback, boldly leaping from peak to peak, to lounging, pedestrian healthfulness. Life is not finical and never thinks of making a moral distinction between health and infirmity. It seizes the bold product of disease, consumes and digests it, and soon as it is assimilated, it is health. An entire horde, a generation of open-minded, healthy lads pounces upon the work of diseased genius, genialized by disease, admires and praises it, raises it to the skies, perpetuates it, transmutes it, and bequeathes it to civilization, which does not live on the home-baked bread of health alone. They all swear by the name of the great invalid, thanks to whose madness they no longer need to be mad. Their healthfulness feeds upon his madness and in them he will become healthy.
>
> In other words, certain attainments of the soul and the intellect are impossible without disease, without insanity, without spiritual crime, and the great invalids are crucified victims, sacrificed to humanity and its advancement, to the broadening of its feeling and knowledge—in short, to its more sublime health.
>
> Thomas Mann, Preface to *The Short Novels of Dostoevsky*, 1945

1. The End of Faustus: Death and Transfiguration

> A work that deals with the Tempter, with apostasy, with damnation, what else could it be but a religious work? What I mean is a conversion, a proud and bitter change of heart . . . (490) [1]

Thomas Mann does indeed belong on the frontispiece of this volume. In furnishing me with the epigraph for this entire study, he has furnished me with much more. All his work, like Leverkühn's *The Lamentation of Doctor Faustus* which he is there describing, is this very sort of "mammoth variation-piece." And Leverkühn's theme, "For I die as a good and as a bad Christian," is essentially Mann's: the heights and the depths of the human reaches, and the unavailability of the middle ranges. All this too is my theme—and Mann has done so much to usher us all into it that I must pay this homage. Thus I dare not yield to the temptation of passing by his work on the grounds that, more than any other of my authors, he has been the subject of extensive—if not exhaustive—commentary both various and brilliant.[2] In view of all this learned work, I cannot start *ab novo* as if nothing had been written before, while my own purposes will not permit me to make this a mere review of scholarship. Yet I must make use of Mann, who is so self-consciously aware

[1] From *Doctor Faustus*, by Thomas Mann, trans. H. T. Lowe-Porter (New York: Alfred A. Knopf, Inc., 1948). Copyright 1948, by Alfred A. Knopf, Inc. All page references are to this edition. Excerpts are reprinted with the permission of Alfred A. Knopf, Inc.

[2] Among the many impressive treatments of his difficult *Doctor Faustus*, as the pages that follow will indicate, I found most illuminating Joseph Frank's "Reaction as Progress: or, the Devil's Domain," *Hudson Review*, II (1949), 38–53; and Erich Heller's "Parody, Tragic and Comic: Mann's *Doctor Faustus* and *Felix Krull*," *Sewanee Review*, LXVI (1958), 519–546, later printed as the last chapter of *The Ironic German: A Study of Thomas Mann* (Boston: Little, Brown and Company, 1958). While the second appeared after my own essay was mainly written, I found many of my ideas reflected and clarified in it.

of the very problems I deal with, indeed who dedicated his work almost exclusively to their exploration. All he wrote is at once a warning against extremity and an acknowledgment not merely of its indispensability for the sake of vision but of its inescapable attractions if you are its man and it is your destiny.

Thanks to Mann, Faustus becomes our last—as he was our first—symbol of modern man as tragic visionary. Since Mann has made him the extreme representative of the morbid tendency of our culture and our history, I cannot claim to carry his theme further. It may seem that Mann has in effect written this book for me, but in his way—which perhaps accounts for our difficulty with his work as novels. His strongly philosophical investigations, while often obscuring his drama, may seem to have treated my subject too discursively and too exhaustively for me to include him and still leave anything for me to do—in other words, for me to include him without appearing to rival him. This would be an act of special presumption since, like all moderns, I have learned endlessly from Mann, and what I have learned has been an indispensable guide to my own probings. Still, most readers would agree that Mann, though often more essayist than dramatist in style and literary conception, is not quite transparent; so that a medium may after all be useful to place him within my conception.

This last Faustus is clearly far more like the first Faustus, that sixteenth-century ill-fated magician of modernism emerging from the dawn of Protestantism, than he is like Goethe's humanistic transformation of him. His world is the world of sin and damnation, of forbidden alchemy and the unyielding door that denies all to affirm human limitations—the lock on aspirations that only transcendent grace, as reward for self-humiliation, can open. It is not the open world that can lead through striving to clarity, the neo-Promethean world that Goethe imposed and justified to find the purely human grace that each can create. For Goethe, man, ejected from the neatly ordered nature posited by simple rationalism—from the mirror-universe of the Enlightenment—can, through subjective assertiveness, exercise dominance over it, bring it once more to order, his order and consequently its. Thus the grand union of subjective and objective, the harmony that was the forward-looking culmination of German humanistic thought by the early nineteenth century. Faustus was rescued from transgression by Goethe only to be urged in the name of heroic zeal to work out his human salvation, with Beethoven's "Ode to Joy" on his lips, by doing all that was forbidden earlier by the orthodox ethic. And the man-god was set to work performing his miracles—the miracles which by the time of Mann destroyed all harmony and threatened to destroy man himself. This turn suggested that perhaps the sixteenth century was righter and that the humanly synthesized harmony was the delusion of prideful excess, of a cursed self-sufficiency. The high point of modern Western culture was a fraud, its promise now mere ashes. Even art must remake the dulling formula that smothers what it promised to liberate. For, as Gide's Michel came to realize in rejecting it, harmony has become the mean and synthesis become the middle way—the way, that is, of the middle class. While it is true, then, that it is the *Faustbook's* Faust rather than Goethe's that is relevant to Mann's, Goethe's is very much there by negation. As others have seen, *The Lamentation of Doctor Faustus* is Leverkühn's instrument to "take back" Beethoven's Ninth Symphony, with his "Ode to Sorrow" the revocation of Beethoven's "Ode to Joy," in the same way as in his novel Mann is taking back Goethe's *Faust*. In that finally satisfying moment in which Faust can rest, in that tribute to human endeavor when he wins land back from the sea on which to found a healthy folk, Goethe indeed seems to have produced the literary equivalent of Beethoven's joyous Ninth. And Mann, musical novelist, calls out with his devilish revoker to revoke.

Having recognized the deceptive optimism in claims that polar extremes can be synthesized through the act of human will, that subjectivity and objectivity can be fused through the postulation of the urgent "I AM," Mann rejects the middle areas, the human areas, in order to cultivate the extremities, the saintly and the diabolical. Refusing to mediate them, he forces them paradoxically to support each other, indeed to reflect each other, finally to become masks for each other. It is here that he turns the sixteenth century upon itself, finding—as Gide found and as later we shall see Melville and Faulkner finding—that the Protestant ethic itself contains the charter for the devil's way. As Leverkühn returns to the archaic to find the authentication of his radically modern musical inventiveness, so Mann bypasses Goethe to return to the original Faust of an outmoded time. And in Mann's case, as in Leverkühn's, it is authentication by parody.

Parody, of course, is the root of Adrian's musical genius and the flower of his musical creations. The devil's gift, it accounts for the inhuman coldness, along with the flaming brilliance, of both. It is the consequence of an anti-harmonic modernism and an anti-harmonic archaism, barbaric in the blending of two anti-humanisms, the post-humanistic and the pre-humanistic—"twice barbaric indeed, because of coming after the humane, after all possible root-treatment and bourgeois raffinement" (243), as Adrian's Mephistopheles guarantees him. It is this new-old barbarism that Adrian's humanistic biographer comes to fear:

> Here no one can follow me who has not as I have experienced in his very soul how near aestheticism and barbarism are to each other: aestheticism as the herald of barbarism. I experienced this distress certainly not for myself but in the light of my friendship for a beloved and emperilled artist soul. The revival of ritual music from a profane epoch has its dangers. It served indeed the ends of the Church, did it not? But before that it had served less civilized ones, the ends of the medicine-man, magic ends. That was in times when all celestial affairs were in the hands of the priest-medicine-man, the priest-wizard. Can it be denied that this was a pre-cultural, a barbaric condition of cult-art; and is it comprehensible or not that the late and cultural revival of the cult in art, which aims by atomization to arrive at collectivism, seizes upon means that belong to a stage of civilization not only priestly but primitive? (373)

Parody, the guise of the newly objective anti-harmonics, is then a complete inversion of the resolution of extremes that Adrian's teacher Kretschmar found in Beethoven's Sonata Op. 111. There is extremity here too, but all finally converts to the blessedness of the human. Let me excerpt painfully from Zeitblom's summary of Kretschmar's performance:

> What now happens to this mild utterance, rhythmically, harmonically, contrapuntally, to this pensive, subdued formulation, with what its master blesses and to what condemns it, into what black nights and dazzling flashes, crystal spheres wherein coldness and heat, repose and ecstasy are one and the same, he flings it down and lifts it up . . . The characteristic of the movement of course is the wide gap between bass and treble, between the right and the left hand, and a moment comes, an utterly extreme situation, when the poor little motif seems to hover alone and forsaken above a giddy yawning abyss—a procedure of awe-inspiring unearthliness, to which then succeeds a distressful making-of-itself-small, a start of fear as it were, that such a thing could happen. Much else happens before the end. But when it ends and while it ends, something comes, after so much rage, persistence, obstinacy, extravagance: something entirely unexpected and touching in its mildness and goodness. . . . It is like having one's hair or cheek stroked, lovingly, understandingly, like a deep and silent farewell look. It blesses the object, the frightfully harried formulation, with overpowering humanity . . . (54–55)

The futility of this musical humanism in Adrian's world or in the world left behind by Adrian is echoed in the lament of Zeitblom, returning to his classical pedagogic devotions after the death of Adrian and of nazism, that he can no longer make meaningful "the cultural ideas in which reverence for the dieties of the depths blends with the civilized cult of Olympic reason and clarity, to make for a unity in uprightness" (505).[3] For

[3] One could easily trace the extent to which the extremity of Adrian as man and as composer is a reflection of the political extremity of Ger-

Adrian refused to synthesize extremes into harmonics and instead, with a savage mockery that reflected the unbending Lutheran ethic, drove them ever farther apart in their purity until, through the paradox cultivated by anti-humanistic irrationalism, the poles, in the purity of their common extremity, were forced to become identical and thus interchangeable.

Thus in his first devilishly inspired work, the sacrilegious jest he called *Marvels of the Universe*, he insists on celebrating God's creation—"the immeasurable extra-human," the infinitude of astronomical heights and the ocean deeps—glorying during his "luciferian sardonic mood" (275) in their inaccessibility, their indifference, indeed their irrelevance to the human universe. In

---

many that leads to nazism. The political discussions of Kridwiss, Breisacher, and company indicate that Leo Naphta of *The Magic Mountain* is still with us. They reveal the same anti-humanism, one which justifies old Zeitblom's closing doubts about the future and "unity in uprightness." Again there is the dangerous circularity, so subversive of human values in its identifying of extremes. Just one of many passages will serve:

> It was an old-new world of revolutionary reaction, in which the values bound up with the idea of the individual—shall we say truth, freedom, law, reason?—were entirely rejected and shorn of power, or else had taken on a meaning quite different from that given them for centuries. Wrenched away from the washed-out theoretic, based on the relative and pumped full of fresh blood, they were referred to the far higher court of violence, authority, the dictatorship of belief—not, let me say, in a reactionary, anachronistic way as of yesterday or the day before, but so that it was like the most novel setting back of humanity into mediaevally theocratic conditions and situations. That was as little reactionary as though one were to describe as regression the track round a sphere, which of course leads back to where it started. There it was: progress and reaction, the old and the new, the past and the future became one; the political Right more and more coincided with the Left. (368)

But, though Zeitblom's every written word is, like the story he tells, conditioned by the historical moment out of which it issues, I shall steer clear of this yet further symbolic level of the complex book since my interest is with Adrian as tragic visionary rather than with the tragic destiny of Western culture through its destructive, avant-garde representative, Germany.

his *Gesta Romanorum* he celebrates the medieval union of the sacred and the obscene, of the pious and the perverse, leading to his Apocalyptic Oratorio, modeled on Dürer, in which Adrian willfully forces a tight, an abstract musical system through the use of the *glissando*, that anti-systematic "barbaric rudiment from pre-musical days" which Zeitblom rejects on "profoundly cultural grounds" (374). This oratorio, Zeitblom tells us, "is dominated by the paradox (if it is a paradox) that in it dissonance stands for the expression of everything lofty, solemn, pious, everything of the spirit; while consonance and firm tonality are reserved for the world of hell, in this context a world of banality and commonplace" (375). And why not? For here the "pandemonium of laughter, of hellish merriment" (378) is made to be a reflection of the unearthly sublimity of the children's chorus: "The passages of horror just before heard are given, indeed, to the indescribable children's chorus at quite a different pitch, and in changed orchestration and rhythms; but in the searing, susurrant tones of spheres and angels there is not one note which does not occur, with rigid correspondence, in the hellish laughter" (378–379). In this "substantial identity of the most blest and accurst, the inner unity of the chorus of child angels and the hellish laughter of the damned" (486), Zeitblom correctly sees the anti-humanistic, the revolutionary and reactionary paradox of Adrian's creative genius: "calculation raised to mystery" (379).

To repeat, this inhuman parody is the devil's gift, although that Adrian was ready for it we know from his earlier *Love's Labour's Lost.* In his life as well as in his music he had been preparing himself for his visitor that climactic night. Indeed, amid the towers of Kaiseraschern and the playful hermetics of his father he had been prepared from the first. After all, was it not in his father's "speculating the elements" that the noxious "Hetaera Esmeralda" made her first bewitching appearance? From Kaiseraschern to the theological mysteries into which the obviously diabolical Schleppfuss initiated him and to the forbidden alchemy of music under Kretschmar. And our Faust, like his original, sprouts under the very shadow of Luther to become an inverted reflection of him. All that is left is for the purity of Adrian's asceticism, leading even to a "distaste for the too great physical nearness of people" (220), to be momentarily identified with the extremity of license. He is ready for the re-entrance of Esmeralda, both his father's butterfly and the devil's agent, the prostitute to whom he is led by "the small-beer Schleppfuss" (142). She at once repels him by her merest touch and challenges him to the all-consuming embrace. So he searches her out and, warned by her of the danger of her disease, is all the more urgent.

> . . . what was it, what madness, what deliberate, reckless tempting of God, what compulsion to comprise the punishment in the sin, finally what deep, deeply mysterious longing for daemonic conception, for a deathly unchaining of chemical change in his nature was at work, that having been warned he despised the warning and insisted upon possession of this flesh? (155)

He never sees her again but is tied to her forever—in the abstinence of his life, in the austere licentiousness of his work, in the chemistry of musical creativity and human destruction bestowed by syphilis. The term *Hetaera Esmeralda*, "her name —that which he gave her from the beginning—whispers magically . . . throughout his work" (155). And the polarities are affirmed in this momentary and devastating union that always commands his fidelity and allows him the brilliant inventiveness of genius. For he has been led to the extremity of license only by the extremity of self-denial and is permanently freed from the sensual only by this single total enslavement to it: ". . . his chastity since then, since that embrace, since his passing contagion and the loss of his physicians, sprang no longer from the ethos of purity but from the pathos of impurity" (220). We are reminded of Schleppfuss' prophetic story of medieval witchcraft, in which the sexton's daughter renders the cooper impotent to all women except her. But the cooper is less faithful than Adrian and has his beloved burned as a witch, hearing in her shrieks "the voice of the Demon, croaking as against his will he issued from her" and recovering "the sinfully alienated free use of his manhood" (109). Adrian's remains "alienated": "Thou maist not love" (248), he is commanded by the devil or by his disease or by the frigidly anti-human dedication of his work and his life. And of course there is no saying how literal or metaphorical his devil is meant to be, whether it was he who summoned Esmeralda and the disease—and with them the superhuman capacities of Adrian's creativity and the limited time for his exercise of it—or whether it was all these that summoned him as their symbolic reduction, their ambiguous incarnation. But, given the brilliance of Mann's symbolism that works both ways, it cannot matter how we answer—any more than in *The Magic Mountain* it matters whether Hans actually has contracted tuberculosis when Mann forces us to define the disease in terms of a certain spiritual condition with which Hans has surely been afflicted.

Impelled by the moral-sensual collision with Esmeralda, which is echoed in the contractual confrontation by the devil, Adrian rejects all to realize the inmost depths which have moved him all along but which have not before claimed his exclusive devotion. He wills his diabolism; but, unlike that other artist Aschenbach, he does not withdraw from art for the demonic but rather presses art into the demonic, that which heightens and even purifies as it dehumanizes it. For Adrian's story is not based on the simple humanistic dialectic of *Death in Venice* which identifies art, austerity, and civilization and opposes them—almost in Settembrinian fashion—to the sensual and the diseased. The new Faustus lives in a world more Janus-faced than this, in which art and disease, austerity and sensuality are one. But of course this is his world because, as Faustus, he lives in hell. And hell is the world without love, the denial of the human and of human claims, the cold identification of equally life-denying extremes. Thus the Adversary can tell him, "Thy life shall be cold, therefore thou shalt love no human being. . . . Cold we want you to be, that the fires of creation shall be hot enough to warm yourself in. Into them you will flee out of the cold of your life. . . ." And Adrian can answer, "And from the burning back to the ice. It seems to be hell in advance, which is already offered me on earth" (249). But even the devil knows he is not wholly responsible, that his injunctions upon Adrian are but fulfillments of what has been latent within his quarry: "A general chilling of your life and your relations to men lies in the nature of things—rather it lies already in your nature; in feith we lay upon you nothing new, the little ones make nothing new and strange out of you, they only ingeniously strengthen and exaggerate all that you already are" (249).

Still something remains in Adrian that seeks to cheat the devil and rejoin humanity. His most natural companion was the cynical, unreliable Rüdiger Schildknapp, who acknowledged no human obligations. Their "laughter-loving friendship . . . rested upon an indifference as profound as it was light-hearted" (171). But always they did not move beyond formal address to the *du*. It is precisely the *thou* which, here as in *The Magic Mountain*, humanizes. Which is why Rüdiger, who could not and would not attain to it, was Adrian's likeliest friend. But there is also the flirtatious Rudi Schwerdtfeger, who wooed Adrian for his *thou* and won a show of affection and the Violin Concerto that Adrian confessed to be his only human work. And there is Marie, whom Adrian loved "out of his own world of musical theology, oratorio, mathematical number-magic" (423), in whom he wished to find "the human content of his future work" (436), through whom he hoped even to overcome death. But the Adversary must take his revenge: through his love for Marie, Adrian blunders into losing them both and destroying Rudi. Or perhaps does not blunder; perhaps it is the devil in Adrian rather than the Adversary himself. For Adrian may have acted not entirely without some subterranean awareness of these consequences (442, 501). At the end there is the beloved Nepomuk and the finally intolerable deprivation, this one not requiring Adrian as accomplice, this one externally and arbitrarily imposed by the *diabolus ex machina* that at last establishes Mephistopheles as a literal reality.

Having with a stroke of underground cunning deprived himself of Rudi and Marie and having with a gratuitously ruthless stroke been deprived of Nepomuk, Adrian is ready to underwrite his inhuman fate by taking back Beethoven's Ninth Symphony. And he translates this conclusion into nonmusical terms as well:

> I find . . . that it is not to be. . . . The good and the noble . . . what we call the human, although it is good, and noble. What human beings have fought for and stormed citadels, what the ecstatics exultantly announced—that is not to be. It will be taken back. I will take it back. (478)

But the *Lamentation* does more than take it back. For we are told that despite its tight and unyielding structure it moves freely in response to subjectivity; that though "a work of extreme calculation, [it] is at the same time purely expressive" (488). Here, then, is the revolutionary-archaic break-through: Leverkühn has not only reversed Beethoven, but in so doing he has surpassed him at his own game. By attaining pure expressiveness, the work is "mellower, more melodious": Leverkühn has managed at last "without parody" (489).

Is not this high seriousness, this "expression as lament," a cheating of the devil and a paradoxically inhuman return to humanity? While Zeitblom is anxious that we do not sense any alleviation of despair in this most despairing of works, he suggests that the mere act of giving despair an aesthetically controlled expression is some kind of human victory over it.[4] For at the end of the *Lamentation* "the final despair achieves a voice":

> . . . it would mean to disparage the uncompromising character of the work, its irremediable anguish to say that it affords,

[4] This notion finds an echo in my final chapter where I try to relate the author's aesthetic transcendence of the dark vision to his thematic transcendence of it.

> down to its very last note, any other consolation than what lies in voicing it, in simply giving sorrow words; in the fact, that is, that a voice is given the creature for its woe. (491)

But, Zeitblom asks, may we not convert the aesthetic paradox—that sees the expressiveness of subjectivity issuing out of extreme calculation—into "a religious one, and say too (though only in the lowest whisper) that out of the sheerly irremediable hope might germinate? It would be but a hope beyond hopelessness, the transcendence of despair—not betrayal to her, but the miracle that passes belief" (491). And our narrator calls our attention to the final note as it dies away:

> Then nothing more: silence, and night. But that tone which vibrates in the silence, which is no longer there, to which only the spirit hearkens, and which was the voice of mourning, is so no more. It changes its meaning; it abides as a light in the night. (491)

So does Adrian change his meaning here at the last. Like the paradoxical light in the night, the echo of sound in silence, he remains with us transfigured in his very dissolution. The limitlessness of his rebellion and of his unrepentance is itself a kind of piety. It is not, then, that he reforms out of even the slightest repentance; it is that he rejects any reformation so utterly as to attain the extremity that, in Mann's world, can become miraculously transformed into its absolute opposite. Thus it is that the last and most desperate Faust, by virtue of his unrelaxed desperation, is transfigured to Jesus.

> A work that deals with the Tempter, with apostasy, with damnation, what else could it be but a religious work? What I mean is a conversion, a proud and bitter change of heart, as I, at least, read it in the "friendly plea" of Dr. Faustus to the companions of his last hour, that they should betake themselves to bed, *sleep in peace*, and let naught trouble them. In the frame of the cantata one can scarcely help recognizing this instruction as the conscious and deliberate reversal of the

"Watch with me" of Gethsemane. And again the Johann's wine, the draught drunk by the parting soul with his friends, has an altogether ritual stamp, it is conceived as another Last Supper. But linked with it is an inversion of the temptation idea, in such a way that Faust rejects as temptation the thought of being saved: not only out of formal loyalty to the pact and because it is "too late," but because with his whole soul he despises the positivism of the world for which one would save him, the lie of its godliness. This becomes clearer still and is worked out even more powerfully in the scene with the good old doctor and neighbour who invites Faust to come to see him, in order to make a pious effort to convert him. In the cantata he is clearly drawn in the character of a tempter; and the tempting of Jesus by Satan is unmistakably suggested; as unmistakably also is the "*Apage!*" by the proudly despairing "No!" uttered to false and flabby middle-class piety. (490)

And in the farewell *apologia* to his friends by Adrian-Faustus—the last-hour scene that echoes the last-hour scene of Adrian's cantata as we have just witnessed it—this note of relentless self-sacrifice, of savior-scapegoat, is sounded again—but again in a way that permits no slightest similarity to the Beethoven-Goethe-humanist way.

Yea verily, dear mates, that art is stuck and grown too heavy and scorneth itselfe and God's poor man knoweth no longer where to turn in his sore plight, that is belike the fault in the times. But an one invite the divel as guest, to pass beyond all this and get to the break-through, he chargeth his soul and taketh the guilt of the time upon his own shoulders, so that he is damned. For it hath been said "Be sober, and watch!" But that is not the affair of some; rather, instead of shrewdly concerning themselves with what is needful upon earth that it may be better there, and discreetly doing it, that among men such order shall be stablished that again for the beautiful work living soil and true harmony be prepared, man playeth the truant and breaketh out in hellish drunkenness; so giveth he his soul thereto and cometh among the carrion. (499–500)

The pure incarnation of our darkest aspects—even as Germany was—Adrian has made a full assumption of our burden of guilt. Thus the saintly—indeed the Christ-like—through the cultivation of the absolutely unmitigated Satanic: light through a totally unenlightened darkness, hope through hopelessness, blessedness that is the other side of damnation, a heaven that is a transcendence—through an utter realization—of hell. This is indeed the universe of what the late Philip Blair Rice termed "the non-Euclidean," "the merging parallels," [5] where the recklessness of abandon impossibly yields the break-through.

Of course, none of this is to be confused with repentance; indeed, the very power of this miracle depends on the refusal to repent. In his initial interview with the devil Adrian argues against his Adversary's insistence that he is already in hell, thanks to his rebellious pride that will never allow contrition. Adrian counters with the claim that there is also a "prideful *contritio*," the "*contritio* without hope, as complete disbelief in the possibility of mercy and forgiveness, the rocklike firm conviction of the sinner that he has done too grossly for even the Everlasting Goodness to be able to forgive his sin—only that is the true *contritio* . . . for Goodness the most irresistible of all" (247). His visitor answers this brilliant sophistry with the claim that the self-conscious, deliberate parodist could never arouse "the single-mindedness, the naive recklessness of despair" needed "for this sinful waye to salvacion" (247), that Adrian's very awareness of the possibility prohibits its accessibility to him. And Adrian merely piles this awareness onto "the most abandoned guilt," thus even improving upon this "last and most irresistible challenge to the Everlasting Goodness."

It may well be that, as Joseph Frank suggests, the desperation produced in Adrian by the ruthless immolation of Nepomuk finally leads him to the requisite "single-mindedness" and "naive recklessness of despair" which are projected outward, "without parody," upon the singularly expressive *Lamentation* and its

[5] From "The Merging Parallels: Mann's *Doctor Faustus*," by Philip Blair Rice, *Kenyon Review*, XI (1949), 199–217.

final tone that "abides as a light in the night." But this sounds dangerously close to true contrition, to a salvation won through a profoundly human love; and Mann could not now allow a resolution that so leans to the simply affirmative, perhaps having learned better from *The Magic Mountain*. And so he must work dialectically to undercut it. At the end of his final scene, his farewell to his companions, Adrian in effect recapitulates the two sides of his original argument with his Mephisto:

> My sin is greater than that it can be forgiven me, and I have raised it to its height, for my head speculated that the contrite unbelief in the possibility of Grace and pardon might be the most intriguing of all for the Everlasting Goodness, where yet I see that such impudent calculation makes compassion unpossible. Yet basing upon that I went further in speculation and reckoned that this last depravity must be the uttermost spur for Goodness to display its everlastingness. And so then, that I carried on an atrocious competition with the Goodness above, which were more inexhaustible, it or my speculation—so ye see that I am damned, and there is no pity for me for that I destroy all and every beforehand by speculation. (502)

And in this infinite regress the dual nature of the extremity is allowed to stand unresolved. It leads to the inversion that identifies grace with damnation to the extent that it is bestowed uniquely upon the sinner whose only repentance is his all-too-conscious rejection, in the manner of Christ's rejection of Satan's temptation, of the divine command to repent. But it is contradiction as well as inversion in that the grace, like the contrition, is every time denied as it is affirmed.

All this equivocal assertion of polarities befits the strange movement from Faust to Faust-as-Jesus, if not a movement from Faust to Jesus. As I have said, this Faust, the other side of Luther still, is indeed our last as he was our first modern man as tragic visionary. In the purity and the extremity of his recognition of his role, there would seem to be no place for the visionary to go beyond him. By assuming his role with full intelligence and self-consciousness, he is taking it all on himself: he is trying to do and say it all, thus obviating the need of another to do it and say it ever again. This farthest expression of the tragic vision can, in Mann's hands and as one of his characteristic paradoxes, convert the tragic vision into something else even as it converts Faust into a strange sort of Christ. As with the role of Nazi Germany in the history of Western culture, the culmination of the movement carries a kind of purification with it, a purge that signals the beginning of another movement. And so, once we leave Mann, the movement of this volume itself must shift from the self-conscious demon to the self-conscious savior, from the visionary as Faust to the visionary as Jesus—with the recognition that the two may after all be one, that so long as the would-be Jesus is only man there remains the Faust within, "elementing" him. But whether or not, as Mann hoped, his Faust—with the light of his darkness—would mean the beginning of something, he seems to have meant the end of something, thanks to a redemption that he in his third coming has so dearly purchased.

2. *The Magic Mountain:* The Failure of "*Spirituel*" Mediation

> But unreasoning love is *spirituel;* for death is the *spirituel* principle, the *res bina*, the *lapis philosophorum*, and the pedagogic principle too, for love of it leads to love of life and love of humanity. Thus, as I have lain in my loge, it has been revealed to me, and I am enchanted to be able to tell you all about it. There are two paths to life: one is the regular one, direct, honest. The other is bad, it leads through death—that is the *spirituel* way. (596) [6]

The facile alternatives and the obvious choice between them in this conclusive oration by Hans Castorp to Clavdia Chauchat,

[6] From *The Magic Mountain*, by Thomas Mann, trans. H. T. Lowe-Porter (New York: Alfred A. Knopf, Inc., 1951). Copyright 1927, Alfred A. Knopf, Inc. All page references are to the 1951 edition. Excerpts are reprinted with the permission of Alfred A. Knopf, Inc.

agent of his corruption and his humanizing, are indicative of the less sophisticated view Mann took of his intransigent oppositions in his earlier book—and of the less sophisticated hopefulness with which he then looked for affirmation. To say this is not to be totally just to the novel since it gets a good deal more troublesome than is promised by the clean-cut reduction of it that I have indicated. It is as if Mann changed his mind while writing his novel and refused to allow the simplification of his increasingly reluctant materials—the simplification with which he may have optimistically begun. The simple dialectic seems to have been planned in the neat Hegelian manner with the usual thesis-antithesis-synthesis arrangement. But just as we seem to have arrived—probably in the all-illuminating chapter, "Snow"—everything proceeds, luckily, to get pretty well messed up. It is questionable, given the uncertainties and inconstancies of direction, whether *The Magic Mountain* ever straightens out satisfactorily, for all the brilliance of its maneuvers. And it may be that the final, the purest, and the most controlled working of these themes had to await the sustained and inexorable mastery of *Doctor Faustus*. Nevertheless, it should be helpful for us to witness the earlier belaborings of these problems so that we may better appreciate the full meaning of their final mature design.

It is immediately apparent that Hans Castorp's involvement with the demonic is continually more tenuous than Leverkühn's. For Hans is unexceptional man while Adrian is mammoth in his uniqueness, the final incarnation of extremity. Hans, unimpressive, essentially commonplace, the not very dedicated, not very practical engineer, is after all no more than a "*Joli bourgeois à la petite tache humide*" (342), as Clavdia characterizes him. Settembrini terms him "life's delicate child" whose "stock-taking" impulses it pleases to experience and experiment. Hans is precisely such a child, passing through many stages and temptations once he is shocked into a full awareness of his Mountain retreat and release, but incapable of an encompassing commitment. He is being initiated into the race, educated by its history, by the dialectical interplay of the alternatives to which it has yielded; he is not himself, like Leverkühn, of a stature or of a madness to create himself as the image of the race, its suicidal, sacrificial redeemer. Thus Hans is the protagonist of a *Bildungsroman* which still bears many features of the freely moving picaresque from which it developed. And he moves—experimentally, tentatively—from position to opposition in search of that which will allow him to live and to live faithfully, with a faith that is earned, earned through a full appreciation of that which quickens life and deadens it, deepens it and drowns it.

Hans is recapitulating, picaresque fashion, the history and the decline of Western culture, in a kind of parody of its major moments. At a single point in time and space, Hans yet wanders spiritually from Europe to Asia, from classicism to medievalism to modernism and to romanticism. Yet each representative of a given moment is a parody, an absurd reduction of that moment —that which convinces Hans of its bankruptcy and of his need to turn elsewhere. It is as if the tendencies which are presently attracting him summon up an incarnation of themselves in their extreme form in order to warn him away by forcing him to see their partiality, indeed their invidiousness.

Originally reacting against the impact of the Mountain with his "Flatland" dullness, he meets Settembrini, the extreme representative of Flatland ethics erected into an ideology. This confrontation, coming as it does in the midst of the anti-humanistic attractions of the Mountain, helps push Hans, out of a kind of "slack" perversity, into a celebration of disease instead of health, sensuality instead of austerity, death instead of life. Under the seductive tutelage of the flaccid and careless Clavdia and the Rhadamanthine Behrens, he comes increasingly to see the humanistic as an enemy of the "human" and the "*spirituel*" way to life, one which is really a way to death. In the Walpurgis-Night—itself an obvious borrowing from Goethe's *Faust*, as was the orgiastic dream of Aschenbach in *Death in Venice* even earlier—Hans turns finally from Settembrini's humanistic pedagogy to his uninhibited celebration of the *thou* with Clavdia. He is moving, in his own modest way, in the direction Adrian later took so wholeheartedly.

But this is as far as Hans can venture before another movement is instituted. For shortly after the Walpurgis-Night this *spirituel* movement calls up its own purified incarnation in that early version of Leverkühn, Leo Naphta. Clavdia, with her human—if deathly—warmth, is gone, and this openly diabolical creature is what Hans faces in her stead. However persuasive, this vision is too much for the still-balanced Hans. He sees in Naphta the logical consequence of his recent direction and must turn aside. But in those several long—too long—debates he witnesses between Naphta and Settembrini, Hans knows that while he may turn in revulsion from Naphta, he has come too far merely to bounce back to the spirit of Carducci. In the last pages before the scene in the snow, Hans comes most clearly to perceive the meaninglessness of their polemics as the extremes meet and cross each other while contradicting themselves. Suddenly Settembrini seems the othodox and Naphta the freethinker as all the categories become confused, identity appears everywhere—especially among opposites—and only the spirit of dispute keeps the pseudo dialogue going.

The critical scene in the snow is needed to move Hans beyond the empty polemics of pompous talkers representing bankrupt extremes. Hans must find his way back to life from death—and through death. He does it in "the anti-organic, the life-denying" snow (480), the "wild inhumanity" (476) of its mathematical perfection threatening his death with the indifferent and infinite fury of the Lawrentian snow we have seen. Hans retraces his oscillations between Naphta and Settembrini, matching an anti-bourgeois impulse to succumb to self-destruction with the humanistic, purely "ethical reaction." And he feels "as often after a colloquy with Settembrini and Naphta, only to a far greater degree: dazed and tipsy, giddy, a-tremble with excitement" (485).

> You went in a circle, gave yourself endless trouble under the delusion that you were accomplishing something, and all the time you were simply describing some great silly arc that would turn back to where it had its beginning, like the riddling year itself. You wandered about, without getting home. (487)

But with his idyllic dream in the snow Hans seems at last to move forward, and toward home. The pastoralism of the scene is pure and purely Apollonian: the "children of the sun" are clearly an answer to the darkly Dionysian release of the Walpurgis-Night. Yet they are no projection of Settembrini's humanism but live in innocence with a simple and yet intelligent immediacy of unsullied sense: "A dignity, even a gravity, was held, as it were, in solution in their lightest mood, perceptible only as an ineffable spiritual influence, a high seriousness without austerity, a reasoned goodness conditioning every act" (492). But the smiling boy who smiles no longer leads Hans with solemn eyes to witness with him the dismemberment of the child by the hags. Hans awakens ready to save himself from the snow, freed from the invertible extremes. He is newly dedicated neither to reason nor to recklessness, neither to humanism nor to terrorism, but to life and love and the human, always recognizing their kinship to death and to the obscene horrors which the sensual and the diseased can lead to even as they lead also to the profound assertion of life. Here Hans would seem to have attained heights far more inclusive, humanly admissible, and durable than those attained during the short-lived Walpurgis-Night. But these are illusory too, however persuasive their dialectical resolution.

The blood sacrifice is shortly played out for Hans in reality as he witnesses the death of the kindly, courageous, upright Joachim, his "large and mild eyes" now "larger and deeper, with a musing, yes, we must even say an ominous expression . . ." (519). As Hans is "disquieted," we know that this is a projection of the snow dream and Joachim a projection of the "lovely boy" whose eyes changed everything for Hans. Now life and love must follow closely too as Clavdia reappears bringing Peeperkorn with her. And Hans's dream begins to fail. The perfection of life that transcends the discursive imperfections of Settembrini and Naphta finds its extension, its distorted incarnation, in the mighty "personality," possessor and bestower of the most sacred *thou*, Mynheer Peeperkorn. In his futility he fails it just as Hans's earlier guides failed their own representations. From now on Hans will come upon much blood sacrifice, culminating in the all-engulfing blood bath at the end, and will come only fleetingly, as in a dream, upon the blessed love of which he dreamed—only long enough to be teased by it and its unattainability.

Even the monumental failure of Peeperkorn, parody of Hans's highest and all-resolving movement, cannot discredit it for him and send him searching elsewhere. As Mann's final words are meant to tell us, Hans still tries to remain true to his dream in the snow. But the world of the Flatlands and of the Mountain are working in other ways. All that is left is *ennui*, unhealthy mysticism, the hysteria of hatred, and the blowup. Ever since the mockery of the snow dream in the bitter reality of the magnificent Peeperkorn, Hans has been sliding downhill on his Mountain until it joins the Flatlands in its universal blood sacrifice: "That historic thunder-peal, of which we speak with bated breath, made the foundations of the earth to shake; but for us it was the shock that fired the mine beneath the magic mountain, and set our sleeper ungently outside the gates" (709). The Mountain was as busy preparing appropriate conditions as the Flatlands were. After all, "The Thunderbolt" follows the Mountain's "Hysterica Passio." The world has caught up with the Magic Mountain. As they meet, we are shown that after all the Mountain was illusory: it always was a rarefied reflection of the real world, an extreme abstraction of the dialectics of its history—like all aesthetic symbols an intensification of reality because it is lived at a higher temperature, at fever pitch. And Mann ends his history, the story of Western culture into the madness of the First World War, on the darkest of all notes, although in his prayerful farewell tribute to Hans and his human capacity for love he tries to manage the kind of inversion of extremities that later, in *Doctor Faustus*, was to allow light to emerge. But how is Hans, without extremity and total commitment, to manage it? Can his simplicity so serve?

The dream of love that Hans dreamed in the snow—of love that comes through death but remains as sovereign over death and in the face of death—seems, for all its promise of conclusiveness, at last no more than dream, and illusory. Unlike Ivan Karamazov, Hans seems prepared to accept God's ticket to paradise despite the blood sacrifice, prepared to become a child of the sun "in silent recognition of that horror" (495). But his subsequent experience cannot sustain this momentary breakthrough. There are moments of recall, but moments only. There is his affectionate and fully comprehending farewell to the heroic Joachim in the soldier's quiet tragedy. There is the *thou* he achieves with Peeperkorn, as he had achieved it with Clavdia, before the pure "personality" announces his futility before Hans and the universe; but Peeperkorn abdicates and Clavdia withdraws. There is the discovery in Schubert's "Linden-tree" of another momentary symbol of his dream of "self-conquest," of returning through death to the "all-too-earthly" kingdom of life with "the new word of love and the future" (653). But "degenerated to a piece of gramophone music played by electricity" (653), it was doomed to fade.

These, then, were the "moments" our narrator speaks of at the close as, using the *thou*, he bids farewell to Hans, marching off into dubious battle—moments "when out of death, and the rebellion of the flesh, there came to thee, as thou tookest stock of thyself, a dream of love" (716). But we have seen how unsubstantial they were, how unlikely this "human," this "*spirituel*" synthesis was, how factitious even if so devoutly to be wished for. But as our narrator withdraws, asking whether "out of this extremity of fever" (and could he not as well have said "out of this fever of extremity"?) "may it be that Love one day shall mount" (716), we must wonder what we have seen in

Hans's meanderings that can make this hope more than a wistfully wishful one. Or is it not a finally empty dialectic that has no dramatic context?

In *The Magic Mountain* we have the recapitulation of the history of one kind of novel, one that is intrinsically secure from the final surrender to extremity that yields the tragic. For in it we have the breadth, the patient expansiveness of the epic that in fiction leads through the picaresque to the *Bildungsroman*. It rejects narrow intensity for maturity with all its tolerance. Addressing Hans at the end, the narrator acknowledges, "We have told [your tale] for its own sake, not for yours, for you were simple. But after all, it was your story, it befell you, you must have more in you than we thought . . ." (715). But does he have enough—even, finally, for Mann? Perhaps Mann's need to create Leverkühn suggests that he does not. It may be that Hans, as "life's delicate child," as the "stock-taking" "*joli bourgeois*," simply has not risked enough to earn the stature needed for vision and for pronouncement. Even at the momentary break-through that Hans is persuaded of under the spell of the "Linden-tree," Mann must make certain concessions:

> May we take it that our simple hero, after so many years of hermetic-pedagogic discipline, of ascent from one stage of being to another, has now reached a point where he is conscious of the "meaningfulness" of his love and the object of it? We assert, we record, that he has. . . . The truth was that his very destiny had been marked by stages, adventures, insights, and these flung up in his mind suitable themes for his "stock-taking" activities, and these, in their turn, ripened him into an intuitional critic of this sphere, of this its absolutely exquisite image, and his love of it. To the point even that he was quite capable of bringing up all three as objects of his conscientious scruples! (651)

Hans remains "simple" and "conscientious," the "critic" to the end. The complexity of his experience cannot subdue him to itself, cannot finally contaminate him. And that Mann returned to create *Doctor Faustus* may be his admission that *The Magic Mountain* is a partial failure, that Hans is not protagonist enough to engage extremity conclusively. "Love" is a big and deep word for the middling Hans, perhaps for anyone less than Adrian—if one is to arrive at even the merest possibility of it without cheating it of its bigness and deepness and so reducing it from the richly and darkly *spirituel* "human" world to the shabbily humanistic one. If this love can be earned, not through synthesis, but only through the miracle of inversion, then only he can earn it who, as exceptional, can summon from within an extremity to match the extremity that is imposed upon him. It takes the uniqueness, the creativity, the willfulness of genius to do what is beyond the simple, ordinary student of experience: it takes one who walks in the tradition of Oedipus more than in the tradition of Odysseus. For the peace of Ithaca is different from the peace of Colonus.

It is significant that *Doctor Faustus* as well as *The Magic Mountain* ends with the narrator speaking lovingly to his protagonist, addressing him with the *thou* that various characters in both novels have worked hard to earn the right to use. In both cases here is evidence of the narrator's final desperation to leave us persuaded of the possibility that has been so undermined by the convincing bleakness of all that has gone before. Coupling Adrian's fate and promise with Germany's as he echoes the silence of the "light in the night," Zeitblom closes with the prayer: "When, out of uttermost hopelessness—a miracle beyond the power of belief—will the light of hope dawn? A lonely man folds his hands and speaks: 'God be merciful to thy poor soul, my friend, my Fatherland!' " (510). But Zeitblom is more than mere narrator, like the nameless voice who speaks to us in *The Magic Mountain*. He is Adrian's oldest and most faithful friend, the Wagner to Adrian's Faust. Appropriately named Serenus, the mildly Catholic scholar of the classics is always mildly humanistic, a markedly qualified version—a dwindling—of Settembrini and Settembrinian presumption. Yet he can always react with the authority of civilization against Adrian's waywardness, even as, through his Boswell-like devotion and admiration, he proves his own devotion—however vicarious—to the demonic. And beyond these functions he supplies, out of all measure to his stature, the love of boundless capacity. In enumerating earlier those who almost lured Adrian back to the human realm, I did not speak of the self-effacing Zeitblom whose presence it is so easy to overlook—as Adrian overlooked it—but who, from his right earned in childhood to use the *du*, can claim a kind of priority of love that his unwavering affection, despite all, extended to the everlasting. For his love, conferred by an almost natural right, was there at the first, lingered even beyond the last, and so was without end.

There is also the simple devotion of Adrian's mother that is there at the first and at the last. She has been the eternal mother, simple and earthy, as his father has been the first representative of the uncanny. These are the oppositions which battle to become his exclusive inheritance so as to claim his exclusive allegiance. And we see from the first how mixed within him they are, his mother's appearance and musicality, his father's migraine and mysticism, and the eyes a blend of the two. Adrian, at his most driven, cannot leave the symbols of home and mother, so that he must find a place to spend his adult life that is a close replica of his family home in Buchel and that provides him in Frau Schweigestill a foster mother who has all the requisite and reminiscent qualities. It is she who utters the last words in Adrian's farewell scene with his companions, words of scorn directed at his shallow and shocked guests and of an unlimited compassion showered upon her errant foster child:

> Let me see the back of ye, all and sundry! City folk all, with not a smitch of understanding, and there's need of that here! Talked about th'everlasting mercy, poor soul, I don't know if it goes 's far's that, but human understanding, believe me, that doos! (503)

This recalls us to Adrian's dispute with the devil, echoed in his last words, in which, on the one hand, the possibility of grace increases with the sinner's depravity and, on the other, the awareness of this strange inversion precludes its accessibility to him—unless, of course, by increasing his depravity it makes salvation even more likely, except that . . . and on and on, round and round it goes, this "atrocious competition" between the sinner's speculation and God's Goodness. As we have seen, it is even further complicated by Nepomuk's death, the final desperation beyond parody, and the "expressiveness" that gives despair a voice. Frau Schweigestill's words suggest that the competitive chain is not infinite after all and that grace will have the last word—the totally and simply human grace of duty and devotion, of an "understanding" that passeth all understanding. It is this "understanding" beyond all reason, this true realization of the *thou*, that fosters Zeitblom's final words of prayer for a mercy that his own compassion has already granted. For Serenus has earlier assured us that this human love—that hears "with the throat," as Kyo says—this love that cannot be affected by what the object of that love "has done" is a version of the Everlasting Love:

> My life, insignificant but capable of fascination and devotion, has been dedicated to my love for a great German man and artist. It was always a love full of fear and dread, yet eternally faithful to this German whose inscrutable guiltiness and awful end had no power to affect my feeling for him—such love it may be as is only a reflection of the everlasting mercy. (452)

It had to be that the "Everlasting Goodness" with its infinite mercy would win the competition since, as everlasting, it necessarily outlasts the depravity that speculation only increases. Still it is only a moderate victory—a victory in retreat from the tragic—that it can win, using such mild instruments of human decency as Zeitblom and Frau Schweigestill. For the giant unrepentant figure of Adrian looms, towering beyond them and their miraculous gift of grace as it towers beyond Hans Castorp and his human hopes, threatening to continue rejecting all as temptation and to continue the competition from beyond the grave, from the underworld that has claimed him as he has claimed it uniquely as his own. So, looked at from the other-than-human side, the competition may not be ended after all, and every human miracle may be dissolved. For in Adrian's "non-Euclidean" world, any retreat from extremity would also be a giving up of the impossible salvation that is the only sort he can accept. The competition between the tragic and the human realms has created the tensions of Mann's most characteristic work; and here at the very end his wisdom must leave it in its irreducible Manichaean dualism. Those persuasive homely pieties, which may have served at the end of Hans Castorp's "stock-taking" education, can be sounded in *Doctor Faustus* only when Adrian is removed from the stage. But even then the classic and human acceptance must compete with the shrill *glissando* echoes of Adrian's immortal music and the tragic perseverance of his speculation that insist still on the mockery of fierce and willful denial.

CHAPTER FIVE

The World of Law as Pasteboard Mask

> Hark ye yet again—the little lower layer. All visible objects, man, are but as pasteboard masks. But in each event—in the living act, the undoubted deed—there, some unknown but still reasoning thing puts forth the mouldings of its features from behind the unreasoning mask. If man will strike, strike through the mask! How can the prisoner reach outside except by thrusting through the wall?
>
> Captain Ahab

1. Franz Kafka: Nonentity and the Tragic

The metaphor of captivity is obviously an apt one for the modern tragic visionary. It establishes him as outlaw, with the ethical world as his enemy and his judge, and fixes his role as the unyielding rebel who must continually try to thrust through the wall with which society contains him. Or his captivity may be viewed as metaphysical, with all of existence seen as an imprisonment within the blankness of enigmatic nothingness that threatens at any moment to strike. Is there a way in which both social and metaphysical levels may be urged at once, with the first seen finally as a symbolic reduction of the second? If so, the rebellion of the prisoner must be seen also as more than anti-legal, as one made not against the rest of us but in the name of the rest of us against the universal imprisoning agent that, implacable, threatens all alike.

The meaning of Kafka's *The Trial* rests precisely on how this issue is resolved: who is the imprisoning agent and in accordance with what law does he imprison? Or we may put it in terms of Ahab's metaphor: how reasoning is the unknown thing and what is its relation to its unreasoning mask? We seem to be offered the choice of approaching the novel politically or theologically. That is, we may view Joseph K. as innocent and the Court as exclusively irrational and unjust; or we may view K. as guilty and the Court as rational and just, even if its rationality and justice are incomprehensible to K. The first approach would seem to neglect the considerable evidence in the novel pointing to K.'s guilt as the second overrides the absurdities and contradictions of the Court as well as the evidence of its rottenness.

Of course, if one tries hard enough, he can manage all the evidence without giving up his hypothesis. Thus the political reader could say that K.'s frequent awareness of his guilt argues for rather than against a political interpretation, that it is not a sign of the Court's justice but a symptom of K.'s brainwashing by the ruthless organization that has badgered him into submission. And whatever hints there may be that the Court knows what it is doing—if they are more than the delusions, distortions read in by K.'s tormented soul—could be seen as suggesting the purposeful and even single-minded malevolence that lurks deceptively behind the seeming indifference of bureaucratic caprice. Thus one interpretation of Ahab's "reasoning thing" that tricks us and even lulls us with "the unreasoning mask." On the other hand, the theological reader could even more simply dispose of all arguments by merely reading all evidence for K. or against the Court as further indications of the inscrutability of the ways of God to man. The more absurd and the more unacceptable, the more conclusive it is in pointing to the Kierkegaardian deity and his trembling subject.

But how finally convincing are these claims? Is it not sophistic to make quite so free with Kafka's feverish insights, to unbend so blithely these involute coils that struggle to project Kafka's tortured imagination? Would he have made the problem of guilt seem so primary and developed it so carefully if he meant it all to be read as mere neurotic distortions? Or would he have shown the Court's contradictions to find expression in a corruptness that takes unquestionably obscene forms if he merely wished to emphasize its apparent absurdities? Are the details of the novel so casual and Kafka's shocking specification so wayward that they allow us to dismiss all indifferently as so many examples either of the cruel toying with K. or the austere baffling of him?

What can be gained by our worrying Kafka's details as if they were significant in their selection? Mainly, in being more attentive we could be more empirical instead of forcing *The Trial*, for all its complexity and, more important, its dramatic urgency, into a prearranged allegorical scheme. The more thoroughly we dwell on these details the more difficult it becomes to translate them convincingly into any single conceptual pattern. But we may be wrong if, seeing the disingenuousness of straining to marshal them to prove an argument, we rather consign them to the miscellaneous absurd that disguises an unambiguous theological commitment or to the senselessness that calls for psychoanalysis rather than criticism. And it is not mere obscurantism to urge that the novel resists systematic interpretation. We learn painfully that our intellect must suffer anticlimax upon anticlimax. Each time we meet someone apparently on the inside, the promise of illumination evaporates once again into the airiness of contradiction. Finally, in the Cathedral, we are certain that the Priest is about to present us with the key—and so he does, except that it locks closed doors instead of opening them. For every possible explanation of a crucial moment in his parable, an alternative and opposed explanation is also advanced. And the two are left standing side by side, so that this scene turns out to be but another version of our earlier disappointments at the hands of well-meaning informants like Huld and Titorelli, whose explanations of the workings of the Court also throw up obstacles to every approach that is confidently undertaken until only the riddle remains before us, unapproachable but still beckoning from afar, still thrusting forth its elusive and delusive emissaries.

Kafka's method is not to be confused with the dialectic of Kierkegaard in *Fear and Trembling* when he tries to approach the inmost secret of the *Akedah*, the Abraham-Isaac story. For there the many possible meanings eliminate each other in order to point to a final interpretation that is to be seen as inevitable. There is a way right up to the parable, and one only. For Kafka there is only the irreducible dramatic complex that is his fable, Aristotelian and not Aesopian. It will not open to any discursive probing. If his terms do not translate into a single answer, it is not because he perversely and mockingly prefers to hide it but because he has not got it. As a poet who thinks in images, Kafka as fable maker sees the maddening nest of possible and yet incompatible relations as somehow being out there in experience, embedded in it, but beyond rational extrapolation. He is not an allegorist, not because he will not be one, but because he cannot. Indeed, it often seems that, unlike many poets, Kafka would have preferred to be one. Perhaps as a would-be allegorist, it is his inability to find a solution that causes the unfinished state of his work, so that in the strange case of Kafka metaphysical incompleteness causes aesthetic incompleteness. Often, as we saw, for example, in Gide with his "state of dialogue," philosophic confusion can, through the tension generated by the conflict, allow the poetic realm its power and its balance. But not so for Kafka, dependent as he was upon an allegory that would not come. Yet it is our blessing that it would not, that his struggles with the mass of paradoxical possibilities only created absurdities beyond which he could not move even as within them he could not rest. For what he thought of as his failure is, by very reason of that failure, of indispensable help to us.

The most serious problem that concerns K.'s guilt must, then, be approached from below, from the details of the novel, and these more from the narrative itself than from mere occasional admissions by K. or continual insistences by the Court. Evidence of the latter sort that stems from direct testimony occurs in abundance from the start: from that time K. seemingly without reason considers the possibility of suicide and blurts out, "But this isn't the capital charge yet," (14) [1] and from the early claims by the not very respectable warders that even the lowest Court officials can make no mistake and "never go hunting for crime in the populace, but, as the Law decrees, are drawn towards the guilty . . ." (10). But we need more narrative support if we are to know how we are to take these apparent confessions and claims, since there is so much in the novel to counteract them. K.'s guilt is most persuasively revealed by his failure of the test he undergoes through the story. He has of course been similarly guilty before his arrest. We must remember that, if the most fearsome characteristic of the Court under which K. suffers is its mystique of hierarchy, this is precisely the characteristic of his role in the Bank that K. has most cherished and throughout the novel tries to protect. After his preliminary interview with the Inspector, K. is left greatly disturbed by the discovery that all has been witnessed by three of his bank clerks and, even more, by the fact that the Inspector refers to them as his "colleagues":

> These insignificant anaemic young men . . . were actually clerks in the Bank, not colleagues of his, that was putting it too strongly and indicated a gap in the omniscience of the Inspector, but they were subordinate employees of the Bank all the same. (21)

It does not occur to him that the Inspector does not bother to recognize these trivial distinctions, perhaps out of a self-importance that characterizes the Court's mystique of hierarchy,

[1] From *The Trial*, by Franz Kafka, trans. Willa Muir and Edwin Muir (New York: Alfred A. Knopf, Inc., 1946). Copyright 1937 by Alfred A. Knopf, Inc. All page references are to the 1946 edition. Excerpts are reprinted with the permission of Alfred A. Knopf, Inc.

against which K. is bitterly to complain and of which his own is a reflection. And later, back at the Bank, he tries to relax:

> Once order was restored, every trace of these events would be obliterated and things would resume their old course. From the three clerks themselves nothing was to be feared, they had been absorbed once more in the great hierarchy of the Bank, no change was to be remarked in them. K. had several times called them singly and collectively to his room, with no other purpose than to observe them; each time he had dismissed them again with a quiet mind. (24)

The dull "aesthetic" routine of K.'s life must be restored, the routine of the Bank and even the routine of the evenings:

> That spring K. had been accustomed to pass his evenings in this way: after work whenever possible—he was usually in his office until nine—he would take a short walk, alone or with some of his colleagues, and then go to a beer hall, where until eleven he sat at a table patronized mostly by elderly men. But there were exceptions to this routine, when, for instance, the Manager of the Bank, who highly valued his diligence and reliability, invited him for a drive or for dinner at his villa. And once a week K. visited a girl called Elsa, who was on duty all night till early morning as a waitress in a cabaret and during the day received her visitors in bed. (23)

It is just this loyalty to his routine role that leads him to betray a rare human impulse. The moment occurs during the nightmarish scene in the lumber room where K. discovers the original two warders about to be whipped, apparently because of his complaint against them. Since K.'s struggle is not with the pitiful creatures but with the Court, he feels called upon to intervene on behalf of Franz and Willem. He tries to bribe the whipper without immediate success. But K. breaks off the possibility of further negotiation when, after Franz shrieks at the first stroke and the bank clerks are about to appear, he slams the door on the scene. And to protect himself further he turns the clerks away, accounting for the noise as "only a dog howling in the courtyard" (110). Earlier in the scene K. had told the whipper, speaking of his concern for the warders, "I could simply leave, shut this door after me, close my eyes and ears, and go home; but I don't want to do that, I really want to see them set free . . ." (109). Of course he does do precisely what he wanted not to do as soon as his intervention threatens to compromise him. After turning his back on the scene, K. laments how, if Franz had controlled himself and thus given K. a few more moments with the whipper, he would probably have succeeded in liberating the warders.

> But at the moment when Franz began to shriek, any intervention became impossible. K. could not afford to let the dispatch clerks and possibly all sorts of other people arrive and surprise him in a scene with these creatures in the lumber-room. No one could really demand that sacrifice from him. (111)

Yet K. is given other chances to commit himself to save those whose punishment he has caused. After the clerks withdraw, he passes the lumber room and almost opens the door once more. But it is too late, he persuades himself, promising to make the Court officials pay for their crimes. Late the next day he does open the door only to find the identical scene as the day before, the whipper ready to whip and the warders ready to plead. But not again for K.: "At once K. slammed the door shut and beat on it with his fists, as if that would shut it still more securely" (113). And he orders the clerks to clean the room out, to introduce into it the order of the Bank that would render it proof to further discomforting invasions. He must have succeeded, for neither he nor we hear further of the warders he has three times denied.

Thus, despite the shock of arrest that disrupts the routine of the Bank executive's career, he yet clings to it, unaware that in its mystique of hierarchy the Bank is essentially allied to the absurdities of the Court that madden him. Nor does he recognize that he cannot protect his role in the Bank without protecting the Court; that he cannot secure the former without helping the latter to destroy all security; finally, that his allegiance to his pre-shock ambitions deprives him of the right to make his self-righteous claims against the mystagogic proceedings of the Court. Yet, contradictory as they seem, K. must desperately hang onto both sets of values—the pre-shock and the post-shock, those of the Bank careerist and of him who would resist the Court. Committed as he is to his defense, he is always regretfully aware of "what an obstacle had suddenly arisen to block K.'s career!" (168) As he thinks of drawing up his plea, he comes to see how much his work for the Bank is suffering at the hands of his work against the Court:

> But at this time when K. should be devoting his mind entirely to work, when every hour was hurried and crowded—for he was still in full career and rapidly becoming a rival even to the Deputy Manager—when his evenings and nights were all too short for the pleasures of a bachelor life, this was the time when he must sit down to such a task! (162)

But the Bank routine does suffer as his distraction grows—and his position at the Bank (and, apparently, before the Court) worsens. Even the submerged aggressiveness of the paranoiac finally reveals itself as K. suspects plots are being laid against him and can soothe himself while thinking of the ascendancy of his rival, the Deputy Manager, only with the promise: "I'm not equal to him just now, but once my personal difficulties are settled he'll be the first to feel it, and I'll make him suffer for it, too" (177).

K. can yet ask, in words that significantly relate the world of the Bank to the world of the Court and that link his guilt at Court to his refusal to abandon his pursuit of the Bank hierarchy:

> While his case was unfolding itself, while up in the attics the Court clerks were poring over the charge papers, was he to devote his attention to the affairs of the Bank? It looked like a

> kind of torture sanctioned by the Court, arising from his case and concomitant with it. And would allowances be made for his peculiar position when his work in the Bank came to be judged? Never, and by nobody. (168)

So the Court's is not the only final judgment whose mysterious source K. must fear. The torture does indeed seem to be sanctioned by the Court, as both torture and test: perhaps every absurdity about the Court becomes a kind of punishment as appropriate for K. as those we find designed for the damned in Dante. For K.'s is not any abstract doctrinal guilt; it is a clearly specified guilt found in his acts and attitudes. We need not restrict ourselves to notions of an original sin shared with all men when the novel furnishes us with a convincing *dossier*—though, of course, it may be a *dossier* similar to those we could make on all men. K. concedes as much when, having determined to bend all his business talents to undertake his own defense and to "eliminate from his mind the idea of possible guilt" (160), he sees that in his first plea "the whole of one's life would have to be passed in review, down to the smallest actions and accidents, clearly formulated and examined from every angle" (162). This is an admission of the extensive possibilities of guilt in what is being charged, and we have already seen in general and in detail how vulnerable K.'s life, like everyone's, is to such austere and exhaustive probing. K.'s anxieties over these hopeless difficulties lead to his collapse before the manufacturer's important business deal, as he gratefully sees it taken over by his hated rival, the Deputy Manager.

We are beginning to see, then, that there is also in K. that which dedicates him to the obsessive pursuit of his case and of his fight against the Court, whatever the cost to his career. For K. is also a special sort of antagonist of the Court—even a rebel against it in his unrelenting guardianship of his "rights" (161) and his dedication to matters of ethical "principle" (107). It is these opposed drives—for the Bank affairs (leading to collaboration with the Court) and against the Court (leading to subversion of the Bank affairs)—that tear K. apart. They can perhaps allow us to make some sense of the paradox that finds K. both utterly unique and a mere common cipher before the Court. Of course many others besides K. have been accused, have presumably been arrested one fine morning without having done anything wrong. The essence of the Court and of the Law, especially as revealed in the bureaucratic form they take in this novel, is to treat man generically rather than uniquely. It must be granted that much of what seems unique in what happens to K. may stem from the fact that his subjective view is all we have, that each case is surely individual to the man on trial, and that for him the question of guilt and injustice is unique. In Malraux's terms—terms that reveal his existentialist bias—K.'s is a voice we hear with the throat rather than with the ears, the voice of "the madman . . . the incomparable monster, dear above all things, that every being is to himself and that he cherishes in his heart" (*Man's Fate*, 59). So in one sense the uniqueness of the commonplace K.—commonplace in the Bank and commonplace before the Court—can be traced, it may seem, to the uniqueness of his existential moment, like those of all of us when viewed by the world of law and reason, but totally unique when viewed subjectively. It is the uniqueness of *his* nightmare that Conrad's Marlow will tell us one dreams alone and cannot communicate. To the extent that we are limited by K.'s view and K.'s subjective awareness, we may be foolish to look here for objective claims about the nature and extent of man's generic guilt.

Yet much of K.'s treatment *is* unique, it seems, even to the special and sometimes loving pains many people connected with the Court take with him, while at the same time it is the impersonal inefficiency of the enormous machine that maddens him. This impossibly messy and corrupt octopus, the ubiquitous Court, is yet one which overlooks no one, loses no documents, "never forgets anything" (199). Left on his own to get to Court that first Sunday, K. is lost in the human wilderness of the building but decides to manage his way himself, confirming—in what is a strange admission—that if as Willem said "an attraction existed between the Law and guilt" (45), then he would necessarily choose the alternatives that would lead him to the interrogation chamber. He asks fruitlessly at door after door for a man whose name he has invented and, with no further questions asked about the man or K.'s quest, is admitted at once and knowingly to the chamber by a woman who tells him, "I must shut this door after you, nobody else must come in" (47). Surely this line echoes menacingly in the priest's parable at the end when the doorkeeper tells the man waiting a lifetime for admittance to the Law, who wonders about all the others who must be seeking similarly, "No one but you could gain admittance through this door, since this door was intended only for you. I am now going to shut it" (270–271).

This network of insolubles is connected to that other which finds in various forms the repeated assertion that, while K. has been arrested for guilt by a Court that has sought him out, the arrest and the trial can take place only through K.'s collaboration: only, that is to say, if he recognizes them as such. The morning of his arrest he makes various small concessions that he feels compelled to make even though he senses with the shrewdness of his business tact that he should not be making them since they constitute an acknowledgment of the rationality and perhaps even the justness of the absurd procedures that have begun to unfold. And he never gets over the feeling that, if he had insisted on his routine that morning and had recognized nothing amiss, all would have evaporated. As he tells Frau Grubach,

> If immediately on wakening I had got up without troubling my head about Anna's absence and had come to you without regarding anyone who tried to bar my way, I could have breakfasted in the kitchen for a change and could have got you to bring me my clothes from my room; in short, if I had behaved sensibly, nothing further would have happened, all this would have been nipped in the bud. But one is so unprepared. In the Bank, for instance, I am always prepared, nothing of that kind could possibly happen to me there, I have my own attendant,

> the general telephone and the office telephone stand before me on my desk, people keep coming in to see me, clients and clerks, and above all my mind is always on my work and so kept on the alert, it would be an actual pleasure to me if a situation like that cropped up in the Bank. (26–27)

The "aesthetic" routine, the very activities at the Bank that his trial totally disrupts and incapacitates him for, could have prevented it all. The security of his own carefully nourished and cherished absurdities, of his own mystique, would have rendered him invulnerable to this assault inflicted by strange absurdities and a hostile mystique. Thanks to his routine and his living "in a country with a legal constitution," with "universal peace" and "all the laws . . . in force" (7), K. needed never to worry beyond the aesthetic: "He had always been inclined to take things easily, to believe in the worst only when the worst happened, to take no care for the morrow even when the outlook was threatening" (7). Yet here he throws over all to recognize the trial, and recognizes it in order to commit himself to total warfare against it, although there remains that in him which would deny it and would rather turn back to the secure mystique of the Bank. In the first interrogation, too, K. insists that "it is only a trial if I recognize it as such" (51), which is what his proud self-assurance leads him to do in order to win his victory. When one week later he loses the Law-Court Attendant's wife to the student at Court and future official, acting on behalf of the Examining Magistrate, K. "recognized that this was the first unequivocal defeat that he had received from these people. . . . he had received the defeat only because he had insisted on giving battle" (73).

His recognition of the trial and his commitment to it—in short, his forcing the issue to be joined—engage him more and more, as he moves from an indifferent acceptance of Huld as his advocate to a total involvement in Huld's activities in his behalf and even beyond to a dismissal of Huld for not being active enough as K. takes the case into his own hands. There is finally that crucial moment in the Cathedral which is a kind of symbolic reduction of the whole trial. K. is about to leave when the priest's voice rolls "through the expectant Cathedral" calling K.'s name in words "unambiguous and inescapable" (263–264). K. has his final choice:

> For the moment he was still free, he could continue on his way and vanish through one of the small dark wooden doors that faced him at no great distance. It would simply indicate that he had not understood the call, or that he had understood it and did not care. But if he were to turn round he would be caught, for that would amount to an admission that he had understood it very well, that he was really the person addressed, and that he was ready to obey. (264)

And as he does everywhere else in the novel, despite his Bank-clerk propensities, he turns to acknowledge all. In so doing he totally abandons hope for "a mode of living completely outside the jurisdiction of the Court" (267) and instead invites the parable of the doorkeeper whose appropriateness his confronting action has affirmed. The priest, as well-intentioned prison chaplain bringing K. this final bitter comfort before execution, closes by confirming the need for the recognition that K. has continually tendered: "The Court makes no claims upon you. It receives you when you come and it relinquishes you when you go" (279). After all, we must remember that in the priest's parable the man seeking admittance to the law "is really free, he can go where he likes . . . When he sits down on the stool by the side of the door and stays there for the rest of his life, he does it of his own free will; in the story there is no mention of any compulsion" (275). And at the last moment during "the odious ceremonial of courtesy" (287), K. knows he must recognize the execution too, and recognize it by collaborating with it: "K. now perceived clearly that he was supposed to seize the knife himself, as it travelled from hand to hand above him, and plunge it into his own breast" (287). He cannot manage it but recognizes his failure and feels profound shame in leaving it to the executioners. His shameful recognition of failure is his recognition of the propriety of the proceedings, the recognition that enables him to accept the execution—and thus to allow it—despite the weakness of his lingering hopes.

One point is crucially clear: K.'s is the only case that we hear of as being brought to a final conclusion, and a final conviction. And this occurs, despite all the alternatives and all the bureaucratic inefficiency, within the incredibly brief space of a single year. For the novel begins with K.'s arrest on his thirtieth birthday and closes with his execution on the eve of his thirty-first. Thus while, as Max Brod tells us, the novel is incomplete and "in a certain sense . . . was interminable" and "could be prolonged into infinity" (296–297), in another sense it is totally finite and finished. For whatever the possible number of intermediate chapters, the end is immovably there setting its limits; and it is, for the Court, an unprecedentedly quick one.

But K. has been a most unusual accused. His attitude in the first interrogation is markedly arrogant, as the Court takes pains to inform him; he struggles with Court officialdom over the Examining Magistrate's woman; he alone does what many have threatened to do but what none have dared do when he dismisses his advocate; and confronted with the more compromising but more tolerated alternatives of "ostensible acquittal" and "indefinite postponement," he seems from all that follows to have determined to pursue nothing less than the unobtainable "definitive acquittal" (192). There is also that Sunday morning in the Court's waiting room where K., feeling himself a mere visitor, believes himself nobly distinguished from the other accused, all of them sitting about so futilely and meekly in patient anticipation of nothing, simply to show their subservience. K. is certain that none of his "colleagues" believe he is one of them and is proud of the dignity he believes misleads them. He treats these meek anticipants disdainfully, high-handedly, and finally with crude violence. Angered that the one he has picked on will not acknowledge the self-possessed K. as an accused, a most unusual accused, K. proudly surmises that he is being taken for a Judge. A short time later K. returns to the hall and to the very man he has mistreated, but he has himself been reduced to a helpless state of near collapse. A more important reflection on this scene is furnished later by Block, the commercial traveler, who disabuses K. of his misinterpretation of that first scene in the waiting room. The submissive suitors at Court reacted to K. as they did, not because they thought he was a Judge or because they were impressed with his fiery resistance to the Court, but because—consistent with an old superstition among the accused—from K.'s face, "especially the line of his lips" (219), they could tell he was shortly to be found guilty. And they reacted with horror. Here, then, is another indication of how uncommon an accused K. is, for surely Kafka is suggesting that it is the grim determination to resist absolutely that the set of K.'s lips must have revealed to the fellow-accused. And K.'s inexcusable actions toward them, together with the haughtiness of motive we see as responsible for these actions, prove the accuracy of the prophecy. Perhaps they are an anticipation of his treatment of the warders in the whipping scene we have examined.

K.'s role as both representative and exceptional—as everyman and as rebel, as man before the Law and as *the* man before the Law—is helpfully conclusive. There is undoubtedly a specialness and an aloneness about K.'s case, besides the uniqueness each accused must feel subjectively about his own. Not only is he outside the vast community of those who have not been accused, but he stands apart from the more limited group of the other accused. What we see of those like the deputy manager of the Bank and K.'s uncle, still living—as K. was before his thirtieth birthday—outside the jurisdiction of the Court, should convince us that they are hardly less guilty than K. If anything, they are less worthy, perhaps with a commonness that nothing could raise to the uniquely human level. We cannot help being irked by the fact that the unaccused do not respond with shock to the strange circumstances of K.'s arrest and the strange kind of Court which is trying him. Like Job's comforters, they all seem to assume that somehow K. must have been guilty to have been arrested. The unaccused are in fact, then, protectors of the Court in that they accept its absurdities as sensible and its Law as rational. They accept K.'s guilt of a crime of which they must be innocent since they have not been accused. And since they have not been accused and *they* know themselves innocent, then the Court must know what it is doing in arresting K.

Undoubtedly K., in the days before he was accused, reacted similarly. Indeed, it is in his reversions to his pre-arrest psychology and in the defense of his pre-arrest respectability and position that K. has been seen to be also a protector of the Court. Those who are unaccused or who have not yet been accused have accepted the absurd as rational simply because it exists and has spared them so that they need not examine it and may rest confident of the justness of its operation. For one to be arrested is for him to be hurled by an external shock into recognizing the absurd as absurd and thus into finding it no longer acceptable now that it has picked on him. The novel thus becomes a metaphor of the awakening to what Marlow will term the "touch of insanity in the proceeding," the "sense of lugubrious drollery" that characterizes worldly caprice.

The accused are the most worthy since in their necessary recognition they reveal themselves as those who are ready for the ultimate and terrorizing confrontation. When Frau Grubach tells K. of his trial, "It gives me the feeling of something very learned . . . of something abstract which I don't understand, but which I don't need to understand either" (26), we recognize the pre-shock complacency of one who can never be tried. But I have said K. is unique also among the accused. We see others pitiably patient in the waiting room, we meet Block at length, and we hear of others. No other trials are reported as finished, no other sentence passed. No other accused has dismissed his advocate, although we learn from Block that in a moment of impatient rebellion he too once entertained the notion of dismissing his advocate. In contrast, however, to those early spirited days, there is the harrowing scene played for K.'s benefit when Block is made to crawl before Huld and is thankful for the opportunity to do so. The other accused, who may, like K., have begun in the spirit of rebellion, have been beaten into submission. They work for their cases continually and so does K; but they work in humility as he works in pride. As K.'s insistence on "definitive acquittal" indicates, he demands, with the firmness of a newly won rational and ethical conviction, nothing but justice. The other accused plead not for justice but for mercy, for grace—which explains why the advocate bears the strange name of Huld and why he cannot serve for K.

Albert Camus was wrong, then, in scornfully linking Kafka with Kierkegaard as among those who leapt blindly to faith instead of revolting in the face of the absurd. For in what has been said about K. we see where Kafka breaks from Kierkegaard. Those accused who bend the knee to embrace the absurd in quest of grace yet know it to be the absurd since they have passed through K's stage of rebellion that follows upon arrest; they are less than K. and are to be contemned. The dogged and destructive rebellion is higher than the leap for Kafka since the leap is induced under pressures that make it a disguise for a "failure of nerve."

In another way too, then, K. is both exceptional and representative. In his "stage along life's way" he shares something with all the others even as he stands alone. There is still in him a remnant of the pre-shock mentality of all the unaccused of whom he has once been one; he is in the early stage of rebellion through which the other accused apparently have passed; and he has open to him the way of meekness taken by the others, to which he is urged but which he rejects. He will not be chastised, not even by the priest and in the face of threats, and remains in the abortive state of rebellion refusing to accept less than legal justice even while acknowledging the possibility of guilt on other grounds. He has chosen for himself the role of everyman-Jesus even though he tacitly but continually rejects the rest of mankind as he is tacitly but continually rejected by them.

We have already seen K. as totally isolated from his kind, first from the unaccused and then from the other accused. But this isolation is a reflection of the isolation of the "aesthetic," pre-shock K. After all, as we see in what we are told of K.'s earlier life and in the scene with the whipper, the pursuit of the Bank values is hardly conducive to the warmth of personal relations. Rather, it forces persons to be reduced to things. Once arrested, however, K. feels the need to seek a new and unprecedented acceptance by others. Without exception he fails. The evening of his arrest he returns home determined to enlist Frau Grubach's sympathies. For some strange reason he is most concerned that she shake his hand, in part perhaps because the Inspector earlier refused to. But, newly accused, he is not so easily to be taken into the human community. Frau Grubach speaks with all the sympathy that is conventionally appropriate, "with tears in her voice, forgetting, naturally, to shake his hand" (27). Considerably dejected, K. at once asks about Fräulein Bürstner in hopes of pursuing another candidate. He lies in wait for her until late in the night when he forces himself upon her in hopes of finding some intimate contact with her. Her weary indifference is beyond tolerance, but he takes advantage of it to assault her with spiritual and physical demands she can neither resist nor meet. When he asks if she is angry, she answers in a way that reveals her total lack of personal discrimination: "I'm never angry with anybody" (38). In the days and months that follow, K. pursues this first night's advantage, but to no avail. Indeed, he never has another chance at her. She has Fräulein Montag move in with her to help keep K. off. K.'s growing paranoia, under the pressure of a groundless accusation that has capriciously singled him out, sees Fräulein Montag as hypocritically malevolent in her designs to keep him ostracized.

There are the other women who befriend him, the Law-Court Attendant's wife and of course Leni. But invariably K. sees in them a promise that they never fulfill. He is astounded at the immediacy with which they offer themselves to him and proffer him help in his case, only in each case to see them turn with casual indiscriminateness to someone else, the Law-Court Attendant's wife to the student pimp of the Examining Magistrate and Leni to Block. Indeed, of Leni we learn that she finds "nearly all accused men attractive" (231). In the scene among K., Block, and Leni, K. is somewhat disturbed at Leni's discussing Block in the latter's presence "as if he were absent." But a moment later she begins to speak to Block and K. must observe, "Now it's my turn to be treated as if I were absent" (227). Throughout the novel, then, K. seeks a unique relation with women, one that can humanize him, and is continually forced to recognize that he cannot move beyond the indifference of thinghood in their eyes. As in Sartre, sexual relations dehumanize, prevent rather than assure any true union of persons. But once again is not K. being punished precisely as he deserves, since surely his earlier relations with Elsa were precisely of this limited and life-denying sort? Once he is arrested, however, even in the limited sexual realm K. is frustrated more than he is fulfilled.

Fräulein Bürstner makes a final crucial appearance in the execution scene at the end—if it is really she, for K. has his doubts. The two executioners walk on either side of K., fastening his arms within theirs. We are told, "K. walked rigidly between them, the three of them were interlocked in a unity which would have brought all three down together had one of them been knocked over. It was a unity such as can be formed almost by lifeless elements alone" (283). We must note ironically that K. has here achieved the only unity he has found in the novel. But K. is not ready to accept a unity of "lifeless elements" and can think only of rebellion, of struggling against them desperately to the end—as he puts it, like a fly on flypaper. And the one consolation: "The gentlemen won't find it easy" (284). Suddenly Fräulein Bürstner appears, or someone very much like her. It matters not to K. so long as "he might not forget the lesson she had brought into his mind" (284). And why should it matter whether it was uniquely she when uniqueness was the one characteristic their relation most lacked, however strongly K. wished for it. The lesson clearly is his realization of the "futility of resistance" about which he has now come to feel there would be "nothing heroic" (284). For what reason could Fräulein Bürstner lead him from rebellion to resignation except that her appearance or the reminder of her forces him to recognize his failure to make any truly human contact? From the beginning she has been symbolic of the futility of communion in the dehumanized world of the Bank which K. has represented. In representing it he has created for himself a burden of guilt which has undercut his right to find a new human relation, to resist the Court and find a new heroism. Having followed her for some blocks while turning his rebellion inward upon himself, he now pursues her no farther since he can "do without her" (285). He yields to his new-found comrades, and the three now walk on "in complete harmony," "in a solid front." K. seems thankful for the union he has achieved, despite its "lifeless" forebodings, and is anxious to do nothing to shake it. When a suspicious policeman threatens to intervene in the proceedings, the executioners are intimidated and stop. But the no longer isolated K. becomes the Court's prime protector by leading them hurriedly away from him and to safety —and, it should be added, to the quarry, the place of the execution which the safety K. has consciously afforded them can now allow them to perform.

But the resolution is more deceptive and the ending more ambivalent than this. We have seen already K.'s inability to manage the final collaboration of stabbing himself. At this point he unlearns his lesson and turns feebly, futilely, back to the humanity which has rejected him as he rejected it, which has thrown him into the unity of "lifeless elements."

> His glance fell on the top storey of the house adjoining the quarry. With a flicker as of a light going up, the casements of a window there suddenly flew open; a human figure, faint and insubstantial at that distance and that height, leaned abruptly far forward and stretched both arms still farther. Who was it? A friend? A good man? Someone who sympathized? Someone

who wanted to help? Was it one person only? Or were they all there? Was help at hand? (287–288)

The impossible if undying hopes for salvation are accompanied by the return of his doubts about the Court. It is this final, almost self-mocking counter-turn that leads K. to acknowledge in his last words that he dies "like a dog" (288). For humanity has *not* stretched forward to him and *he* has not stretched forward to embrace his fate, one which might allow him to transcend his unreceptive fellow man and himself as unreceptive creature. Further, his admission that he dies like a dog must recall that early scene with the whipper when he traded human compassion for Bank respectability by insisting to the clerks that Franz's shriek "was only a dog howling in the courtyard" (110). Having slammed the door then, how could K. expect now that the window would open and the human figure stretch forward in his behalf?

In the earlier scene, in order to keep himself disinvolved with either the lumber-room atrocities or the curious Bank clerks whom the noise has summoned, K. tries to be preoccupied by opening and leaning out of the window into a little courtyard, through the darkness of which he tries to pierce to find something. So there it is K. who leans out of the window, but, we must note, in order to turn his back on humanity, not to stretch forward to it. For what he looks for in the courtyard has just offered itself to him in the lumber room and he has rejected it. Consequently, he is in effect looking only toward the final scene (as perhaps the presence of the hand-barrows in the courtyard testifies), acting out the role of the leaning figure of false promise seen by the prostrate K. At another crucial moment toward the end Kafka uses windows as an isolating force, however deceptive may be their transparence, or the ease with which they open, in promising a way for human beings to stretch forward to one another. At the start of the final chapter, as K. is summoned to join his executioners, he pauses in his room to look out of his window at those opposite. What he sees should persuade him—even before the lesson Fräulein Bürstner is to teach him—that the inhumane way of his world dooms man, for all his stretching forward, never to grasp another to himself:

> Nearly all the windows at the other side of the street were also in darkness; in many of them the curtains were drawn. At one lighted tenement window some babies were playing behind bars, reaching with their little hands towards each other although not able to move themselves from the spot. (282)

No wonder, then, that K. later makes one final gesture of desperate futility in response to that figure stretching forward from the window far away and far above him: "He raised his hands and spread out all his fingers" (288). It is a gesture that matches the figure's in its abortiveness. Together the figure and K. are the babies "playing behind bars," although the prisoner K. is now played out, since it is at this moment that the dog's death is inflicted upon him.

There is yet another point of union between the final scene and the earlier one, in which we found K. escaping the whipper and the Bank clerks by looking out of the window. The courtyard into which the window opens seems all too much like the one in Gide that we have twice seen with Michel at Biskra. For while looking, K. becomes aware of the "faint reflection of the moon" (111). He cannot, of course, be aware of its deathlike qualities, of the fact that his actions at this moment are helping to deprive him of any right to resist the Court or to hope for human aid, are leading him to that moonlit scene at the end. In view of his lack of awareness, of the indirect relevance of these early actions, and of the distance he has to travel to his doom, no wonder this early moon is faint and is reflected (reflected, we must remember, by the closed, darkened windows). Following upon K.'s momentary reconciliation in the final scene, the moon—again as in *The Immoralist* and also as in Gerald's death march in *Women in Love*—is in full control, dissolving all complexity: "The moon shone down on everything with that simplicity and serenity which no other light possesses" (286). But K.'s indecision returns us to complexity, except that his actions during that earlier scene under a fainter and reflected moon allow him no claim to complexity, but only the death of a howling dog—the dog he created—under an awesome simplicity that has looked down unshaken.

Is this symbolic use of the moon and is this final conviction of K. to be taken as evidence that after all the Court is just and straightforward, so that the confusion is all the product of K.'s finitude and his guilt? From what I said at the start, obviously I cannot believe it is as simple as this. For we have had sufficient indication that at many points, instead of representing the purity of a demanding transcendent reality, the Court is a fearfully complex reflection of the absurdities of life that are revealed when the shock strikes. Its only purity is the purity of the distillate: the Court seems to be the extreme form of hierarchical and mystagogic absurdity pursued for its own sake, in its many-faced (or many-masked) inscrutable intention defying comprehension. This is the hierarchical and mystagogic absurdity that revenges itself on those who have unconsciously been practicing it but are keen enough to recognize the consequences of arrest. It illuminates the inanities, not of a transcendent realm, but of our sublunary one.

And what else should we expect when all we see of the Court are its tireless and wearisome activities in this world? Indeed, like a secret death it lies hidden in the very bones and marrow of the world. "There are Law-Court offices in almost every attic" (206), Titorelli tells the astounded K., who can only remember all the pre-arrest days when, with an obliviousness he shared with all the unaccused, he never knew of the Court's existence at all. Now he must recognize that, as the painter has also told him, "everything belongs to the Court" (189). It is the doom that the world, with the cruelty of worldly existence, bears within itself. To be arrested, then, is to be forced to see through to it and, with hindsight, to be horrified at what life is as it is refracted and purified in the Court. So K., even as he fights the absurdity the Court calls logic with his own logic—the "principle" he has discovered and must now champion—is also struck by the absurdity of the Court as a way of life, the Bank's way of life with people scrambling for position in the mystique of hierarchy when, unknown to them, the fatal and transforming arrest can strike at any moment. For it is the arrest that reveals the unexamined way of life to have been a way of death.

But how can the Court be no more than the obscene bureaucratic monster that reflects the obscenity, bureaucracy, and monstrosity of K.'s world when we have ample and unquestionable testimony of its infallibility, its absolute care and ultimate efficiency, even its justness? Surely there is some perfect authority beyond the lowly ones we hear so much about. The Higher Court that somehow stands behind the Lower is one K. does not see and none of his well-initiated informants can report knowing about. If Huld or Titorelli speaks of higher officials, he must hasten to add something anticlimactic like "higher officials of subordinate rank, naturally" (149). Clearly, then, the Higher Court is one that transcends the phenomenal world hereabout, the social-political world that suffers from Bank-sickness. Clearly, too, its justice must transcend the shabby and arbitrary pretences of its worldly reflection—or rather distortion—in the corrupt Lower Court. We must grant so much to the theological interpretation: as the Lower Court represents the impersonal, often capricious, often cruel, and sometimes methodically irrational operations of worldly law, so the Higher Court must represent the ultimate and ultimately sublime rationale of God. Thus K. must be at once legally innocent—and in this sense he has been wrongly and capriciously seized upon—and yet in some more essential way guilty, as we all are. This guilt, I must repeat, is in the novel: not just the abstract notion of original sin but what we find reflected in his actual commission of inhumane actions, in his very assumption of an inhumane way as his way of life. Thus K.'s arrest may stem from the typical blundering of worldly officialdom, the wrongful accusation that is one of the faces of existent moral evil, so that the Lower Court is in error and is viciously stubborn in refusing to acknowledge it. But it turns out that after all they really need not bother to, that from the supra-legalistic Higher Court view, a view that watches K. being tried through the novel, K. has been guilty after all, so that the Lower Court need never bother specifying its charge. K. specifies it for them continually from the moment of his arrest.

From the Higher Court view, then, K. is as guilty as the legally guilty, so that he has no grounds for a defense based on his innocence. K. senses as much when he plans the writing of his plea and knows he shall have to defend his every action as man. Yet he cannot accept this irrational notion of theological guilt—the guilt of a man who has broken no laws "in a country with a legal constitution" and with "all the laws . . . in force" (7). The other unaccused, persuaded of their own innocence and thus of the justness and orderliness of the rule of law since as innocent they are also unaccused, must maintain the rational assumptions that underlie their security by assuming the guilt of K. since he *is* accused. They will not distinguish between the lower and higher levels of the Court or, for that matter, between this Court and the normally constituted legal courts.[2] But K.,

[2] The greatest obstacle for the critic who would trace without a leap the movement in *The Trial* from the literal to the symbolic levels is Kafka's failure to relate in any workable way "the Court in the Palace of Justice" to "the one with the skylight" (131). K.'s use of these terms acknowledges the distinction, as does Huld's comparison between "an Advocate for ordinary legal rights and an Advocate for cases like these" (236). I am unable to do more than dodge this obstacle since I am unable to clear it. Here is the point where Kafka's aesthetic incompleteness shows, where the pure symbolist and the allegorist *manqué* struggle with each other inconclusively in the mist. How much more promising, for example, is the arrangement with which Dickens begins in *Bleak House*, where the legal court and the absurd court merge in the impossible actuality of Chancery. The world of social-economic reality and of nightmarish fantasy, the political and metaphysical levels have a single narrative source full enough to sustain both at once. We feel the symbol of Chancery as Dickens creates it supports an equal sense of cogency on either level.

forced to apply the rational faculty his successful career at the Bank has sharpened, erects his reasonableness into an ethical principle that resists the unreasonable demand of the Court. While sensing continually that his past way of life is somehow relevant to the question of his guilt, he yet cannot concede this relevance. Having committed no crime against society's law, he must maintain his innocence. No more guilty than the unaccused, nor differently guilty from them, he must claim to be bullied and must fight the injustice of an absolute power whose power cannot, for K., make it right. His attitude, at its strongest, approaches that of Ivan Karamazov, who rejects God's world, who returns the ticket to His paradise rather than accept it at the price of worldly injustice that defies and destroys human reason.

But this rooting of the symbolic level in the bedrock of a detailed social reality comes at a cost. For Rick Carstone, Chancery is more than just an oppressive social institution capable of reform; it is rather an unshakeable and suprahistorical curse upon the human condition. Totally irrational, bathed in the accretion of fogs of many generations, run by an enormous machinery of dehumanized creatures who justify what they cannot control, this monstrous collection of debris asserts itself upon the suitor before the court—born into the case or thrust into it—with the promise of a total resolution that it cannot help but frustrate and a bright future that it cannot help but blight. Its monumental absurdity that promises the clarity of order attracts irresistibly, feeds slowly and long, destroys utterly. It functions as this more than social evil, as this sphinx, for Rick, for Miss Flite, for Gridley, and for countless others, even as such symbols of the court as Krook and Mr. Tulkinghorn considerably exceed mere human dimensions. Yet there is in *Bleak House* another possible attitude toward the court, that of John Jarndyce, which can ensure freedom from it. Though a part of that great memorial of Chancery practice, Jarndyce and Jarndyce, by birth, "he has resolutely kept himself outside the circle" (Scribner's, 1897, II, 101). Unlike the others, he simply stays away from court and takes no interest. And it works, for he remains unaffected.

But is one free, once so totally involved, merely to wash his hands? Rick, once dragged in, insists that Chancery "taints everybody" (II, 101) with no possibility of exemption. To be born into an unsettled case is to be thrust into a senseless world that one must struggle to straighten out before the leisure of living can begin. And if the nature of the court precludes the chance of anything ever being settled, then the struggle is a

Like Ivan's, K.'s right to rebel is sullied by his own guilt: as Ivan reveals a hatred that is responsible for parricide, so K. reveals an inhumanity that has sanctioned the injustice that now threatens him. But he does not allow any humility, any acknowledgment of his creatureliness that his history should lead him to, to supersede his arrogant defiance, nor—apparently—does Kafka want him to, if we may judge from the pitiable ones who have given over their willfulness.

We must return to examine the grounds of K.'s charges against the Court. Having said what I have about the Lower and Higher Courts, what must I say about the way Kafka relates them? How can the corrupt and inefficient Lower Court be

---

desperate and ill-fated one but cannot be abandoned on that account. For one is not free to abandon it. Thus Chancery grows into a metaphysical entity reflecting the nature of existence as much as the legal tangles and abuses of Victorian England. But then along comes John Jarndyce to short-circuit this significance. Through the force of his virtuous will, though continually challenged he does stay outside successfully and does well to do so. All who follow him, like Esther and George Rouncewell, don his coat of invulnerability, finally manage what K. thought of as "a mode of living completely outside the jurisdiction of the Court," and with it manage a happy ending. A happier ending for all will come, presumably, when the court system is reformed.

Is the court an inevitable intrusion upon the human condition, then, or is it just an actual court and no more, one that can simply be ignored by the wise and changed by the well-meaning? It cannot be both as Dickens seems to make it. His difficulty may arise in large part from his rooting the court in reality. This raises the always delicate problem of creating symbolic levels without threatening the literal believability of the actuality from which they spring. Kafka evades the problem by postulating pure fantasy from the start, by separating his Court from the courts embedded in society. It is an easier way but a more troublesome and less satisfying one than Dickens' could have been had he resolved his problem more consistently. Of course, one must admit that these imperfections in *Bleak House* may not mean that Dickens could not resolve his technical problem so much as that he wanted to appease the tastes of Victorian readers and so inserted the sentimental story of Esther Summerson to compensate for the gloom and the terror of Rick's tragic involvement. Unfortunately, the serenely happy ending of the one totally reduced the immense capacities for vision in the other.

claimed to be an emanation of the sublime and infallible Higher Court? How can it represent the foulness that the social interpretation of the novel finds Kafka complaining about, even as it represents the austere authority that the theological interpretation finds Kafka univocally proclaiming? Yet clearly it must be and must do all this. Somehow the Lower Court is sanctioned by the Higher, even though the two seem to present such contradictory faces. Or, rather, the Higher Court presents no face but is seen only as wearing the mask of the Lower Court that contradicts it. It is, then, the "reasoning thing" that puts forth the "unreasoning mask"—an action that drives the Ahabs mad and the Ivans and the K.'s as well. They cannot rebel against the mask without rebelling against the thing that wears it; and their prideful reason allows them no alternative to rebellion. ("I'd strike the sun if it insulted me. For could the sun do that, then could I do the other . . .") Prisoners all—of their reason and of an unreasonable universe through which a reasonable God arbitrarily insists on challenging them—they must strike through the wall.

The Lower Court in all its caprice is part of the cosmic scheme, then, in the sense that all worldly happenings, at their worst as at their best, are. For, at least from the human view, evil does exist in God's world. The Higher Court is testing K., trying him through the bungling Lower Court which it in a sense sanctions as God in a sense sanctions evil by allowing it to exist. Not only does the Higher allow the Lower Court to operate, but it even stands by the latter's decisions. And K., guilty even as in any worldly terms he is innocent, must struggle—from Kafka's point of view is obliged to struggle—and must fail to take the "leap" which requires the suspension of his reason and his pride. The legal, of course, is the supreme expression of the ethical. And the Court, by identifying the contradictory Lower and Higher levels and by having the one flow from the other, is insisting that the universal sway of *its* Law be seen as absolute. But K. has by his arrest been forced from his casual "aesthetic" existence to an ethical of his own.

A most practical and reasonable Bank executive, he has now been forced to use his talents in his own behalf, to defend himself against an absurd attack. And the well-trained rational man responds with a doggedness that his business head cannot shake, a doggedness that converts him into scapegoat. Once arrested, K.'s "aesthetic" blinders have been stripped away, leaving the absurdity of what before seemed rational and thus to be accepted as unavoidably *there*. It still insists on his reverence for it as *the* rational, since the Court's ethical claim, held to be absolute, cannot give way to man's. Still K. pits his ethical against an absurd ethical to which he just cannot submit. The essence of the ethical is its universality but, newly isolated as newly ethical, K. is left as mere individual with his ethical claims reduced to mere personal pretensions, even presumptions. His unyielding logic, held by a private and embattled arrogance, leads beyond the ethical. In refusing to yield to another logic that it cannot accept, his, like Satan's logical refutation of God's absurd demands in the Garden, leads to spiritual pride and its consequences. Though in embracing the rational K. most fervently embraces ethical "principle"—the very principle, Kafka ironically counterposes, that is responsible for the whipping of the warders (107)—yet he finally can claim no more (or less, K. would insist) than the demoniacal. For it is completely *his* logic, and thus unsanctioned, while his own moral history reveals his unfitness to claim an utter sovereignty from which to launch charges. And yet, as Kafka presents it, the object of his charges calls for them: the face of justice that is this frightening and this shabby even if it is the "pasteboard mask" for some (finally just?) inscrutable intention. The Kafka of *The Trial* may be religious, but he does not love his God, indeed is hardly ready to call him "his." For despite his disapproval of K.'s normal human failings and despite the way K. dies, Kafka will not join the Court in condemning him, out of his great contempt for the alternatives to K.

Of course all this approaches overstatement in that K. is hardly up to Satan or Ahab or Ivan. Unlike self-conscious demons or too conscientious moral saviors, K. begins as ethically neutral, uncommitted, if indeed he has any ethical sense at all. Further, we have seen at length and repeatedly how inconsistent his rebellion is, with what unadmirable longing he seeks to return to his most prosaic past, how his partial devotion to conformism makes suspect his fiery zeal for rebellion. We must fear even that were his rebellion to win out, he would return to the conformism of the Bank, cocky about his businesslike common sense that has put the upstart absurdity in its place. A full consideration threatens to reduce K. from a self-appointed pseudo Jesus to everyman and his vision from the tragic to the merely ironic. He never completely loses his routine and commonplace character, however drawn he is to extremity and however resolute he remains in the face of it. He is closer to Hans Castorp than to Adrian Leverkühn, closer to the Homeric than to the Sophoclean, except that for Kafka these figures come closer to merging through a mutual reduction. K. is everyman whose logical persistence, earned in the most unromantic of affiliations, enables him to recognize extremity when it strikes —the extremity that shocks him into becoming the exceptional man who, as a would-be Jesus in search of freedom or crucifixion, rules on the courts of this world and the other world. Yet he paradoxically remains everyman to the extent of wanting to carry on in the old way which is itself Court-like. So his rebellion is keen but sporadic; he is everyman still but everyman-as-rebel. For his rebellion is the other side of his dullness; it is even the consequence of that dullness challenged and found unyielding.

His uncertainty persists even at the close when at the last moment he turns away from the grand climax and his single transformation. He cannot manage the final acceptance he has decided upon; but Kafka, lest he mislead us into overestimating K.'s heroism, makes us feel this counter-turn as stemming from weakness rather than strength, as a turning aside from conclusiveness, as an abdication. This despite our association of the greatest weakness with those who have yielded to acceptance.

Still Kafka in his honesty wants us to recognize this choice as one between weaknesses, with his preference for K.'s arising from the fact that he so persists in the dull worldling's weakness as to convert it, in his struggle with the Court, into a kind of strength. An immovable object, he can only be removed. In this mechanized and bureaucratic world, K. is as close as Kafka dare get to an Ivan. It is a world in which heroism is so reduced in strength and stature that this piece of machinery, this cipher, this nonentity clerk, victim as he is abuser of hierarchy, must become our most satanic representative. Yet he turns out to be man too and even exceptional man in that he has the recognizing power—enough of it so that, when catapulted by extremity, he makes it to the state of the tragic visionary, however reduced a version. His vision, through diminution, is almost stopped at the boundary of the ironic, the merely pathetic and not quite comic. But thanks to the magnitude of his occasional but persistent daring, it finally slides beyond.

2. Albert Camus: Beyond Nonentity and the Rejection of the Tragic

If Joseph K. barely makes it into the tragic realm, Meursault, Camus' "Stranger," never comes close—or perhaps passes far beyond. If K. has tried less manfully than other prisoners in our literature to thrust through the wall, Meursault takes his only prideful consolation in his refusal to try his hand against it at all. It is not that he accepts it; he is further from acceptance than is K. It is just that, like Melville's Bartleby, who also ends up a literal prisoner looking at a blank wall (essentially the same wall that, as figurative prisoner, he allowed to close in his world when society still thought him free), Meursault, yawning at such metaphysical problems as acceptance or defiance, simply would "prefer not to" and stares blankly.

Not that he has rejected life; far from it. Indeed, he accepts it far more exclusively, although with no more illusions, than does the tragic visionary. It is that Camus speaks from beyond the farthest reach of the tragic vision and is trying to make a return in spite of its vision and his total awareness of it. It is as if he has got off the express of the hell-bent literature that has been concerning me and speaks to us out of its wake or, better yet, out of its exhaust fumes. His very consciousness of these fiery apocalyptic visions leads him, out of a kind of spite, to find a return to living that without self-deception may yet be naturalistic and liberal. He turns against the spirit of this very volume I work upon. If I were to imagine him watching me here and commenting upon my objectives, I would see him as having to say something like the following, but in the distinguished prose that characterizes his work: "That's the very trouble. Your very absorption with this vision forces it to a level of self-consciousness which destroys the possibility of that very authenticity which your visionaries have given up all to affirm. We have seen too many of them, these driven demoniacs. One cannot suddenly find himself being driven when he is aware from his reading and his existentialist analysis that he is supposed to be driven. And without the spontaneity of pure driven-ness this entire movement of the self is *ersatz*, an artificial, put-up job that hypocritically justifies a hatred of man and the political reaction that follows from it. Indeed, has not this essential insincerity, this lack of self-candor, always characterized your underground man? Has he not, after all, merely replaced the unauthentic mask he had before shown to himself as his true self with an anti-mask that could claim no more final authenticity for all its destructive powers?"

Thus in *The Fall* we have a shocking parody of the novels I have been treating. Clamence, his pride destroyed by the self-mockery that follows a cowardly failure to act, goes through the appropriate movements of my protagonists, so that we find him with great ardor dwelling upon, indeed celebrating, his sense of guilt. But it is all a fraud: in his self-consciousness Clamence is a pseudo visionary speaking out of a pseudo humility that in its perverse arrogance is more insufferable than the pre-shock pride with which we began. For he condemns himself in order to condemn us all; and in the monologue spoken to us he must have the upper hand since, in his lamentations about self, he is more aware of human guilt than we can be. His self-abnegation becomes his weapon to hate us all, to force us to hate ourselves, and to contemn us for having less awareness than he of our depravity. Yet, of course, we are powerless against him, can have no response, since all we are confronted by is the face of humility that will multiply any accusations we can make. Thus the parody of the tragic vision that turns it on itself. As always, the parody has the advantage of understanding the psychology of its victim (and its model) and of using the very tactics that its victim has used on its enemies.

In Camus' brilliant gambit his intention is to deny what I have seen Kafka as leaving us. I mean not merely Camus' version of Kafka who with Kierkegaard embraces the absurd, but even my version of Kafka who holds out against the absurd although he acknowledges our guilt. For Camus refuses to allow guilt to man since, following upon the tragic vision that relies upon claims to human guilt, our consciousness of it incapacitates us for the action which Camus' naturalistic liberalism requires. All this is relevant also to *The Stranger*, although only implicitly so in this early work, unsophisticated by philosophy as it is. Indeed, it is this work's dramatic directness that makes it the most aesthetically valid of Camus' novels and thus the most valuable for my purposes. Of course I must admit also that its use of the metaphor of imprisonment as its central symbol for the human condition makes it especially convenient.

Like K., Meursault has a most routine occupation. Commentators have universally noted that, as a clerk, he is the pure symbol of Sisyphus-man. Totally implicated in routine, indeed totally dependent on it, Meursault finds Sundays unbearable, with their uncharted freedom that demands more inventive energy than he cares to bother expending. And the greatest torture of his early imprisonment is his need to "kill time," his need to make his way through one interminable Sunday. Meursault's pre-prison life is largely an automatic one, then, with his only satisfactions—indeed his only consciousness—arising from various physical sensations. The rest simply does not matter. He is the least willful of men, as if insisting that nothing at all matters. Of course it is precisely this constitutional unassertiveness that prevents any approximation to the tragic. Insufficiently active to attain to the recognition that was crucial to K.'s trial, in his passivity Meursault does not join the issue. There can be no driven-ness for one who will not commit himself to his drives.

Meursault's only assertion is his constant one that nothing is worth asserting. All alternatives come to the same thing for him, and he cannot be persuaded, cajoled, or bullied into making a rational choice as if it mattered. All things are one and *rien n'importe*. To look or not to look at his mother's dead body, to smoke or not to smoke while sitting with it, to join or not to join with Raymond in his vendetta against his unfaithful mistress, to transfer or not to transfer to the Paris office, to marry or not to marry Marie, to return or not to return to the dangerous scene with the Arabs, to shoot or not to shoot—in each case Meursault is aware of the alternatives and dismisses the choice as meaningless. In each case he chooses and means to choose thoughtlessly, either in accordance with his momentary fancy—his immediate appetites or his mild desire to take the easiest way out in personal relations without having to bother with explanations—or seemingly for no reason at all, automatically, out of a total lack of respect for the occasion that seems to force an insignificant choice upon him.

The Saturday evening before the murder Meursault encounters the "little robot" woman in the restaurant (56).[3] The pure automatism of her being so fascinates him that he follows her out of the restaurant. She appears in the novel once again when Meursault spots her as she inexplicably appears at his trial, with her eyes fixed upon him. The reason for their mutual

[3] From *The Stranger*, by Alfred Camus, trans. Stuart Gilbert (New York: Alfred A. Knopf, Inc., 1946). Copyright 1946, Alfred A. Knopf, Inc. All page references are to this edition. Excerpts are reprinted with the permission of Alfred A. Knopf, Inc.

curiosity is clear: she is a reflection of the indifferent egalitarian universe in which he lives, indeed is a reflection of him. Just before Meursault sees her the first time he has had two interviews, one with his employer and one with Marie. His employer has offered him the Paris transfer, expecting to excite him with it, only to be confronted by Meursault's blankness, which he cannot comprehend. Marie has offered him marriage and can respond to his maddening unconcern only by "staring at [him] in a curious way" (53). He leaves her to dine at Céleste's and at once is joined by the "little robot." When we see him display a curiosity toward her that resembles that which Marie has just shown toward him, we suspect that in the "little robot" he has encountered a more extreme version of himself, a pure reflection of that spiritless mechanical world in which he has chosen to live.

The "little robot" also helps us answer the question that asks whether Meursault is a pure automaton or a pure feather of caprice; for somehow, in his indifference that leads to the utter equivalence of all things and people and thus in his rejection of rational control in his actions, Meursault seems to be both at once. The puppet-woman reveals to us what we, with Meursault, are to learn later more explicitly: that in the routine world of Sisyphus, where all is fated and all are alike condemned in advance, the seeming caprice of mere thoughtless response is the mask for the automatic. In declining to play a conscious role, he turns his strings over to Pattern, which finds his way for him. And so it is with Meursault's refusal to discriminate among things and people or to recognize choice in the many alternatives presented to him.

But history is irreversible, so that what reads forward as chance reads backward as purpose, if not inevitability. And all those disjunctives, in regard to which Meursault's reactions were mere tropisms, turn out at the trial to matter very much indeed. The prosecutor comments, with an irony that shouts his disbelief, "that in this case 'chance' or 'mere coincidence' seemed to play a remarkably large part" (120). He parades forth Meursault's casual choices as in horror we watch them form an elaborate and damning network of apparent cause and effect. Meursault's very refusal to care is now revealed to have been necessary at each point for Chance to have it all its own way in order to weave itself into what a conventional and guilt-conscious humanity will see as Pattern. So every decision was important and Meursault should have been ever on the alert.

There is, however, one more movement to this dialectic, which concludes it in an endlessly bitter irony that confirms the whole cruel joke. After he is sentenced to death, Meursault occasionally allows himself to hope for some way to escape his fate. Perhaps chastened by the fact that the trial seemed to reveal that choices do matter, he has been humanized, or at least partly conventionalized. "The only thing that interests me now is the problem of circumventing the machine, learning if the inevitable admits a loophole" (136). Through this discussion there runs the suggestion of the exertion of human powers to find a way out, to cheat "their bloodthirsty rite," to rebel against "the rattrap," "this brutal certitude" (136). So Sisyphus is rejecting the "machine," the automatic world he never questioned. But the chaplain's visit turns him a final time, and violently. He rejects hope as dishonorable and recognizes the certainty of death, the certainty (and the hopelessness of certainty) that apparently he always had and that must have conditioned the floating, unconcerned nature of his life. And he knows that his has been the proper way after all, that choices did not matter and that all came to the same thing in the end, to man's condemnation and execution one fine dawn.

> I'd been right, I was still right, I was always right. I'd passed my life in a certain way, and I might have passed it in a different way, if I felt like it. I'd acted thus, and I hadn't acted otherwise. I hadn't done *x*, whereas I had done *y* or *z*. And what did that mean? That, all the time, I'd been waiting for this present moment, for that dawn, tomorrow's or another day's, which was to justify me. Nothing, nothing had the least importance, and I knew quite well why. He, too, knew why. From the

> dark horizon of my future a sort of slow, persistent breeze had been blowing toward me, all my life long, from the years that were to come. And on its way that breeze had leveled out all the ideas that people tried to foist on me in the equally unreal years I then was living through. What difference could they make to me, the deaths of others, or a mother's love, or his God; or the way a man decides to live, the fate he thinks he chooses, since one and the same fate was bound to "choose" not only me but thousands of millions of privileged people who, like him, called themselves my brothers. (151–152)

So the trial, the verdict, and the execution, which seemed to make most important those automatic decisions that Meursault originally claimed had no importance, have themselves no importance after all. The breeze from the future, ensuring the murder of man, leveled these with the rest. Meursault has come full circle, except that his experience has brought to him a consciousness and a rational justification of the way of life he had aimlessly drifted into. During the painful procession at his mother's funeral at the start, a nurse for no special reason says to him, "If you go too slowly there's the risk of a heatstroke. But, if you go too fast, you perspire, and the cold air in the church gives you a chill." Meursault adds, "I saw her point; either way one was in for it" (21). During his early imprisonment, before the trial, he suddenly recalls these words and he echoes, "No, there was no way out . . ." (101). Now at the end, in his final outburst, Meursault understands the full meaning of what was being said and its consequences. Though more conclusively limited by the mechanical universe, by the machine that admits no loophole, he has yet proved himself more than robot, more than Sisyphus, in his realization of man's condition and his willful decision neither to struggle against it nor to bend his knee to it but rather to will himself a Sisyphus man, the microcosmic reflection of the macrocosmic apparatus.

Feeling in the universe an indifference that matches his own, he can only hope to be greeted at his execution "with howls of execration" (154). Almost all readers have noticed in these final words the parody of the crucifixion. The parody is single-edged only: it seems to be nothing but bitter mockery. Yet as parody it is more appropriate than most readers have discovered. Meursault detests sympathy since in spending it upon him the sympathizer is keeping himself from recognizing that he shares Meursault's fate and that Meursault represents the total awareness which the sympathizer fears. Thus Meursault hopes for hatred, which will assure him that he is intolerable to those who hate, the indifference of his way of life a revelation they must bury with their "howls." Throughout the novel, and especially after the murder, Meursault's way has been found intolerable, fearfully so, by one "respectable" man after another, all of them morally outraged perhaps in order to hide their terror at what the world must look like through Meursault's eyes. Their howls, like those about two thousand years ago, will assure their victim that his way is believed to be a unique way, one that is hated with a fear that is the other side of admiration. The parody of the New Testament reveals also that this victim is as much a reflection, indeed an incarnation, of his cosmic order as the other one was of his rather different and happier one. Meursault parodies Christ also in his strange insistence on the indiscriminate equality of all men before the cosmic leveler. All men are brothers in being equally "privileged," in having the universal privilege of damnation. Cosmic indifference allows all to be members of "the privileged class" (152), and the belief in it makes men free, even as Meursault's mother, shortly to die, "must have felt like someone on the brink of freedom, ready to start life all over again" (154). For, Meursault must assume, so close to death, she must have had the illumination he has had, the illumination that, in bestowing the belief in the indiscriminateness and sameness of all things, also bestows indifference, brother to the indifference of the cosmos. And the indifference in turn bestows freedom, freedom from will, from values, from distinctions, and most of all from guilt.

Indeed, for Camus there is no guilt. Meursault is convicted by a guilt-ridden humanity that loathes his "callousness." Tried for murder, he is found guilty also of matricide (though his mother died of natural causes) and parricide (though it was not his father, and the son who committed it was to be tried the next day). The prosecutor draws these inferences:

> "This man, who is morally guilty of his mother's death, is no less unfit to have a place in the community than that other man who did to death the father that begat him. And, indeed, the one crime led on to the other; the first of these two criminals, the man in the dock, set a precedent, if I may put it so, and authorized the second crime. Yes, gentlemen, I am convinced"—here he raised his voice a tone—"that you will not find I am exaggerating the case against the prisoner when I say that he is also guilty of the murder to be tried tomorrow in this court." (128)

The speech cannot help reminding us of Dostoevsky, of the dark Christianity in him that so painfully worked out Ivan Karamazov's guilt for his father's murder. He "authorized" it in the same way, and in so doing exemplified Father Zossima's claim about the responsibility of each for the sins of all. Here is parody too, then, as Camus reduces the notion to absurdity, making Dostoevskyan Christianity into a kind of villain. Viewed through Meursault's indifference, man's guilt cannot exist as a primary evil, and condemnation is visited upon man in his essential innocence. At the end Meursault, in absolving himself, absolves all equally: the man who, "after being charged with murder . . . [was] executed because he didn't weep at his mother's funeral . . . That little robot woman was as 'guilty' as the girl from Paris who had married Masson, or as Marie, who wanted me to marry her. What did it matter if Raymond was as much my pal as Céleste, who was a far worthier man?" (152–153) He could have added the perpetrators of the frightful crime in Czechoslovakia that he read of with fascination in the newspaper scrap he found in his cell or, of course, the parricide.

The primary evil, then, is natural rather than moral evil. It arises out of the absurd universe and not out of man. Indeed, it is rather visited upon man. Man, then, as condemned, is the victim rather than the source of evil to which in his native innocence he must respond with the dignity of indifference. This dignity chooses, not the self-pity that consolingly calls the universe evil, but the self-control that insists, whatever the nature of the universe, on calling it brother and its universal curse the privilege—bearer of freedom—that "benign indifference" can confer. Thus Camus ends in the atheist's humanism. Whatever there is of moral evil he sees as derivative, stemming from an improper reaction to the absurd, to the natural indifference we may wrongly term evil—improper in the strength with which it defies or in the weakness with which it embraces. As *The Stranger* unravels largely "to justify" the ways of Meursault, so like much of the work of Camus it was written largely to justify the ways of man. Camus' essential liberalism leads him to be angry with those who heap condemnation upon a creature already condemned by his universe. But, as Kafka has shown us, to deprive man of guilt is also to deprive him of the chance for vision. Those of our authors who are less humanistically limited could claim, in Ahab's terms, that man has more dignity, the dignity of fearless self-knowledge, when the unreasoning mask that imprisons him hides a thing of unknowable reason whose justification finds a shadow in the grudging prisoner's soul. It is this shadow that, through a dual vision, enables him to condemn himself as demon while he rebels as demigod.

CHAPTER SIX

Joseph Conrad: Action, Inaction, and Extremity

1. The Varieties of Extremity

HEART OF DARKNESS

I saw on that ivory face the expression of somber pride, of ruthless power, of craven terror—of an intense and hopeless despair. Did he live his life again in every detail of desire, temptation, and surrender during that supreme moment of complete knowledge? He cried in a whisper at some image, at some vision,—he cried out twice, a cry that was no more than a breath—

"The horror! The horror!"

. . . And it is not my own extremity I remember best—a vision of grayness without form filled with physical pain, and a careless contempt for the evanescence of all things—even of this pain itself. No! It is his extremity that I seem to have lived through. . . . I like to think my summing-up would not have been a word of careless contempt. Better his cry—much better. It was an affirmation, a moral victory paid for by innumerable defeats, by abominable terrors, by abominable satisfactions. But it was a victory! (169–170, 171–172) [1]

[1] From *Heart of Darkness*, in *Youth and Two Other Stories*, by Joseph Conrad (New York: Doubleday & Company, Inc., 1910). All page references are to this edition.

Thanks to Mr. Kurtz, Conrad's magnificently proportioned Marlow never need pay the full price himself for so costly a victory and a vision. And this is the debt to Kurtz that he acknowledges and that he meets, however modestly, in that cautious ethical realm which Marlow clasps for his safety. For, having lived through Kurtz's extremity, Marlow can retain his own more yielding—and more compromising—resistance to extremity, more fearful than ever of its consequences but now fully aware of the vistas it opens onto for him who dares embrace it. And Marlow can move beyond his own "vision of grayness." Kurtz has, at great expense, made the tragic vision available to his less venturesome but still sensitive fellows: in his relation to Marlow, he is an allegory of the role that the visionary and the literature in which he figures are to play for those of us who are interested but not ourselves committed totally. And where the tragic visionary is concerned, of course totality is all.

Heart of Darkness is effective as an ideal archetype of the literature of the tragic vision, giving us an exemplary version of the relations between representatives of the ethical and of the tragic realms. The categories it so clearly schematizes frame most of Conrad's work and reach beyond to many others'. For this reason I use it here, before moving on to the novels that are my central concern, even though Kurtz in his open and wildly vicious defiance is closer in spirit to those visionaries with which I began in my early chapters.

As I have here posed the ethical-tragic relation, it would seem that it is in the ethical resistance to the tragic that moral strength resides. But it is just the paradoxical nature of this strength that constitutes the central problem of *Heart of Darkness*. The key to the novel turns on Conrad's complex attitude toward the twin classical qualities that Marlow terms "innate strength" and "restraint." Two points seem immediately clear: as surely as Marlow does have them, Kurtz does not; and these qualities are severely tried—and especially needed—in Africa, that is, in the primitive reaches of pre-civilization or in the Dionysian darkness of pre-consciousness. We must examine the sources of Marlow's inner strength and of Kurtz's lack of it. The problem is perhaps most neatly posed in the passage in which Marlow, sailing down the river, is attracted and tempted by the frenzied dancing and howling of the natives on the banks. Will he join them? (This, after all, is to be the essence of Kurtz's sin.) Marlow admits that he feels a stirring deep within him, feels a call to his primitive humanity in the spectacle. He cannot ignore the call, but rather rejects it in full realization of its significance and its attraction. And he explicitly gives his listeners the reasons for his rejection:

> Let the fool gape and shudder—the man knows, and can look on without a wink. But he must at least be as much of a man as these on the shore. He must meet that truth with his own true stuff—with his own inborn strength. Principles? Principles won't do. Acquisitions, clothes, pretty rags—rags that would fly off at the first good shake. No; you want a deliberate belief. An appeal to me in this fiendish row—is there? Very well; I hear; I admit, but I have a voice too, and for good or evil mine is the speech that cannot be silenced. Of course, a fool, what with sheer fright and fine sentiments, is always safe. Who's that grunting? You wonder I didn't go ashore for a howl and a dance? Well, no—I didn't. Fine sentiments, you say? Fine sentiments, be hanged! I had no time. I had to mess about with white-lead and strips of woolen blanket helping to put bandages on those leaky steam-pipes—I tell you. I had to watch the steering, and circumvent those snags, and get the tin-pot along by hook or by crook. There was surface-truth enough in these things to save a wiser man. (110)

Previously, in much the same spirit, Marlow has told us,

> When you have to attend to things of that sort, to the mere incidents of the surface, the reality—the reality, I tell you—fades. The inner truth is hidden—luckily, luckily. But I felt it all the same; I felt often its mysterious stillness watching me at my monkey tricks, just as it watches you fellows performing on your respective tight-ropes for—what is it? half-a-crown a tumble—(106)

Again, it is with much the same view that Marlow later seizes upon a very commonplace seaman's manual.

> The matter looked dreary reading enough, with illustrative diagrams and repulsive tables of figures, and the copy was sixty years old. I handled this amazing antiquity with the greatest possible tenderness, lest it should dissolve in my hands. Within, Towson or Towser was inquiring earnestly into the breaking strain of ships' chains and tackle, and other such matters. Not a very enthralling book; but at the first glance you could see there a singleness of intention, an honest concern for the right way of going to work, which made these humble pages, thought out so many years ago, luminous with another than a professional light. The simple old sailor, with his talk of chains and purchases, made me forget the jungle and the pilgrims in a delicious sensation of having come upon something unmistakably real. (112–113)

The source of Marlow's restraint, then, is finally just a healthy practicality, a preoccupation with the most worldly of things because these are explainable, are tangible causes for tangible effects. This notion of diehard practicality persists through the story since it is what is lacking in Africa and what Africa most challenges. The many incidents which befall Marlow on his trip to the scene of action are all fearful indications of the same omen: the cause-and-effect pragmatics of civilization has been replaced by a nightmarish futility. The shelling of the coast by the man-of-war, the landing of soldiers, the "objectless blasting," the bustling activity, all seem pointless and ineffectual. It is like "some sordid farce acted in front of a sinister blackcloth" (69), with "a touch of insanity in the proceeding, a sense of lugubrious drollery" (70). The surf and the Negroes rowing boats are comforts. They have a meaning: "For a time I would feel I belonged still to a world of straightforward facts" (70). Significantly, when the natives later attack Marlow's boat, they are dispersed by nothing so fitting as gunfire but rather by something as seemingly unrelated as the sound of the steam whistle. The world of European efficiency cannot absorb the jungle's unreality into itself. Modern equipment gives us especially eloquent testimony. The farthest accomplishments of the reasonable and utilitarian world, this equipment, sent literally to *real*ize Africa, lies all around, rusted, decayed, broken, as we are continually reminded. Finally one kind, rivets, emerges as an important symbol.

For one thing, rivets save Marlow. He seems almost overcome by the Kafka-esque nightmare of Africa. Desperately challenged, Marlow tries to subordinate everything to his desire to repair the steamboat, and for a significant reason. "In that way only it seemed to me I could keep my hold on the redeeming facts of life" (86). The prime requisites for the repair job, however, are rivets. And the well-balanced Marlow becomes quite passionate in relating his need for them.

> What I really wanted was rivets, by heaven! Rivets. To get on with the work—to stop the hole. Rivets I wanted. There were cases of them down at the coast—cases—piled up—burst—split! You kicked a loose rivet at every second step in that station yard on the hillside. Rivets had rolled into the grove of death. You could fill your pockets with rivets for the trouble of stooping down—and there wasn't one rivet to be found where it was wanted. We had plates that would do, but nothing to fasten them with. (95)

Week after week passes and he cannot get delivery of this small quantity of these petty things. Their full symbolic importance becomes inescapable when Marlow adds, "what I wanted was a certain quantity of rivets—and rivets were what really Mr. Kurtz wanted, if he had only known it" (96). Thus what counts is not merely their pettiness, not merely their identification as a species of European machinery, but also their precise function: they hold "things" together which otherwise, in the words of Yeats, "fall apart." Symbolically as well as literally, then, Marlow, like any European who would keep his sanity, must fight for his rivets. The merest expectation that rivets may arrive leads Marlow and his foreman to behave "like lunatics." Marlow recklessly tries a jig, they caper loudly on the iron deck. Perhaps this is the counterpart to the wild native dance that we have seen Marlow so sturdily resist. For Marlow's is a dance dedicated out of a kind of desperation to those unyielding sources of European resistance to savage intemperance. Elsewhere Marlow lists several of these superficial binders which maintain the balance of civilization, as he insists on the inability of his audience to understand the moral enigma that is Kurtz:

> You can't understand. How could you?—with solid pavement under your feet, surrounded by kind neighbors ready to cheer you or to fall on you, stepping delicately between the butcher and the policeman, in the holy terror of scandal and gallows and lunatic asylums—how can you imagine what particular region of the first ages a man's untrammeled feet may take him into by the way of solitude—utter solitude without a policeman—by the way of silence—utter silence, where no warning voice of a kind neighbor can be heard whispering of public opinion? These little things make all the great difference. When they are gone you must fall back upon your own innate strength, upon your own capacity for faithfulness. Of course you may be too much of a fool to go wrong—too dull even to know you are being assaulted by the powers of darkness. (132–133)

We should see by now that Marlow's conception of strength takes a strangely paradoxical nature: it consists in the relentless retention of artificial props. To hold onto one's crutches brings the restraint that makes him strong; to try courageously to walk without them results in the lack of restraint that we are so often told weakens Kurtz. The problem is hardly a simple one. There is, for example, the problem of "the fool" whom Marlow has just defined for us. If the mere retention of the props of modern society constitutes strength, then the paragons of strength in the tale are such nonentities as the company manager or that "miracle," the chief accountant (he of the "high starched collar, white cuffs . . . snowy trousers

. . . varnished boots . . . green-lined parasol . . . penholder behind his ear" (77) who was annoyed at the sick because their groans impaired the efficiency of his computations). Clearly these are the fools Marlow spoke of who are too insensitive to be aware that there is any problem, any temptation in their situation. And of course these men cannot be expected to understand Kurtz at all. Thus they reject him completely but uncritically, and reject him in the practical rather than in the moral realm, since for them he can be evil only insofar as he represents a threat to their interests, their "aesthetic" pursuits. As beings who do not partake of the ethical, they can hardly be said to possess moral strength; for this strength can hardly exist where there is ignorance of moral alternatives. Marlow, on the contrary, is completely aware of the alternatives, their respective claims and consequences. His rejection of Kurtz, made in the moral realm, is yet critical of itself, so that it reveals both admiration and sympathy together with its repulsion. Marlow chooses the crutches, knowing them to be crutches, and thus knowing also that his choice must shut him off from areas of vision which are Kurtz's. He has chosen morally, but the moral criterion remains worldly and pragmatic: it just wouldn't do to act otherwise and would constitute a breach of civilized faith. By so choosing, he has insured himself against the tragic—but insured himself against the glory of its vision as well as the horror of its devastation.

Kurtz's vision and the value that even Marlow places on it reveal the final complexity of this question of strength. Of course the full meaning of Kurtz can be apprehended only in the context of the idealized imperialism he represents. Speaking, at the outset of the tale, of the Roman conquest of England and of the brutality of imperialism generally, Marlow tells us: "What redeems it is the idea only. An idea at the back of it; not a sentimental pretense but an idea; and an unselfish belief in the idea—something you can set up, and bow down before, and offer a sacrifice to. . . ." (57–58) The use here of the language of primitive religion is significant: it is Kurtz who, bowing down before progressive Western man's rationalization for imperialism, sacrificing himself to it, allows himself—in a perverted service of it—to become the god himself and thus to be bowed down before and sacrificed to. After all, it is Kurtz—"emissary of pity, and science, and progress" (90) and member of "the gang of virtue" (90)—who is responsible for the symbolic painting that shows the bearer of light into darkness as herself blinded and as herself rendered sinister in the light of her torch. It is he who, writing the report for the International Society for the Suppression of Savage Customs, acknowledges the role of the whites in Africa as "supernatural beings . . . with the might as of a deity" (134). Of course, writing as "an exotic Immensity ruled by an august Benevolence," Kurtz pleaded in behalf of altruism for this power to be used for civilizing, the sole salvation. Yet it is this plea that without warning is interrupted by the fearful imperiousness of the command, "Exterminate all the brutes!" just as his self-conscious mission is transformed into the unlimited "ivory-grubbing" and the insistence on adoration of self and with it the sacrifices of idolatry.

When Marlow was speaking of the inborn strength that led him to resist the dancing natives and traced its source to the devotion to practical necessity, he insisted—man of the world that he is—that "Principles won't do. Acquisitions, clothes, pretty rags—rags that would fly off at the first good shake" (110). And so it was with Kurtz. But his story would allow Marlow to go further: the slavish devotion to principle is finally an identification with it, allowing one to make oneself into the god, the embodiment of what he has worshiped. The rest, of course, is demonism and destruction, the overassertion of self finally without even the pseudo humility of the idealistic claim to have lost oneself in service. So Kurtz, relentless as he is in his pursuit of absolute integrity of motives, becomes a pure representative of the force of imperialism that in its arrogance victimizes itself: he becomes what he is at last as a symbol of that impure mask of disinterested virtue which disguises the ugliness of man playing god before man. However lofty the initial undertaking, in the extreme it must lead to the bowing down and the sacrificing by those supposedly being served.

Marlow is too wise and sensitive an ethical man to trust utterly to principle, or to trust utterly to anything. This innate distrust in anything more pretentious than those modest, routine details that bind life to itself is the source of Marlow's resistance to extremity just as Kurtz's abandoned embrace of principle forces his rejection of anything less than extremity. But Marlow does recognize the visionary powers of extremity that accompany its socially destructive powers. And the tribute he pays to Kurtz—the quotation with which I opened this chapter—is impressive testimony indeed. I believe it is worth quoting more fully here.

> I have wrestled with death. It is the most unexciting contest you can imagine. It takes place in an impalpable grayness, with nothing underfoot, with nothing around, without spectators, without clamor, without glory, without the great desire of victory, without the great fear of defeat, in a sickly atmosphere of tepid skepticism, without much belief in your own right, and still less in that of your adversary. If such is the form of ultimate wisdom, then life is a greater riddle than some of us think it to be. I was within a hair's-breadth of the last opportunity for pronouncement, and I found with humiliation that probably I would have nothing to say. This is the reason why I affirm that Kurtz was a remarkable man. He had something to say. He said it. Since I had peeped over the edge myself, I understand better the meaning of his stare, that could not see the flame of the candle, but was wide enough to embrace the whole universe, piercing enough to penetrate all the hearts that beat in the darkness. He had summed up—he had judged. "The horror!" He was a remarkable man. After all, this was the expression of some sort of belief; it had candor, it had conviction, it had a vibrating note of revolt in its whisper, it had the appalling face of a glimpsed truth—the strange commingling of desire and hate. And it is not my own extremity I remember best—a vision of grayness without form filled

> with physical pain, and a careless contempt for the evanescence of all things—even of this pain itself. No! It is his extremity that I seem to have lived through. . . . I like to think my summing-up would not have been a word of careless contempt. Better his cry—much better. It was an affirmation, a moral victory paid for by innumerable defeats, by abominable terrors, by abominable satisfactions. But it was a victory! (171–172)

In this passage Marlow establishes Kurtz as both morally vicious and morally victorious. Marlow may have the strength and the righteousness, Kurtz the weakness and the satanic appetite; but the insight and ultimate victory (that accompany the crime and the self-induced fall), necessarily denied Marlow because of his very strength, are Kurtz's—and Marlow knows it. The paradoxical nature of Marlow's strength and Kurtz's weakness is thus acknowledged by our ethical strong man himself. The self-candor of this acknowledgment leads Marlow to pay his debt to Kurtz by speaking the lie whose corruptness he hates to the woman whose purity he cherishes. This is Marlow's concession to his experience or, more precisely, to his vicarious involvement with Kurtz's experience. For, as always, Marlow is able to compromise, to save what he can. This is his tie to life and his rejection of extremity.

As at once the sensitive and the normal man who has both been shown by Kurtz and been horrified by him, Marlow is our ideal lens and narrator even as he becomes the protagonist of a kind of *Bildungsroman*. And he willingly pays for his education. Normal enough to see the need to reject Kurtz but sensitive enough to qualify his rejection and to see the even greater need to be captivated by Kurtz, Marlow can sensitize us to the phenomenon of Kurtz as he appreciates it, because we can trust him ethically as "one of us." Given Kurtz himself directly, we would simply be repelled by him. Marlow can prevent us from pooh-poohing Kurtz so blandly, without seeing any problem in him that touches us; he can prevent us from being "the fool," the fellow he scorns whose tie to the world is so secure as to render him morally tone-deaf. Thus, less than Marlow in the full breadth of our allegiances and sympathies (and which of us possibly could match him in this?), we perceive vicariously through him as he does through Kurtz. Our own need enables us to understand his—and to accept his willingness to pay for having it satisfied, to acquit himself of his debt to Kurtz by something surely less than identification with him but uneasily approaching it in the totality of its moral involvement. But Marlow has cracked our moral austerity enough for us to countenance all this, even if—through the example of Kurtz—he has made us distrustful of that other, that self-appointed immoral austerity as well. With him we can fear extremity while knowing that some of us who are more daring must embrace it —for our sakes. And for what they reveal we are in their debt.

Marlow's attachment to the workaday world is strong enough for him to cry for rivets and to depend upon them for his salvation. But he also sees them as limitations upon action—limitations that are justified by the example of a Kurtz and that yet cry out for this example lest they stifle the errant soul of man that they in propriety contain. And so Marlow's attachment to the world is also tenuous enough for him to see these necessary limitations as themselves sadly limited. He cannot be confused with those fools who take their blinders for reality and who limit man's vision to what practicality permits. Innocent or dangerous—the high-starched collar of the accountant or the intrigues of the manager—these are "too dull even to know [they] are being assaulted by the powers of darkness" (133). Nor is there any moral awareness in them. On the contrary, Marlow is all awareness, perhaps too much awareness to allow any final commitment—except to the compromising unidealistic world that scorns commitment. The limitations on even this commitment explain why he is open to the extremity of Kurtz, while his refusal to abandon the commitment (to noncommitment) explains why he remains in need of Kurtz.

Since Marlow is incomplete even while he is comprehensive, he cannot furnish the answer to Kurtz. Marlow has no answers: he cannot even quite dare to ask Kurtz's questions. He shows us that we cannot afford the vision of Kurtz if we are to manage, as social beings, to struggle along in our daily drudgeries. But neither can we do without it unless we are to become enslaved to these drudgeries and thus take them as our reality. In seeing the weakness within his own strength, the moral mediocrity that must cling to him so long as he clings to that last rivet, Marlow—sensitively liberal as he is—defines the requisites of the tragic vision, what makes it at once indispensable and intolerable. But if the structure of ethical insights were to be complete, there would have to be some level beyond that of worldly morality from which Kurtz could be judged absolutely: a level which would include Kurtz's vision—and with it would soar beyond a parochial pragmatism—but which would have passed beyond this vision to a final other-worldly affirmation. To stop short of the profoundly religious vision is to rest in demonism; yet to proceed to it is not to deny the existential authenticity of the tragic. It should be clear, however, that a retreat to the dogged insufficiency of Marlow will not do even if Conrad shows us nothing else that will. For if we view Marlow as actor rather than merely as narrator—the observant representative of our own best selves—his position seems hardly adequate to the awesome data of experience organized by the tragic vision or, ultimately, to the affirmation of the earned religious vision to which the tragic may very well be the gateway. I reserve until my final chapter the question of whether we can any longer ask literature (if we ever could) to yield so ultimate a vision as the religious. But if I may once again sound a familiar note, I suggest that this is to ask for tragedy when, as a modern, Conrad at his most authentic cannot reach beyond the tragic vision.

LORD JIM

Very funny this terrible thing is. A man that is born falls into a dream like a man who falls into the sea. If he tries to climb out into the air as inexperienced people endeavour to do, he drowns—*nicht wahr*? . . . No! I tell you! The way is to the destructive element submit yourself, and with the exertions of your hands and feet in the water make the deep, deep sea keep you up. (184) [2]

But the call to willful triumph in the last of these words of Stein is soon muted. The victorious "shadow," speaking with confidence from the unreality of the "shapeless dusk"—existing outside "this concrete and perplexed world" (184)—returns to the light and can pursue his fervor no longer: ". . . his twitching lips uttered no word, and the austere exaltation of a certitude seen in the dusk vanished from his face. . . . The light had destroyed the assurance which had inspired him in the distant shadows" (185). Ironically, taking the symbolic form of light, the reality proves itself as the destructive element by destroying the shadowy dream that claimed to have found the way to overcome it. And Stein senses his ultimate defeat, despite the heroic resilience seen in his biography. It is his romantic self-assertion, his ability to "follow the dream" in the face of failure, that he bequeathes to Jim, but his self-delusion—perhaps recognized in this scene—will be Jim's also, and Jim will also come to a recognition of it, a far more costly one.

Yet the sea in Stein's metaphor appears to represent the dream rather than reality, so that the dream rather than reality would appear to be the destructive element. However, to the romantic—as Stein conceives him and as Jim realizes him even more completely than Stein did—the dream *is* the reality, the existence into which he has been capriciously hurled. As, for the modern existentialist, man suddenly wakes up to find himself catapulted into existence and proves his humanity by the strength of his response to the meaninglessness of the challenge,

[2] From *Lord Jim*, by Joseph Conrad, ed. Robert Heilman (Rinehart Editions; Rinehart & Company, Inc., 1957). All page references are to this edition which I use because Professor Heilman has labored over the textual problem and has compared the standard collected American edition with the three other principal texts: the first American edition, the first English, and the collected English (see Textual Note, pp. 365 ff.).

so Conrad—through Stein—sees as the critical moment of man's existence his awakening to the sealike, dreamlike quality of the life into which he has fallen and which now claims him. And we must remember the dreamlike, indeed the nightmarish, atmosphere which pervaded "the night of the first ages" (109), the irrational unconscious symbolized by Conrad as the *Heart of Darkness*. There, we were told, it is the nightmare which is the terrifying reality that, as we have seen, must be purposefully ignored in the interest of sanity: "When you have to attend to things of that sort, to the mere incidents of the surface, the reality—the reality, I tell you—fades. The inner truth is hidden—luckily, luckily" (106). And Marlow has earlier acknowledged the Kafka-esque quality of this inner truth and of the invulnerable solitude with which one is overcome by it as a reality-principle as well as a dream:

> It seems to me I am trying to tell you a dream—making a vain attempt, because no relation of a dream can convey the dream-sensation, that commingling of absurdity, surprise, and bewilderment in a tremor of struggling revolt, that notion of being captured by the incredible which is of the very essence of dreams. . . .
>
> . . . No, it is impossible; it is impossible to convey the life-sensation of any given epoch of one's existence,—that which makes its truth, its meaning—its subtle and penetrating essence. It is impossible. We live, as we dream—alone. . . . (94)

As a visionary Lord Jim may hardly seem to be enough like Kurtz to justify my using *Heart of Darkness* to shed light on the longer novel. For Jim may seem to have found his salvation—within the total resolution that allows tragedy—by sacrificing himself to what society may demand of the hero, while Kurtz has sacrificed society to his own satanic appetites. But the stories have more in common than the presence of Marlow, though it is surely true that my treatment of *Heart of Darkness* should help illuminate his role in *Lord Jim*. It is rather that his very presence and the similarity of his role suggest something in common between the two men he tries to save and fears to judge.

Quite clearly *Lord Jim* revolves about what Stein calls the "romantic" attitude, which tells us that our protagonist is one of that uncompromising tribe that seeks and finds extreme situations.[3] At the beginning Jim is filled with schoolboy notions of honor and sees himself as uniquely chosen for the courageous and the sacrificial deed: "always an example of devotion to duty, and as unflinching as a hero in a book" (4). But the trials of exacting necessity find him wanting. He has two seemingly insignificant failures before that major catastrophe on the *Patna*. Each time the world, suddenly transformed, presents him with its terrifying aspect. It is this that paralyzes him into inaction. In his first failure at training school the gale blows

> with the strength of a hurricane in fitful bursts that boomed like salvoes of great guns firing over the ocean. . . . Jim had threatening glimpses of the tumbling tide . . . There was a fierce purpose in the gale, a furious earnestness in the screech of the wind, in the brutal tumult of earth and sky, that seemed directed at him . . . (4)

Before he fails again, Conrad tells us:

> There are many shades in the danger of adventures and gales, and it is only now and then that there appears on the face of facts a sinister violence of intention—that indefinable something which forces it upon the mind and the heart of a man, that this complication of accidents or these elemental furies are coming at him with a purpose of malice, with a strength beyond control, with an unbridled cruelty that means to tear out of him his hope and his fear, the pain of his fatigue and his longing for rest: which means to smash, to destroy, to an-

[3] For a discussion of an earlier, a related but weaker—if more optimistic—attempt by Conrad to deal with this sort of protagonist, see my "Conrad's *Youth*: A Naive Opening to Art and Life," *College English*, XX (1959), 275–280.

> nihilate all he has seen, known, loved, enjoyed, or hated . . . (7–8)

Despite the openness of nature's challenge—its frank revelation that it will not cooperate with his dream of glory—the lad complains that he has been caught "unawares." That night on the *Patna*, however, he is not given so open a view of universal malevolence. Instead, nature shows only a pleasant and tranquil face and so beguiles him into a false security. That fateful night Jim "was penetrated by the great certitude of unbounded safety and peace that could be read on the silent aspect of nature like the certitude of fostering love upon the placid tenderness of a mother's face" (13–14). Marlow later comments, "And all the time it was only a clouded sky, a sea that did not break, the air that did not stir. Only a night; only a silence" (99). As Jim returns to his high heroic dreams, he feels "something like gratitude for this high peace of sea and sky" (16) unaware that he is to be repaid at once and not in kind. The nightmare reality that Stein later sees as the "destructive element" has engulfed Jim, and only out of a kind of stubbornness does he resist his complete destruction.

After the inquiry he persists, not quite "shirking his ghost" or "facing him out," although something of each. The opportunity Stein finds for him in Patusan (a name which is obviously meant to echo the *Patna*) Jim answers brilliantly. He never allows himself to be caught unawares here, so that heroic act follows heroic act in a faithful service that surely seems more than atonement enough for his faithlessness to those other non-Europeans who staked all on the white man's loyalty. He seems indeed to have immersed himself in the destructive element without succumbing to it: precisely Stein's formula for the "romantic" who would yet manage life. Instead of the alienation forced upon him by his earlier failure, he not only has integrated himself into the Patusan world but has reconstructed that world about him.

Why is it, then, that Marlow still has his doubts, that he

fears that the "opportunity which, like an Eastern bride, had come veiled to [Jim's] side," may still be veiled? What is there about Jim's situation in Patusan that is still so profoundly unsatisfying? Now that he has reversed his earlier incapabilities and has surely realized everything that a hero of schoolboy romance could ask, what nagging thing mars it all?

To begin with, about the entire affair of the *Patna* lurks an intangible mystery, a circle of moral ambiguities, in light of which no answer like the simple about-face in Patusan can satisfy Marlow—or us. Referring to the elusiveness of the *Patna* episode, Jim says:

> It was not a lie—but it wasn't truth all the same. It was something. . . . There was not the thickness of a sheet of paper between the right and wrong of this affair. . . . Suppose I had stuck to the ship? . . . In thirty seconds, as it seemed certain then, I would have been overboard; and do you think I would not have laid hold of the first thing that came in my way? . . . I would have meant to be [saved] . . . And that's more than I meant when I . . . jumped . . . (112)

This impalpability helps draw Marlow into the situation. As he witnessed the questioning of Jim at the inquiry, he saw Jim's helplessness as he tried to unmask the true reality of what happened that night. Nor can the mere facts help. Those least of all: "They demanded facts from him, as if facts could explain anything!" (23)

> The facts those men were so eager to know had been visible, tangible, open to the senses, occupying their place in space and time, requiring for their existence a fourteen-hundred-ton steamer and twenty-seven minutes by the watch; they made a whole that had features, shades of expression, a complicated aspect that could be remembered by the eye, and something else besides, something invisible, a directing spirit of perdition that dwelt within, like a malevolent soul in a detestable body. . . . his mind positively flew round and round the serried circle of facts that had surged up all about him to cut him off from the rest of his kind . . . (24–25)

Perhaps Marlow recalls his own words out of another of his tales. For Jim, thrust into a dream that constitutes his reality, echoes the full sense of what we have already heard Marlow, in Stein-like tones, tell his listeners in *Heart of Darkness*:

> . . . it is impossible to convey the life-sensation of any given epoch of one's existence,—that which makes its truth, its meaning—its subtle and penetrating essence. It is impossible. We live, as we dream—alone. . . . (94)

Conrad distrusts facts since they deceive us: the utter intimacy of personal experience is incommunicable, and this insulation belies the smug and pretentious claims of facts to tell us about the human history of each of us. The effect Conrad achieves may remind us of that other weaver of sea stories who cultivated the mystic, unsharable sanctity of personal experience—the Herman Melville of *Benito Cereno*. Here we—with Captain Delano—are presented with an obvious, and often obviously misleading, mystery. Suddenly it seems to have cleared, the facts have been straightened out. And then, just to be certain there are no misunderstandings, Melville gives us endless excerpts from Don Benito's deposition in the court records. The facts are laid out again and again, in inexhaustible and repetitious detail. But ironically, the real mystery has not been solved; it has only deepened. For the more Delano knows, the farther he is from capturing the heart of that darkness which fills Don Benito's soul and sends him to his death. Indeed is this not much of what Melville is about when, in *Moby Dick*, he burdens his narrative with the often puzzlesome cetological intrusions? Does not the multiplication of exposition's facts, drawn from many descriptive studies, still leave us infinitely removed from the whale's fullest significance? Hence Ishmael's weariness with his data even as he dare not give up these only contacts with the reality of the whale that obsesses his pages. And we are perhaps reminded finally of Shakespeare's impatience, in his Sonnet 116, with the finitude of fact as he seeks to define love as the star

> Whose worth's unknown, although his highth be taken.

Indeed, the complex manipulation of Conrad's point of view and time sequence is not a mere virtuoso display. Rather, it is yet another attempt to indicate how unreachable Jim's problem is. The course of events is gone over again and again, in all varieties of chronological order and from all varieties of points of view. Seemingly crucial bits of information are added here and there as revelation always seems beyond the next turning. But the heart of the matter still remains just beyond grasp. Thus the enumeration of Jim's heroic actions is something less than immediately convincing.

The haunting theme of common guilt also serves to cloud Jim's success in Patusan. It is a theme that has been with us from the beginning. It helps explain, for example, why Marlow becomes so obsessed by Jim's case that he manages to get to all the sources of information and of different attitudes that he needs to tell his story. For Jim is "one of us," as Marlow often says, so that Marlow is profoundly troubled that as "one of us" Jim should be involved in the ugly business of the *Patna*.

> Why I longed to go grubbing into the deplorable details of an occurrence which, after all, concerned me no more than as a member of an obscure body of men held together by a community of inglorious toil and by fidelity to a certain standard of conduct, I can't explain. You may call it an unhealthy curiosity if you like; but I have a distinct notion I wished to find something. Perhaps, unconsciously, I hoped I would find that something, some profound and redeeming cause, some merciful explanation, some convincing shadow of an excuse. I see well enough now that I hoped for the impossible—for the laying of what is the most obstinate ghost of man's creation, of the uneasy doubt uprising like a mist, secret and gnawing like a worm, and more chilling than the certitude of death—the doubt of the sovereign power enthroned in a fixed standard of conduct. It is the hardest thing to stumble against; it is the thing that breeds yelling panics and good little quiet villainies; it's the true shadow of calamity. Did I believe in a miracle? and why did I desire it so ardently? Was it for my

> own sake that I wished to find some shadow of an excuse for that young fellow whom I had never seen before, but whose appearance alone added a touch of personal concern to the thoughts suggested by the knowledge of his weakness—made it a thing of mystery and terror—like a hint of a destructive fate ready for us all whose youth—in its day—had resembled his youth? I fear that such was the secret motive of my prying. I was, and no mistake, looking for a miracle. The only thing that at this distance of time strikes me as miraculous is the extent of my imbecility. I positively hoped to obtain from that battered and shady invalid some exorcism against the ghost of doubt. (42–43)

Somewhat later Chester, Conrad's version in this novel of the insensitive "aesthetic" fool, says of Jim:

> Takes it to heart? . . . Then he's no good . . . You must see things exactly as they are—if you don't, you may just as well give in at once. You will never do anything in this world. Look at me. I made it a practice never to take anything to heart. (139)

And he offers to bury Jim on a guano-filled island. Marlow's reaction, as he rejects the proposal, is significant:

> To bury him would have been such an easy kindness! It would have been so much in accordance with the wisdom of life, which consists in putting out of sight all the reminders of our folly, of our weaknesses, of our mortality; all that makes against our efficiency—the memory of our failures, the hints of our undying fears, the bodies of our dead friends. (149–150)

With Brierly, ironically one of the judges at the inquiry, this awareness of common guilt is fatal. Temperamentally much like Jim, in his romanticism at least, Brierly has been an unequaled and continual success. Jim's trial so unnerves him, so persuades him to identify himself with the culprit, that he tries desperately to send Jim away before its conclusion—a reminder of Marlow's remarks about burying him to keep him out of our way and out of our awareness. About Brierly's subsequent suicide Marlow has few questions. During the inquiry, he tells us, Brierly "was probably holding silent inquiry into his own case. The verdict must have been of unmitigated guilt, and he took the secret of the evidence with him in that leap into the sea" (49–50).

In view of these universal fears, we can hardly expect Marlow to be utterly convinced—as convinced as Jim wants him to be—by what he sees on his last visit to Lord Jim's domain. In answer to Jewel's fears, Marlow is forced to admit to her, whose admiration for Jim will not allow her to believe it, that Jim will never leave her for the outside world that drove him there "because he is not good enough." But his moral sensitivity leads him to add, "Nobody, nobody is good enough" (276). Jim reveals his own dissatisfaction in a similar lament:

> Is it not strange . . . that all these people, all these people who would do anything for me, can never be made to understand? . . . What more can I want? If you ask them who is brave—who is true—who is just—who is it they would trust with their lives?—they would say, Tuan Jim. And yet they can never know the real, real truth . . . (264)

And then he confronts Marlow with the key question, on which he never does get Marlow's reassurance: "But all the same, you wouldn't like to have me aboard your own ship—hey? . . . Only . . . you just try to tell this to any of them here. They would think you a fool, a liar, or worse" (265). Nobody is good enough, Jim no more so than the rest, and his growing awareness of this truth gives him a maturity which demands more than the schoolboy heroism he can now turn on at will.

When at the end Marlow visits Stein and there sees Tamb' Itam and Jewel, the disappointed, even disgusted report of Jim's last actions ("He would not fight") is meant to delude us into believing that the *Patna* episode has occurred again, that Jim's hard-won heroism has crumbled. He seems superficially to have come full circle to a paralysis that destroys a sacred trust. Yet he promised Marlow, that last time, to be "faithful" (290); and although Jewel bitterly charges him with being "false," Stein's assurance is unquestionable as he tells Jewel, "No! no! Not false! True! true! true!" (304). Of course, "true" here can only mean faithful in the appropriately chivalric context of knighthood. Marlow himself, finally the unromantic ethical man with a worldly commitment—a commitment to "a fixed standard of conduct" (43)—but not one exclusive enough to mar the all-embracing sympathy he requires as narrator, is almost persuaded despite some lingering doubts that he dare not give up. After describing the "proud and unflinching glance" (362) with which Jim accepts his death, Marlow suggests this to have been Jim's moment of vision in which the veil was raised and the face of the Eastern bride, his opportunity, finally revealed. And why not? We remember that after the *Patna* episode Jim insisted on rejecting the temptation of death:

> Sick of life—to tell you the truth; but what would have been the good to shirk it—in—in—that way? That was not the way. I believe—I believe it would have—it would have ended—nothing. . . . No! the proper thing was to face it out—alone for myself—wait for another chance—find out . . . (114)

When he allows himself to decide in favor of death in Patusan, we realize that this last act is no failure and that he *has* found out. He now can accept the punishment he earlier wanted and sought but had to resist, because the act which now brings it about is one of profound courage, however similar it may seem to that earlier act of cowardice.

There are two interlocking justifications for this final action. One of them relates to Jim's new-found and fully exploited capacity for action. Having reversed his initial inability to act so that he has fulfilled all that bravery could demand, he must now commit the supremely brave act of choosing not to act. The redemption Jim so long sought and finally thought he found in Patusan was based only upon the deed, and the deed was proved by the respect it engendered from the society it served. But we have seen that the satisfactions it provided Jim were but superficial. He has discovered as only relative that which he must have as absolute, since he has lost so much in its name. This painful relativism Jim had to be aware of as he witnessed himself worshiped in Patusan and despised as unworthy of trust in the world beyond. It would seem, then, that the deed, the applause, and social service cannot be final moral criteria for him. He must reject the simple schoolboy code and the conforming obligations under which it placed the would-be hero in order to meet a wider obligation. And whatever the final cost, this final action is a victory over relativism in that he has consciously chosen the inaction that lets down his people and even forces them to execute him in a death he rushes to accept.

But of course this is no willful anti-social perversity. There is reason enough why he should have let them down precisely this way—which leads us to the second justification for this action, based on yet another modulation of that ubiquitous theme of common guilt. The criminal Brown, who in talking Jim out of destroying him talks him into his own destruction, seems instinctively to touch Jim's sore spot. Turning upon Jim's moral pretensions as defender of Patusan, Brown challenges him in just the right way:

> And what do you deserve . . . you that I find skulking here with your mouth full of responsibility, of innocent lives, of your infernal duty? . . . I came here for food. . . . And what did *you* come for? . . . I won't ask you what scared you into this infernal hole . . . (333–334)

Brown seems to make their fellowship more intimate with every word he speaks:

> When he asked Jim, with a sort of brusque despairing frankness, whether he himself—straight now—didn't understand that

> when "it came to saving one's life in the dark, one didn't care who else went—three, thirty, three hundred people"—it was as if a demon had been whispering advice in his ear. "I made him wince," boasted Brown to me. "He very soon left off coming the righteous over me. He just stood there with nothing to say, and looking as black as thunder—not at me—on the ground." He asked Jim whether he had nothing fishy in his life to remember that he was so damnedly hard upon a man trying to get out of a deadly hole by the first means that came to hand—and so on, and so on. And there ran through the rough talk a vein of subtle reference to their common blood, an assumption of common experience; a sickening suggestion of common guilt, of secret knowledge that was like a bond of their minds and of their hearts. (337)

And who is this Brown with whom Jim identifies himself? He is not only an indiscriminate murderer, but one who has chosen his profession out of utter misanthropy, out of purely diabolical spite. Yet Brown for Jim is also "one of us": "These were the emissaries with whom the world he had renounced was pursuing him in his retreat. White men from 'out there' where he did not think himself good enough to live" (335–336).

Jim as romantic must still insist on extremity: he cannot close the circle and so limit those who are one of us, not even to exclude one such as Brown. He cannot stop with surface similarities as can Marlow or even the ill-fated Brierly, or the daring captain in the more optimistic *The Secret Sharer.* As extremist Jim must now embrace the dream as his element in a final, full awareness of its destructive quality. And Stein's recognition, with which we began, is now Jim's too. So Brown comes to be the case for common guilt a fortiori, as a gratuitous murderer the very worst possible of his kind. But, ironically, Jim must disdain moral hierarchy and see likeness rather than difference. As Brierly saw himself in Jim—and not utterly without reason—Jim goes the full length and beyond all reason and sees himself in Brown. Mere ethical judgment becomes impossible when the judge sees himself in the accused, finds the same dirt on his hands. When Jewel asks Jim if these men are very evil, Jim answers significantly, "Men act badly sometimes without being much worse than others" (344).

Only paralysis, the refusal to act, can follow from this seemingly Christian insight. And yet he is being faithful in the way he promised Marlow on his last visit; not in any merely racial way though it may seem—as it must have to Doramin—that he has chosen the worst of his kind over the best of Doramin's. But such a view stems only from the reasonable ethical judgment which equates men (as Kyo would put it) with what they do; and Jim has moved willfully beyond. In a more profound sense he is being faithful to the world outside, the world which has judged him and before which he must still prove himself in a way beyond the possibilities for action afforded by his Patusan domain. It is a world of more subtle moral awarenesses than the self-enclosed, ruthless, and finally vengeful demand for self-preservation of Doramin's people, a demand that the still embattled Jim was earlier too young and too ethically eager to question. The faithfulness for which—out of an act of ethical and social treachery—he turns his back on all is, then, a faithfulness, what Marlow at the end calls an "eternal constancy," to "a shadowy ideal of conduct" (362) surely Western and very likely Christian.

We must note finally that this ideal of conduct, while formed in the very shadows from which we heard Stein's formula for victory with which we began, finds itself—like Stein's formula—tested in the light. Here at the end, "within the coast that under the western sun looks like the very stronghold of the night" (362), we find that we have not really left the *Heart of Darkness* after all. But we saw Stein reduced to twitching uncertainty as he moved from the shadows to "the ring of faint light" and into "the bright circle of the lamp" (184–185). Emerging from the dark "into the light of torches" (361), Jim carries his "shadowy ideal of conduct" with him still, and just as firmly. In surrendering "himself faithfully to the claim of his own world of shades" (363), Jim—more than the successful Stein ever could—has earned his right to the "proud and unflinching glance" "sent right and left at all those faces" (362) whom he has so fearlessly and irrevocably betrayed.

But as a solution to the moral dilemma Jim's tentative alternative proves to be a delusion: as Doramin's rage reveals, the Christian refusal to act is also, alas, a form of action and doomed with the others. Thus closes another door on the existential trap, confirming the claims of Axel Heyst, the protagonist of *Victory*, that all action—Jim's as well as Kurtz's—is the devil's work but adding what Heyst's career, in flying from action, attests: that inaction is as deadly as the rest and with fewer satisfactions. It opens no door out of the dilemma but only one that leads in again to the tragic.

2. *Victory:* Pseudo Tragedy and the Failure of Vision

> I suppose I have done a certain amount of harm, since I allowed myself to be tempted into action. It seemed innocent enough, but all action is bound to be harmful. It is devilish. That is why this world is evil upon the whole. (54)
>
> "There must be a lot of the original Adam in me, after all."
>
> He reflected, too, with the sense of making a discovery, that this primeval ancestor is not easily suppressed. The oldest voice in the world is just the one that never ceases to speak. If anybody could have silenced its imperative echoes, it should have been Heyst's father, with his contemptuous, inflexible negation of all effort; but apparently he could not. There was in the son a lot of that first ancestor who, as soon as he could uplift his muddy frame from the celestial mould, started inspecting and naming the animals of that paradise which he was so soon to lose.
>
> Action—the first thought, or perhaps the first impulse, on earth! The barbed hook, baited with the illusion of progress, to bring out of the lightless void the shoals of unnumbered generations!

"And I, the son of my father, have been caught too, like the silliest fish of them all," Heyst said to himself. (173–174) [4]

The baron's dismal view has been justified by what we have seen elsewhere in Conrad. Its validity should be persuasive, as it was for Heyst, faithful son and disciple of a father who seemed to have learned his Conradian lesson well. But Conrad has also made it clear that the inevitability of moral failure does not alter the comfortlessness of avoiding engagement. Nor, we have seen, is inaction ultimately an avoidance of engagement so much as just another sort of engagement. Rather, for Conrad risk is all—risk even in total awareness that there is little to gain and that integrity, for which the risk is taken, consumes itself. And the fullness of risk involves the fullness of commitment, and with these, extremity. Always, however, the need for commitment is balanced by the vision of its futility: as the first reveals the inadequacy of Heyst's position, so the second justifies it.

Victory is all too clearly designed to prove Heyst wrong. Indeed, this design is what will give us trouble since what Conrad has shown us elsewhere demonstrates, not that Heyst is wrong but that he is intolerable, not that his refusal to bend to life is in theory invalid, but that it is in fact untenable for the morally sensitized man. The sequence of events and its significance are obvious enough. Apprentice to his father's philosophy at the start, Heyst is dedicated to resist all human involvement. As he tells us, ". . . he who forms a tie is lost. The germ of corruption has entered into his soul" (199–200). The furthest concession his father would make to the temptations of "flesh and blood" is a disinterested pity:

> You still believe in something, then? . . . You believe in flesh and blood, perhaps? A full and equable contempt would soon

[4] From *Victory*, by Joseph Conrad (New York: Doubleday & Company, Inc., 1939). Copyright 1915, Doubleday & Company, Inc. All page references are to this edition. Extracts are reprinted with the permission of the Trustees of the Joseph Conrad Estate, J. M. Dent and Sons, and Doubleday & Company, Inc., New York.

> do away with that, too. But since you have not attained to it, I advise you to cultivate that form of contempt which is called pity. (174)

Even the father himself, acknowledged by Heyst to have been "very ruthless," was yet "not without pity" (196). Thus the "form of contempt which is called pity" becomes the point of vulnerability for him whose person is temperamentally incapable of accepting the dictates of his cynical reason. And so it is with Heyst. Pity betrays him to Morrison, and pity keeps him tied to Morrison until the latter's death releases him once more, but only with the consequence of slander which—with his own feelings of guilt—ties him to the memory for good.

> In past years, in moments of doubt that will come to a man determined to remain free from absurdities of existence, I often asked myself, with a momentary dread, in what way would life try to get hold of me? And this was the way! (202)

It is, ironically, the very indifference of Heyst, "the most detached of creatures in this earthly captivity," that enables him to assume for Morrison the role of "an agent of Providence" (199). He appears as providentially for Lena in what seems a similar and a similarly disinterested act:

> It was the same sort of impulse which years ago had made him . . . accost Morrison, practically a stranger to him then, a man in trouble, expressively harassed, dejected, lonely. (71–72)

But clearly his pity cannot be so purely related to contempt in this case, since it can hardly remain so continuously detached: ". . . this was another sort of plunge altogether, and likely to lead to a very different kind of partnership" (77). His commitment to it continually threatens to become total but remains limited by his temperamental reticence. The invasion of his domain by the allegorical figures of evil finds him "disarmed" as always, despite his new sense of responsibility. Lena, however, is free to act and cherishes the opportunity to prove their union to be a worthy object of total dedication. Her sacrificial victory conquers Heyst's reticence as well as their enemies. And before adding his sacrifice to hers, he recites the inevitable lamentation: "Ah, Davidson, woe to the man whose heart has not learned while young to hope, to love—and to put its trust in life!" (410) So Heyst acknowledges the error of his ways. He stands corrected by Lena in a mutual consecration of their union which, were Heyst otherwise, might have defied the fates as he had hoped.

We have our narrator's word for it that Heyst too is a "romantic": "Not that we were two romantics, tingeing the world to the hue of our temperament, but that both of us had been acute enough to discover a long time ago that Heyst was" (51). And Davidson adds, remarking on Heyst's precipitate flight with Lena in words that mark Davidson as a later version of Marlow, "I shouldn't have had the pluck. . . . I see a thing all round, as it were; but Heyst doesn't, or else he would have been scared" (51). And it is his strangely romantic propensity that enables Heyst not to be scared.

> Truth to say, Heyst was not one of those men who pause much. Those dreamy spectators of the world's agitation are terrible once the desire to act gets hold of them. They lower their heads and charge a wall with an amazing serenity which nothing but an indisciplined imagination can give. (77)

As a romantic—though of a kind quite different from Lord Jim [5]—Heyst shares Jim's need to manage his relation to reality. His father's desperate teachings have transformed the world into mere delusion and put themselves in its place. At the philosopher's death, the son feels the burden of his nihilistic legacy descend upon him, claim his fidelity, and deprive him of

[5] Morton Dauwen Zabel distinguishes most helpfully between the Jim-form and the Heyst-form of romanticism in his "Joseph Conrad: Chance and Recognition," *Sewanee Review*, LIII (1945), 1–22.

the world: "The rooms, filling with shadows, seemed haunted by a melancholy, uneasy presence which could not express itself" (176). The very objects left Heyst by his father assert themselves upon the son to keep his normal reality in shadow:

> It seemed as if in his conception of a world not worth touching, and perhaps not substantial enough to grasp, these objects familiar to his childhood and his youth and associated with the memory of an old man, were the only realities, something having an absolute existence. (176)

We should not be surprised, then, when Heyst explains to Lena his insufficiency of presence and of action before Mr. Jones and Ricardo by saying, "I believe you are very plucky. . . . I . . . am so rebellious to outward impressions that I can't say that much about myself. I don't react with sufficient distinctness" (316). And a bit later in this conversation: "I have lived too long within myself, watching the mere shadows and shades of life" (318). It is fitting that Mr. Jones, against whom he is so powerless, should be almost literally a ghost, a shade, and thus to Heyst representative of inimical humanity at large:

> I've said to the Earth that bore me: "I am I and you are a shadow." And, by Jove, it is so! But it appears that such words cannot be uttered with impunity. Here I am on a Shadow inhabited by Shades. How helpless a man is against the Shades! How is one to intimidate, persuade, resist, assert oneself against them? I have lost all belief in realities. . . . (350)

But the sacrifice Lena takes upon herself shakes the strange security of his cynicism; it acts as the shock to propel Heyst to a new sense of dream and life. Heyst stands as witness to the tableau of victory: the sensual and violent Ricardo, now disarmed, worshipfully seated at the feet of Lena, who has his knife (and masculinity?) buried harmlessly in the folds of her dress between her knees. The seemingly defenseless girl, Heyst's helpless dependency whom he has protected so woefully, has now in unmanning Ricardo unmanned Heyst as well:

> Doubt entered into him—a doubt of a new kind, formless, hideous. It seemed to spread itself all over him, enter his limbs, and lodge in his entrails. He stopped suddenly, with a thought that he who experienced such a feeling had no business to live—or perhaps was no longer living.
>
> Everything—the bungalow, the forest, the open ground—trembled incessantly; the earth, the sky itself, shivered all the time, and the only thing immovable in the shuddering universe was the interior of the lighted room and the woman in black sitting in the light of the eight candle-flames. They flung around her an intolerable brilliance which hurt his eyes, seemed to sear his very brain with the radiation of infernal heat. . . . A great shame descended upon Heyst—the shame of guilt, absurd and maddening. (391–392)

And what were shadows now become his reality as the symbols of his father's negations fade:

> Heyst stumbled into the room and looked around. All the objects in there—the books, the gleam of old silver familiar to him from boyhood, the very portrait on the wall—seemed shadowy, unsubstantial, the dumb accomplices of an amazing dream-plot ending in an illusory effect of awakening and the impossibility of ever closing his eyes again. (403)

It was at the beginning of the Lena episode, however, that his grasp on his inherited sense of reality—or unreality—weakened. Our narrator has told us of the early Heyst:

> The young man learned to reflect, which is a destructive process, a reckoning of the cost. It is not the clear-sighted who lead the world. Great achievements are accomplished in a blessed, warm mental fog, which the pitiless cold blasts of the father's analysis had blown away from the son. (91–92)

And we have already been told that he was suffused in this fog as he contemplated the desperate rescue upon which, through this symbol, Conrad is clearly bestowing his blessing:

> Formerly, in solitude and in silence, he had been used to think clearly and sometimes even profoundly, seeing life outside the flattering optical delusion of everlasting hope, of conventional self-deceptions, of an ever-expected happiness. But now he was troubled; a light veil seemed to hang before his mental vision; the awakening of a tenderness, indistinct and confused as yet, towards an unknown woman. (82)

Of course Heyst's father was correct in estimating the enmity of the world, the prospects of failure in it, of being overcome by it. Its unreasoning, disorderly, anti-human qualities are discovered in the immeasurable haze of the reality to which Heyst has opened himself once he has opened himself to Lena. The pageant upon which the primal, Eden-like, and yet daring conjunction of the lovers converges is an apocalyptic one played on high rocks overlooking the sea under the tropical noontime sun:

> They moved, silent in the great stillness, breathing the calmness, the infinite isolation, the repose of a slumber without dreams. They emerged at the upper limit of vegetation, among some rocks; and in a depression of the sharp slope, like a small platform, they turned about and looked from on high over the sea, lonely, its colour effaced by sunshine, its horizon a heat mist, a mere unsubstantial shimmer in the pale and blinding infinity overhung by the darker blaze of the sky. (190)

We are once again among the abstract, life-denying snows of Lawrence and Mann. Lena senses the enmity of the scene and shrinks before it: "That empty space was to her the abomination of desolation. . . . '. . . I look at all that water and all that light . . . It seems as if everything that there is had gone under' " (190–191). Here the apocalyptic element is made explicit as Heyst sees in her vision "the story of the deluge . . . The vision of a world destroyed." (191)

The deluge, we shortly discover, is the destructive moment that awaits in all lives, the explosive shock to the well-established, secure comfort of one stage of existence and the revelation of a cosmic caprice that will hover menacingly over all man's noblest delusions which would construct a life of ordered integrity. Thus when Lena describes the sudden and traumatic ending of a hopeful and pleasantly routine interlude in her childhood, Heyst merely choruses, "The deluge." This conversation is omen as well as commentary: it finds an echo in the final and fatal scenes in which, as summoner of the deluge, "the thunder growled distantly with angry modulations of its tremendous voice, while the world outside shuddered incessantly around the dead stillness of the room where the framed profile of Heyst's father looked severely into space" (401). Once again the imposition of an infinite, untamed, hazy reality upon the rigorous clarity of the mere shadows and shades of pure negativism. And the choice: the destruction of a life affirmed or the total denial of life. But in the earlier moment of apocalyptic vision, the newly committed Heyst must acknowledge that, even in the wake of the deluge, the happy people in the world destroyed are "they specially who ought to have been congratulated" (191). Thus he indicates this early the formula for tragedy that he confirms at the end, when, under the tutelage of Lena, he awakens finally to a new reality that demands his destruction. The formula is plain, and it is finally affirmative: total dedication to a delicate microcosm in awareness of the constant menace of the macrocosm which finally sends the deluge that leaves a "world destroyed" in which, however, the totally dedicated are specially to be "congratulated."

The more hopeful Lena, shaken by her view of the sea and the fearful vision it brings, is hardly restored by the ensuing conversation. She is newly disturbed by a final glimpse:

> The flaming abyss of emptiness, the liquid, undulating glare, the tragic brutality of the light, made her long for the friendly night, with its stars stilled by an austere spell; for the velvety dark sky and the mysterious great shadow of the sea, conveying peace to the day-weary heart. (216)

But if an intimation of the consequences of her new attachment to life and hope seems momentarily to frighten her into Heyst's shadows, the challenge of the invaders leads her to embrace the brilliant and terrifying realities that end, like the fire, by consuming her—and her Heyst. At the moment of her triumph over Ricardo, as she reaches for the knife Ricardo offers her, "there was a flash of fire in her mysterious eyes—a red gleam in the white mist which wrapped the promptings and longings of her soul." (399)

The communion of the lovers above that fearful expanse of sea has yet another telling reverberation. Heyst cries "Sail ho!" as he notices a boat in the distance. He dismisses it, unaware that it is the boat that the sea is collaborating with Schomberg to send to accomplish their destruction. Its appearance at this moment is proof of the justness of Lena's symbolic reading of the scene. It establishes the identification of the scene with the shadowless, sun-filled, fire-filled reality that asserts itself—even if destructively—upon the Heyst who is renegade to all his father shadowed forth. And it confirms far more than Heyst knows the comparison he is about to draw to the deluge: it converts the comparison into prophecy, making far more precise the apocalyptic "vision of a world destroyed." Stein's metaphor of the sea as "the destructive element" is here extended almost to the literal level, which is to say it achieves the density of symbol. For with the boat—borne on the "flood" beneath them—moving under their very eyes, it is the destruction of their own world that they see.

Nor is even this all there is to this intricate network. From the deluge the talk runs on to Heyst's "neighbour," the "good-natured, lazy fellow of a volcano" (193), as Heyst calls him. From the beginning it has been characterized as "indolent" and has been personified as a companion to Heyst who is somehow similar to him—"also a smoker" (4). Of course in part this is fair warning to look out for the equally inactive Heyst in whom smoldering fires also continually threaten the heat and violence of explosion. But more significantly, the seeming indolence of the volcano is as deceptive to Heyst as the deep peace of the sea was that night on the *Patna* for Jim. For the boat, being carried by the deluge whose agent it becomes, is to be guided to its oblivious victims by this very volcano. When Ricardo expresses his fears that he and his partners may miss their objective, Schomberg gives them an inescapable target: "What do you think of a pillar of smoke by day and a loom of fire at night? There's a volcano in full blast near that island—enough to guide almost a blind man. What more do you want? An active volcano to steer by!" (168–169) Schomberg is proved correct, we later learn. The voyagers were almost overcome, almost totally lost "when they caught sight of the smoke of the volcano. It nerved them to make an effort for their lives. Soon afterwards they made out the island" (240). This is the object Heyst turns to after the deluge—an object, he seems to think, less pregnant with ominous significance. But, having already seen the role it has been assigned, we rather recognize it as co-conspirator. It is fit neighbor, not for Heyst his father's son, but for the Heyst who plunges—even if into the abyss.

And who are these "envoys of the outer world" (329)? That they are allegorical figures is plain enough—if anything, too plain. Even Heyst concedes their function. Mr. Jones, the ghost, is pure evil, the intellectual evil that is disembodied. His misogyny, necessary to the concluding action, is consistent with a dehumanization so complete as to be free of the most basic of our drives. The suggestion of Satan ("I am he who is" [317]) is continually clear, if tentative, as Conrad's dramatic good sense forces him to play coy in mute acknowledgment of his overcommitment to allegory. Ricardo, the jungle cat, is sensual evil. His vulnerability to women reveals the physical absorption of the beast of prey, while his dislike of whisky only confirms it by suggesting that, like the beast, he needs no artificial stimulant. Ricardo himself significantly relates his feelings about drinking to Mr. Jones's misogyny when, speaking of women as creatures to be either desired or avoided and of the more extreme attitude of Mr. Jones, he says, "I'm hanged if I don't think they are to him what liquor is to me" (161). Pedro ("The brute force is at the back" [329]) is indeed kept in the background. As merely subhuman in his bestiality, he hardly supplements the others. He seems to have been included only because Conrad, requiring more than a single villain for his plot, preferred to have the mystic number of three rather than the two he needed.

Mr. Jones cannot help reminding us of that other scoundrel with the commonplace name, Brown in *Lord Jim*, in that he too judges his victim by reducing him to his own immoralism. Of course he is armed with the slander of Schomberg that persuades us about the fateful consequences of Heyst's involvement with Morrison. Thus Mr. Jones answers Heyst's impatience with their failure to act against him:

> Not everybody can divest himself of the prejudices of a gentleman as easily as you have done, Mr. Heyst. . . . We are—er—adequate bandits; and we are after the fruit of your labours as a—er—successful swindler. It's the way of the world—gorge and disgorge! (383–384)

And as Lord Jim's precious Jewel was mistaken by the outside world for a priceless gem, an emerald, so the infatuated Ricardo—deserting his "gentleman"—identifies Lena with Heyst's supposed loot: "But there is plunder stowed somewhere that's worth having? . . . And who cares? . . . It's you who are my treasure. It's I who found you out where a gentleman had buried you to rot for his accursed pleasure" (396). And yet, again in a way reminiscent of Brown, the invaders are in part self-appointed agents of the deluge. Jones tells Heyst:

> In one way I am—yes, I am the world itself, come to pay you a visit. In another sense I am an outcast—almost an outlaw. If you prefer a less materialistic view, I am a sort of fate—the retribution that waits its time. (379)

If such are his enemies—the perverse "rebel . . . coming and going up and down the earth" (317–318) and the cat to whom "life was not a matter of passive renunciation, but of a particularly active warfare" (260)—there is also his supposed ally, the servant Wang who represents, not malevolence, but the total indifference of amoral practicality: "Heyst envied the

Chinaman's obedience to his instincts, the powerful simplicity of purpose which made his existence appear almost automatic in the mysterious precision of its facts" (181). He is a man always armed in the sense that Heyst has been "a disarmed man all [his] life" (404). When he is sufficiently impressed by the threat of Jones and Ricardo, Wang deserts immediately, methodically, of course taking with him Heyst's gun—as if it could have done his master any good anyway.

> His Chinaman's mind, very clear but not far-reaching, was made up according to the plain reason of things, such as it appeared to him in the light of his simple feeling for self-preservation, untrammelled by any notions of romantic honour or tender conscience. (307)

Clearly Wang is Chinese for a significant reason. The inheritor of a closely integrated culture, he easily merges with Alfuro society on the island so that, never isolated, he is assured of a refuge when danger strikes. And when he so simply refuses Heyst and Lena sanctuary, we are to recognize in the act the destructive indifference of the organized community that efficiently pursues the general welfare. It is in the same matter-of-fact way that he puts Heyst's gun to use, casually killing Pedro when the chance arises. Of course Wang's "mysterious precision," his casual efficiency, remain peculiarly Eastern in being mysterious and casual. They seem to proceed, not from a rationalist's dedication to a manageable finite world, but from a resignation to the cosmic indifference of an unindividuated infinity. He may remind us of Mann's—or at least Settembrini's—notion of what it is to be "Eastern"; and in his inhumane, if automatic, decisions, he confirms the diagnosis: he becomes another reflector of the disinterested, glimmering infinity of the sea out of which, by way of thunder, issues the destructive god.

But totally purposeful against the threat is Lena, who was so helpless against Schomberg and who complained, "real bad people that you can see are bad, they get over me somehow.

. . . I am afraid of wickedness" (207). But now the role she envisions for herself in her conjunction with Heyst makes her "a human being who counted" (292); it frees her to act where Heyst, whose paralysis persists, cannot. She even glories in Heyst's incapacities because of what they leave only her to do—for him and for the sanctification of their union. Thus the sublime quality of her victory which, even in death, breaks the shell of Heyst's lingering resistance to total dedication. Yet it is finally only a symbolic—indeed a token—victory. For she has split the villains and set Jones against Ricardo by her mere presence, so that she has won before her final disarming of Ricardo. The disarming itself only has the ironic function of assuring that her victory be a tragic one by putting her in the way of Jones's bullet, and that it be—in terms of usefulness—an ineffectual one since the knife can be put to no use, least of all by her, as she acknowledges. All this futility perhaps strengthens the devastating effect her victory has on Heyst.

Heyst himself is at the start already beyond the reach of the ethical, or rather is in full retreat from it, from the light of common and communal reality. The novel traces his return to the human communion, first through his semi-commitment to Lena and then suddenly, thanks to her sacrifice, through a belated affirmation that demands his own unqualified gesture of total commitment to the warmth that destroys. Whereas Jim could break through only by yielding up his union with Jewel and with it his service of the ethical, Heyst must break back through to the ethical he earlier abandoned, thus negating his negation.

Of course Heyst's original rejection was more an empty retreat than a defiant surpassing. Anything but demoniacal, he was Kierkegaard's despairing man who cautiously willed not to be himself rather than the more common despairing man who, like most of our protagonists, recklessly willed to be himself.[6]

[6] From *The Sickness unto Death*, by Soren Kierkegaard, trans. Walter Lowrie (Princeton, N.J.: Princeton University Press, 1941), Part First, *passim.*

So, confronted by Jones and Ricardo, "He considered himself a dead man already" (354). For "His very will seemed dead of weariness" (390). It is this state in Heyst that allows the opposed alliances to become confused, so that the active and heated member of each pair, Ricardo and Lena, apparently in league through Lena's shrewd duplicity, are opposed by their lifeless partners as Heyst allows himself to be led by his apparent kinsman, the ghostly Mr. Jones. He comes fully to life only to add his death to Lena's in a tribute to life that a self-inflicted death can alone articulate. He takes fire, but only to realize the metaphor; for fire consumes what it gives warmth to.

If Heyst had been less preoccupied with his will-lessness, he would have noticed how inconclusive the threat is with which the world is challenging him. For all the menace that issues from them, Jones and Ricardo turn out after all to be inefficient and generally unimpressive antagonists. Only Heyst could be overcome by them since he overcomes himself—with shockingly little help, except from a stray bullet that miraculously finds an unintended target. Heyst is presented with several chances to turn the tables on the invaders, especially after Mr. Jones learns of Lena's presence and becomes anxious for his gentleman friend Heyst to join with him in his pathological aversion to the "Mud souls, obscene and cunning!" (392) Conrad pointedly shows us how much simpler it would be for Heyst to disarm Mr. Jones than for Lena to disarm Ricardo as she does. Now it is true that this difference in their capacity to act is crucial to Conrad's theme. It follows, then, that the threat sent them by the world could, by a healthier attitude, have been effectually dismissed; that the clouds could, by a sunnier disposition toward life and hope, have been dispelled before they brought the deluge. But if there is nothing more substantial, indeed more inevitable, than this about the ruinous consequences of involvement, then Conrad's brilliant symbolism has clearly overstated his case; and all we have learned from his other work we must unlearn, since it now evaporates under the pressure of a blithe optimism. For we have earlier learned from Conrad what

Heyst's father learned: that commitment and the action to which it leads are fatal. But now we learn that they are fatal only to Heyst who, because he has earlier turned his back on them, is unable—after running off with Lena—to accept them totally enough or consistently enough. Had he done so, had he been able to join fully with Lena, there would have been no defeat, no deluge.

It is one thing to counter Heyst's father and to celebrate commitment and risk despite all we know that he knows. But it is another to insist that all we have been shown by Conrad and all that the symbolism in *Victory* shows us—that the vision of Heyst's father and of the paralyzed Heyst—can be dissolved into airy phantoms, seen as a crank's delusions, if we merely summon a faith in human communion. This is to deny the driven-ness of the visionary in his extreme situation. It is a retreat from the tragic to the sentimentally ethical that asks for blind faith in life and love and for the comforting cinematic outburst, "Together we can lick the world, baby." For so they could have, Heyst and Lena, had Heyst seen his errors and found the courage to be resolute before it was, perchance, too late.

Perhaps it is that the later Conrad, more mature and anxious for reconciliation, was no longer content with the tragic vision which, we have seen through Marlow, always made him most uncomfortable—as well it should have. So he tried to move beyond to full tragedy. But he had no place to go—nothing both post-ethical and post-tragic to affirm—and had instead to come back, to retreat to the pleasant prospects of ethical existence whose delusions his characters had long before seen through. These prospects can be reasserted now only by denying those earlier denials. And yet even in this novel we can see how persuasive these tragic denials are, so that the later recantation seems a betrayal of Conrad's dramatic powers.

Not only does Conrad try to reach the upper limits of tragedy through the unqualified affirmation given us through Heyst and his sacrifice, but he even tries to build his catharsis right into the *dénouement*. For Heyst dies by fire, a rite in which he converts the house he and Lena shared into a funeral pyre for the lovers. Davidson justifies the act for Heyst and, we are to assume, in the Heystian spirit: "fire purifies everything" (410). It is, then, a ritual purgation and a cue to the thematic catharsis toward which Conrad is straining. But the content of the ritual, the gods whom it celebrates, belie the gesture. Conrad's limitations are too severe to permit a break-through, and the data of his world will support nothing that he gives us in its stead. As author Conrad has himself run a risk: unwilling to abide with the tragic vision and able only to withdraw before it since he cannot go beyond, he has still dared to try high tragedy. Instead of achieving more he has achieved less, his pseudo tragedy destroying the authenticity of the vision it tried to surpass. But Conrad's risk was a worthy and admirable one, even if futile and perhaps foredoomed. If it makes him an imperfect or even, at moments, a foolish novelist, it makes him a daring one, and thus a fit companion for the reckless if erring heroes he so profoundly chronicled.

CHAPTER SEVEN

The Perils of "Enthusiast" Virtue

1. Melville's "Enthusiast": The Perversion of Innocence

> For in tremendous extremities human souls are like drowning men; well enough they know they are in peril; well enough they know the causes of that peril;—nevertheless, the sea is the sea, and these drowning men do drown. (357) [1]

This language and this metaphor tell us at once that in *Pierre* we are in a universe bordering or even overlapping Lord Jim's. It is just as obvious that this is the universe which has been mine throughout this study. This relevance alone can justify my using a novel whose often incredible weaknesses—indeed whose horrors—would seem to argue conclusively against its being taken seriously. The shrieking melodramatics of style and action are beyond excuse or apology. Yet even Melville's alternative title, *The Ambiguities*, expresses his central concern with the cleft consciousness that I have emphasized as characterizing the tragic sense. Here, perhaps, we approach the essential cause of Melville's difficulties with this novel: his failure to hold con-

[1] From *Pierre; or, The Ambiguities*, by Herman Melville, ed. Henry A. Murray (New York: Farrar, Straus & Cudahy, Inc., 1949). Copyright, L. C. Page & Company, Inc. All page references are to the 1949 edition.

sistently to the distinction between himself and his disorderly hero. In contrast to Gide and his Michel, for example, the distance between Melville and Pierre, demanded by the objectivity of Melville's role—by his need to contain Pierre's divisive vision within an aesthetically harmonious structure—frequently comes close to vanishing altogether. And as it vanishes so, of course, does the aesthetic power of his novel: as he yields uncritically to the absurdities of his hero, so we refuse any longer to yield to him. Melville, here as in *Moby Dick*, is himself trapped by the order-destroying despair that is his theme. But he fails here to do what he did in *Moby Dick* in the face of his dark vision: in the language of Mann, he fails to transcend despair by giving it an aesthetically controlled voice. Instead, its chaos brings on his own by undermining his art.

Thus the very source of Melville's failings in *Pierre* strengthens its claim to being thematically urgent to my undertaking. The aesthetic justification for excluding it reveals my thematic need for it as almost indispensable. This is the furthest extent of my apology for the time I must spend on so unreadable a work. Its special usefulness to me stems from the nature and the direction of Pierre's enthusiasm. Not, of course, from the mere fact of his enthusiasm, for we have been moving from one total "enthusiast" to another throughout. But Pierre's enthusiasm falls upon him in a state of literally paradisiacal innocence. Seen by him as morally pure, it is totally conditioned by his moral inexperience even as it initiates him into its corrupt world quickly and roughly. In Pierre's original and youthful motives there is nothing of Ahab's drive to make vengeful war upon that in the world which has dared to wrong him, humiliate him, and thus to finish with him, leaving him as "the insulted and the injured." Pierre's situation is more casuistic, indeed, is truly polar: untouched himself, his innocent Eden still open to him, he must give his newly awakened moral sensibility full rein to confront and consecrate the one flaw he has discovered. He must disinterestedly champion righteousness absolutely and sacrificially in an attempt to restore a world of perfection unflawed, to convert all to the transcendent good that has until now flowed above and through his world unchallenged. Under the binding dictate of this moral intuition, he must at whatever cost to himself and others become the agent of this divine goodness, of whose undisputed dominion he has always been assured. He must now counter the vision of evil that he has found lurking beneath, tauntingly reminding him in the ambiguous portrait of his father that it has been there openly staring at him all along. Shaken out of his pre-ethical "aesthetic" bliss, he must trade his innocence, which unquestioningly assumed a natural perfection, for the moral striving for a newly human perfection. As we see the natural traded for the moral-human, the "aesthetic" for the ethical, the state of innocence for the state of experience, the "naive" for the "sentimental," we see again the sublime humanistic objective whose dangerous futility Mann was later to trace—as Melville traces it here—the creative synthesis urged by Blake, by Schiller, by Goethe, by Emerson.

There is no resting on this side of total awareness and total commitment, of so thorough an identification with the godhead as to become its image. There is to be no compromise for the sake of simple human obligations that allow the dutiful routine of every day whose need persists despite the shattering seizure and the extremity it brings. As Pierre's late and despairing vision reveals, the God-enfolded world demands that the homely catnip be overwhelmed by the pretentious amaranth:

> But here and there you still might smell from far the sweet aromaticness of clumps of catnip, that dear farm-house herb. . . . that plant will long abide, long bask and bloom on the abandoned hearth. Illy hid; for every spring the amaranthine and celestial flower gained on the mortal household herb; for every autumn the catnip died, but never an autumn made the amaranth to wane. The catnip and the amaranth!—man's earthly household peace, and the ever-encroaching appetite for God. (405)

But to what god does this relentless appetite lead? To the Titanic, the anti-Olympian bringer of chaos, Enceladus. For in his vision Pierre assumes the godhead, becomes the image of this divine undoer. His original transcendental identification with Christ has been thus perverted in the nightmare he now lives through, in that "ideal horror" that reflects his "actual grief" (407). Nietzsche, we may remember from my first chapter, placed the chaotic Titanic temperament significantly within the tragic framework as the pre-Dionysian antagonist of the Apollonian. Surely this is a long way from the easy grace of the natural world or its sublime transformation into the chivalric Christian world.

It was the latter that Pierre's haughty mother dreamed of at the start as she tried to reconcile her desire for his heroism with her fear of the willfulness needed to achieve it.

> Now I almost wish him otherwise than sweet and docile to me, seeing that it must be hard for man to be an uncompromising hero and a commander among his race, and yet never ruffle any domestic brow. Pray heaven he show his heroicness in some smooth way of favoring fortune, not be called out to be a hero of some dark hope forlorn;—of some dark hope forlorn, whose cruelness makes a savage of a man. (22)

Thus her hope that "he remain all docility to me, and yet prove a haughty hero to the world" (22).

This prayer for epic rather than tragic greatness proves to be too much to ask, so that his mother's slight apprehensiveness proves prophetic: his dedication to sacrificial heroics moves him to haughtiness against her as well, in her eyes surely "makes a savage" of him. His movement to the choice of a self-aware moral greatness follows upon the permanent destruction of his idyllic pre-ethical world. It was the unshadowed world, the naturally and socially rich world of blithe optimistic acceptance —one which could persuade the knightly apprentice to Christian gentlemanliness to mock at the possibilities for earthly sorrow: "Well, life's a burden, they say; why not be burdened cheerily?" (25) This is the Pierre who has "not wholly escaped" the "amiable philosophers of either the 'Compensation,' or 'Optimist' school," those who "deny that any misery is in the world" (325); the Pierre who has not known grief and can "half disbelieve" (47) in it. The idyl of Pierre and his queenly Lucy seems to persuade our author as ironist (for *he*, at least, knows what is coming) to raise his voice with theirs in almost hysterical celebration:

> Oh, praised be the beauty of this earth, the beauty, and the bloom, and the mirthfulness thereof! The first worlds made were winter worlds; the second made, were vernal worlds; the third, and last, and perfectest, was this summer world of ours. In the cold and nether spheres, preachers preach of earth, as we of Paradise above. . . .
>
> Oh, praised be the beauty of this earth, the beauty, and the bloom, and the mirthfulness thereof! We lived before, and shall live again; and as we hope for a fairer world than this to come; so we came from one less fine. From each successive world, the demon Principle is more and more dislodged; he is the accursed clog from chaos, and thither, by every new translation, we drive him further and further back again. Hosannahs to this world! so beautiful itself, and the vestibule to more. (36–37)

Yet it is to be Pierre himself who becomes Enceladus, the demon principle emanating from chaos. In this early stage no break in natural perfection can seem to Pierre to signal its permanent destruction. The hallelujah which Melville, echoing his ecstatic hero, has just shouted for us, has told us that whatever in this fair world is less than "the true fair" (to use the appropriately Platonic notion of Spenser's lovely Sonnet 79 from the *Amoretti*), whatever reveals a not totally exorcised demonism, can be used to translate this world into one yet closer to the heavenly, "the true fair," and to complete exorcism. All leads upward, then, for the enthusiast, who responds to the shocking confrontation by evil with a renewed enthusiasm that, through the moral striving of the man-god, can transform all. It is no wonder that at first Pierre shudders at the threat of the "far profounder gloom" (47) which he senses in Isabel's face, that under its spell he turns in fear away from Dante, "Night's and Hell's poet" (48). Of course it turns out to be Dante who later supplies him with the ambiguous epigraph to comment on what the revelation of his father's sin has really done to him:

> Ah! how dost thou change,
> Agnello! See! thou art not double now,
> Nor only one! (100)

Melville himself, in a more candid moment, acknowledges that what the shock of truth about his father has shattered in Pierre is permanently and irreparably shattered: "Ay, Pierre, now indeed art thou hurt with a wound, never to be completely healed but in heaven; for thee, the before undistrusted moral beauty of the world is forever fled . . ." (75). It is the end of the "aesthetic" and the invitation to the dangerously deceptive ethical that can never allow the restoration and the satisfaction it promises. Of course, Melville's indication of this deception and the consequent self-deception reveals the extent of his distinctness from Pierre, his freedom to judge Pierre.

There is clearly much that is Emersonian—or at least what was popularly thought of as Emersonian—in Pierre's attitudes to the natural world and moral sentiment. We know of Melville's impatience with the facile consolations of transcendentalism, so that as we find Pierre subject to them we may expect to find him opening himself to the revenge of a dark irony. Thus we ought to fear the worst as we see him react to the vision of intimate evil where he had most faith in virtue. He reacts with unquestioning confidence in his moral intuition and its divine source as well as in his own ability to remain spotless even while indulging his willfulness. For he claims his will to be subservient to the "divine commands" (125) with which he so assuredly identifies himself. To prove himself "divinely dedicated" (125), to guarantee his freedom from self-interest, he must hurt—perhaps destroy—himself and his: ". . . he was almost superhumanly prepared to make a sacrifice of all objects dearest to him, and cut himself away from his last hopes of common happiness, should they cross his grand enthusiast resolution . . ." (125). And of course they must cross it.

In turning away from "all common conventional regardings" (125), he must disdain mere human opinion out of deference to "the Christ-like feeling" (125) that answers "the inflexible rule of holy right" (126). And in proper transcendentalist fashion he will turn from the impure conformist world to the natural universe itself, inspirited throughout by the goodness of divinity:

> This day I will forsake the censuses of men, and seek the suffrages of the god-like population of the trees, which now seem to me a nobler race than man. Their high foliage shall drop heavenliness upon me; my feet in contact with their mighty roots, immortal vigor shall so steal into me. (126)

But that evening, as Pierre moves toward his first meeting with Isabel, the friendly Eden on which he has been depending is severely transformed—perhaps Melville's ironic comment on Pierre's bland security in nature's goodness and receptivity. It is a strong and fearsome picture:

> In that wet and misty eve the scattered, shivering pasture elms seemed standing in a world inhospitable, yet rooted by inscrutable sense of duty to their place. . . . [the mysterious mountain masses] shaggy with pines and hemlocks, mystical with nameless, vapory exhalations, and in that dim air black with dread and gloom. At their base, profoundest forests lay entranced, and from their far owl-haunted depths of caves and rotted leaves, and unused and unregarded inland overgrowth of decaying wood—for smallest sticks of which, in other climes many a pauper was that moment perishing; from out the infinite inhumanities of those profoundest forests, came a moaning, muttering, roaring, intermitted, changeful sound: rain-shakings of the palsied trees, slidings of rocks undermined, final crashings of long-riven boughs, and devilish gibberish of the forest-ghosts. (128–129)

Here is a new and different nature, bereft of innocence. Here is the hellish instead of the heavenly, the "inhumanities" that should warn Pierre of what he forsakes and what he invites when he forsakes the human. And this is what he does as he heads toward Isabel. Is it perhaps not a warning also that, under pressure from the "rotted" world to which he is now to be exposed, Pierre's innocence will go the way of nature's and eventuate in the human equivalent of this forbidding picture? If it is such a warning, Pierre can hardly be said to sense it very strongly. For following this bleak natural prospect, as he approaches Isabel's door, Pierre's transcendental assurance seems to be totally without shadow:

> Infallibly he knows that his own voluntary steps are taking him forever from the brilliant chandeliers of the mansion of Saddle Meadows, to join company with the wretched rush-lights of poverty and woe. But his sublime intuitiveness also paints to him the sun-like glories of god-like truth and virtue; which though ever obscured by the dense fogs of earth, still shall shine eventually in unclouded radiance, casting illustrative light upon the sapphire throne of God. (131)

The downward path taken by Pierre's innocence is traced in his movement from Christ to Enceladus, from an almost gratuitous benefactor to an almost gratuitous murderer, from the disinterested agent of *Agape* to the tortured agent of *Eros*—in short, from the light-bearing transcendentalist to that devotee of darkness, Captain Ahab. Melville originally comments on Pierre's desertion of everyone's interest but the unknown Isabel's, on his desertion of every duty but his abstract duty to "Truth" and "Virtue," with an ardor to match Pierre's: "Thus, in the Enthusiast to Duty, the heaven-begotten Christ is born; and will not own a mortal parent, and spurns and rends all mortal bonds" (125). This ardor, stemming from our sometimes critical author, should assure us—and perhaps does—except that in retrospect, in light of the fall which follows, it should assure us only of the savage irony it conceals. We are of course to remember this when we see Plinlimmon, the pragmatic preacher of "virtuous expediency," specifically condemn the imitation of Christ by "inferior beings" as leading to their eventual involvement in "*unique* follies and sins, unimagined before" (250). And so it is to be with Pierre who, as the best and worst of men, has courageously but fatally chosen to break Plinlimmon's injunction to man: "he must by no means make a complete unconditional sacrifice of himself in behalf of any other being, or any cause, or any conceit" (251).

In calling the one duty to which Pierre enthusiastically responds the "abstract duty to 'Truth' and 'Virtue' " and in opposing it to the simple human duties, the immediate, individual, and personal duties that in his history he has helped to accumulate day by day—duties to family, to his beloved, to himself, and to history—I have meant to suggest the point of weakness in this "amaranthine" identification with godhead. It is what a Personalist like Berdyaev, in the existentialist tradition, terms "objectivization." And it is, as we have seen from the first in this volume, the inescapable demonizing consequence of the ethical stage pursued overzealously, the consequence of Hegelian (or Emersonian) immanence claiming our too enthusiastic allegiance, which means our abandonment of everything less abstract, of all that touches us and warms our flesh. Thus just before Melville ambiguously identifies Pierre with "the heaven-begotten Christ," we are told that his new call to enthusiasm and duty, his undeviating pursuit of virtue and truth as these are dictated by his moral intuition, "in its mature development, when it should at last come forth in living deeds, would scorn all *personal* relationship with Pierre, and hold his heart's dearest interests for naught" (125, my italics).

This prideful assumption of the absolute is most dangerous, as Plinlimmon tells us. We must remember further that the source of true *Agape* is not in an impersonal abstraction but in a capacity for immediate, individual, personal love endlessly and indiscriminately multiplied. It cannot be produced by inverting all normally discriminated attachments, damning them, and seizing upon their opposite. For the latter, however sacrificial its consequences, has also been carefully discriminated, however inversely so. Pierre himself early senses the upside-down character of his inner revolution as he speaks of the "reversed idea in my soul," "profoundly sensible that his whole previous moral being was overturned" (102). It becomes painfully clear that inversion of this sort, exclusive and destructive as it is, only too easily becomes perversion as the pretension to disinterestedness fades to reveal the wild passion that has been underneath motivating all.

There is additional evidence of his decision to be an indifferent savior of those who have been socially outcast as a consequence of sexual waywardness. After having defended Delly Ulver as a matter of Christian principle before his mother and the Reverend Falsgrave, he reacts typically to Isabel's first mention of Delly's difficulties: ". . . I am still uncertain how best it may be acted on. Resolved I am, though, to succor her" (183). And so he does, including Delly in that bizarre—even absurd—threesome who that night take their quixotic flight. Her addition to the party serves no purpose so much as it does the demonstration of the indifferent, all-embracing ethical principle whose champion Pierre has become. Yet in embracing all he must touch none—which shall lead him ultimately to reject all.

It is through touch that his underground, incestuous motive is revealed, and, having been revealed, undercuts whatever sanctions his actions—questionable at best—may have claimed and leads him to a meaningless, uncontrolled, and almost random annihilation at the end. Having begun his crusade so much more on the side of the angels than Ahab was—or so it seemed—he ends on the other side even beyond Ahab, who, we must remember, to the end had some poor remnant of his "humanities." When, tortured by his thankless struggle to live the truth and write the truth, Pierre is comforted by the warm grasp of his sister Isabel and is asked whether his torments have been removed by her touch, he answers in startled desperation, "But replaced by—by—by—Oh God, Isabel, unhand me!" (321)

And he acknowledges the changed aspect of virtue, even as we saw the changed aspect of nature earlier. He is overwhelmed by the ambiguous dual principle:

> Ye heavens, that have hidden yourselves in the black hood of the night, I call to ye! If to follow Virtue to her uttermost vista, where common souls never go; if by that I take hold on hell, and the uttermost virtue, after all, prove but a betraying pander to the monstrousest vice,—then close in and crush me, ye stony walls, and into one gulf let all things tumble together! (321)

He half-seriously questions whether Isabel is his sister and warns the gods to look out for the heavenly fires which they inspired in him, for now that heaven and hell are no longer separated the fire will roar uncontrolled in its transformed fury to do its worst. He concludes his tirade by reducing virtue and vice to "two shadows cast from one nothing" (322). With this assertion of nothing as the sole "substance," the atheistic existentialist has discovered himself.

Pierre has been a long time making this total confrontation. He has had evidence enough even before he undertook the actual flight with Isabel. In announcing his final plan to her he insists again and again on his moral purity and on the purity and harmlessness of the plan, a plan to which "heaven itself did not say Nay" (226). All this over-protestation as he seeks to justify their need to live before the world as man and wife! Yet Pierre himself seems shocked at the plan and expects Isabel to be literally floored by it, so that perhaps he is not as convinced of its purity and his as he must protest he is. He holds Isabel up and whispers it to her:

> The girl moved not; was done with all her tremblings; leaned closer to him, with an inexpressible strangeness of an intense love, new and inexplicable. Over the face of Pierre there shot a terrible self-revelation; he imprinted repeated burning kisses upon her; pressed hard her hand; would not let go her sweet and awful passiveness. (226)

So the game was really up before it started, although despite this "self-revelation" Pierre forges ahead and does not draw his inevitable conclusions, personal and moral, until the later scene of painful caresses.

Yet his self-deception in his supposed service of his ideal is made clear even earlier. Pierre has sworn to "know nothing but Truth; glad Truth, or sad Truth; I will know what *is*, and do what my deepest angel dictates. . . . From all idols, I tear all veils . . ." (76). His search for truth shows him the limits of his mother's prideful love and the importance of beauty in the blissful life he has passed. He answers this recognition in an unfortunate imitation of Lear:

> Welcome then be Ugliness and Poverty and Infamy, and all ye other crafty ministers of Truth, that beneath the hoods and rags of beggars hide yet the belts and crowns of kings. And dimmed be all beauty that must own the clay . . . (106)

But Melville is obliged also to face the naked truth and to "tear all veils." And unhappy as he is ("Save me from being bound to Truth, liege lord, as I am now" [126]), he must outdo his hero by acknowledging his weakness as well: though Pierre was "charged with the fire of all divineness, his containing thing was made of clay" (126). Melville must follow this with the admission of Isabel's beauty and its profound attraction for Pierre. Surely we are to recall Pierre's invocation to ugliness as we read our author's uneasy concession that

> womanly beauty, and not womanly ugliness, invited him to champion the right. Be naught concealed in this book of sacred truth. How, if accosted in some squalid lane, a humped, and crippled, hideous girl should have snatched his garment's hem, with—"Save me, Pierre—love me, own me, brother; I am thy sister!"— Ah, if man were wholly made in heaven, why catch we hell-glimpses? (127)

It should be no surprise, then, to find Melville upbraiding high-minded "self-imposters"—Plato, Spinoza, Goethe, "with a preposterous rabble of Muggletonian Scots and Yankees, whose vile brogue still the more bestreaks the stripedness of their Greek or German Neoplatonical originals" (244). Undoubtedly Emerson is among the "Yankees." We have seen that Pierre too has caught "hell-glimpses," enough of them to make him turn in anger upon these affirming philosophers who have deluded him. Though more hysterical, he echoes his author in having about the same cast of villians:

> Now I drop all humorous or indifferent disguises, and all philosophical pretensions. I own myself a brother of the clod, a child of the Primeval Gloom. Hopelessness and despair are over me, as pall on pall. Away, ye chattering apes of a sophomorean Spinoza and Plato, who once didst all but delude me that the night was day, and pain only a tickle. Explain this darkness, exorcise this devil, ye can not. Tell me not, thou inconceivable coxcomb of a Goethe, that the universe can not spare thee and thy immortality, so long as—like a hired waiter—thou makest thyself "generally useful." (356)

Actually it is Vivia, the author-narrator of Pierre's book, who writes this, although we are told that Pierre is speaking through him. Is this not a likely hint that in much the same way Melville is speaking to us through Pierre? Too much so and too often so, there is reason to feel. And the similarity of their maledictions against the "amiable philosophers" is significant evidence.

Despite these realizations, Pierre is able to welcome Lucy's incredible gesture when she comes to Pierre and Isabel to sacrifice herself to them. Her reason—"I feel that heaven hath called me to a wonderful office toward thee" (365)—has all too familiar a ring to us, as it should have to Pierre. Apparently Pierre's enthusiasm is contagious! Lucy answers her mother's pleas with Pierre-like confidence:

> What she was doing was not of herself; she had been moved to it by all-encompassing influences above, around, and beneath. She felt no pain for her own condition; her only suffering was

> sympathetic. She looked for no reward; the essence of well-doing was the consciousness of having done well without the least hope of reward. (384)

By now Pierre should know better; he should appreciate the final irony in the fact of Lucy's saintly commitment just after he has himself seen the final futility of his own commitment. Instead, he responds to her as indeed a divine agent and decides to defend her mad resolve against all comers. Assured of her purity, he worries only whether his dismal quarters could be "the place that an angel should choose for its visit to earth" (366). The language used by Melville suggests even he may share this judgment. Yet the story carries its own judgment of her self-dedication: for it is her decision and Pierre's stalwart defense of that decision against those it hurts that set off the grotesque torrent of blood with which the novel closes.

Perhaps Melville has been too candid about Pierre. With a too great relentlessness he has traced how "the heaven-begotten Christ" has changed to Enceladus, how Pierre's dedication to an immanent, all-absorbing moral order has changed to his Ahab-like, hell-bent war against the hostile, amoral chaos. One could not have begun meaning to have more purity of intention or have ended with less. As unique as the open generosity of his original motive are those secret "unique sins" into which existential logic perverts it—which is what the coldblooded, "non-benevolent" Plinlimmon predicted. Melville clearly finds the sensible, unsympathetic Plinlimmon distasteful ("there was still something latently visible in him which repelled" [341]), but he faces the unhappy and necessary truth of Pierre, the grandly noble alternative. Nor can the final blame rest elsewhere than with Pierre, not even with that detestable, Plinlimmon-like society whose own inhumanities challenge Pierre to take too much on himself. Melville has promised to be "more frank with Pierre than the best men are with themselves"—surely more frank than Pierre himself can be until it is far too late—even though as a consequence of Melville's frankness

Pierre "shall stand in danger of the meanest mortal's scorn" (127). So let us be careful with Pierre, who is meant to be among the very "best men," lest we become as scornful as Plinlimmon and reveal ourselves to be among the "meanest" of mortals. Melville himself suffered from a divided and uncertain allegiance to Pierre that often brought him also to an overzealous rage which consumed the aesthetic possibilities of his work. Perhaps Pierre was too extreme a case, tracing too extreme a movement. Yet in coming toward the end to the demoniacal stage we by now well recognize and in occupying it so fiercely, he should be instructive to us even if he was hopelessly elusive for Melville.

2. Dostoevsky's "Idiot": The Curse of Saintliness

> Though Christ encountered woe in both the precept and the practice of his chronometricals, yet did he remain throughout entirely without folly or sin. Whereas, almost invariably, with inferior beings, the absolute effort to live in this world according to the strict letter of the chronometricals is, somehow, apt to involve those inferior beings eventually in strange, *unique* follies and sins, unimagined before. . . . What man who carries a heavenly soul in him, has not groaned to perceive, that unless he committed a sort of suicide as to the practical things of this world, he never can hope to regulate his earthly conduct by that same heavenly soul? . . . he must by no means make a complete unconditional sacrifice of himself in behalf of any other being, or any cause, or any conceit.
>
> Plotinus Plinlimmon (249–251)

If Pierre has committed the unique sins, Dostoevsky's Myshkin is guilty of the unique follies—in their way, perhaps, as destructive in their consequences. The critic cannot begin to talk about the problem of Myshkin without citing Dostoevsky's famous claim, "My intention is to portray a truly beautiful soul." And this claim would seem clearly to remove Myshkin from consideration as a tragic visionary in my sense. It would rather argue that Dostoevsky has here transcended the tragic vision and, in portraying a true saint, has reached to a considerably more sublime vision. It would argue consequently that the inevitable half-darkness in which I have seen all these extreme protagonists to be wandering may be unequivocally and divinely lightened, that the duality which characterizes their moral life may—given enough innocence and purity—reach a higher reconciliation. In arguing for this exalted affirmation, it would, in other words, argue against my claim for the inescapability of the tragic vision within the conditions of extremity and the aesthetic and existential demands for authenticity, as our crisis-novelists have conceived these. And since one can hardly dispute Dostoevsky's passion for extremity or the fierce candor of his authenticity, I must find a place for even his sublimest work or else qualify my general contention considerably. I have chosen *The Idiot*, then, as the most difficult of his works to bring within my context and as perhaps the most crucial of all novels from the standpoint of my dialectic. I see it as the case against my view a fortiori, with its protagonist at the end of the spectrum toward which I have been shading constantly, the seemingly angelic end farthest removed from the open demons with which I started. It remains to be seen whether this spectrum returns upon itself so that, as our intermediate novels seemed to be prophesying, we end much where we began and moral progression is finally illusion.

In this one case, then, I must use this second novel of the chapter, not as a nontragic (or a less than tragic) analogue, but as an even more critical example of the tragic. Not, of course, that any sensible reader could even for a moment see Myshkin as being transformed into a demoniacal creature. He is surely not to be confused with Pierre. Both are self-sacrificing enthusiasts, but while Pierre's dedication to virtue stems from a prideful and highly self-conscious assumption of righteousness, Myshkin takes up the burdens of humanity with a humility that makes no pretensions for his role—indeed that would deny any which others would make for him. Pierre is a self-appointed Jesus while Myshkin would shrink from any such imputation, although his actions, combining personal disinterestedness with lack of pronouncement, based on love of persons rather than love of principle, seem far more Christ-like. Thus this comparison would suggest that, as Dostoevsky intended, Myshkin approaches the Christ parable without its obvious perversion into parody—a perversion we have frequently witnessed, if nowhere more forcefully than in *Pierre*. But if I know better than to try to transform Myshkin into one of that rebellious group of visionaries of whom Pierre is our most recent and most extreme example, neither can I allow his goodness to remain unquestioned by casting all blame for his unhappy end upon a fallen and uncomprehending world that cannot tolerate the divine simplicity of innocence. I must hope it is not merely the cold unyielding eye of Plinlimmon I am using as I claim to find the novel casting some of the blame on Myshkin through the very presumption upon the rest of humanity that his humility inversely asserts.

It may of course be that Dostoevsky did not totally succeed in his attempt "to portray a truly beautiful soul" or at least it seems likely that he was not totally satisfied with the results. If he were satisfied, would he have felt the need to pursue the problem of saintliness and worldliness in the more careful and qualified way he did with Zossima and Alyosha in *The Brothers Karamazov*? Zossima's saintliness seems unquestionable, but it is dramatically inconclusive in that he had to retire from the world to achieve it. He is transfigured from a licentious worldling only through the monastery, which is the safeguard against extreme situations because it forbids human involvement. Zossima appears to recognize as much in summoning Alyosha to a more difficult saintly mission:

> . . . this is not the place for you in the future. When it is God's will to call me, leave the monastery. . . . I bless you for great service in the world. Yours will be a long pilgrimage. And you will have to take a wife, too. You will have to bear *all* before you come back.[2]

[2] From *The Brothers Karamazov*, by Feodor Dostoevsky, trans. Constance Garnett (New York: The Macmillan Company, 1912), p. 76.

It seems, then, that Dostoevsky may have felt some sense of failure with Myshkin, leading him to try again with Alyosha to explore the possibilities of sainthood operating with the necessary limitations of its human agent within a fallen world. And Dostoevsky was too much of a Christian not to insist that the fallen world would somehow have to be reflected in its saintly but human intruder, and that the intruder would have the humility to accept and assert this fact. So Zossima sends forth Alyosha to a danger and a suffering perhaps beyond what he could trust himself to undergo. The story as regards Alyosha was left unfinished by Dostoevsky and, although the children are cheering him at the close of the novel, many doubts are left about how he would have made out in the unwritten sequel—with the Aglaia-like, sick figure of Lise lingering in the background casting many of them. Given his Karamazov name and Dostoevsky's honesty—as well as my own theory about the tragic—I remain at least as skeptical as Eliseo Vivas is in his essay [3] whose persuasiveness allowed me to turn back to *The Idiot* with confidence. I am skeptical finally because all I have really to go on is the earlier failure of Myshkin, a failure Dostoevsky took seriously enough to try again in *The Brothers Karamazov*, even if he could not bring Alyosha far enough for us to judge whether he can do better, indeed whether man can do better. So it still must be Myshkin's career we examine to find Dostoevsky's detailed study of the consequences of man as Jesus.

There is Zossima as well as Alyosha in Myshkin. His retirement in the Swiss sanitarium both before and after the action of the novel is clearly his withdrawal from human involvement, his monastery where his modest sanctity goes its way in peace. He is, like the saint, unfit for society, which will not understand him, labels him "idiot," and keeps him apart in forced solitude. When he recovers enough superficial similarity to his fellows

[3] "The Two Dimensions of Reality in *The Brothers Karamazov*," by Eliseo Vivas, in *Creation and Discovery* (New York: Noonday Press, 1955), pp. 47–70.

to get by, he returns to society where his essential position remains the same, his ideas "idiotic" and his language gibberish. But his involvement brings the darkest of troubles to others and himself, and he shall have to withdraw again to his sanctuary where he can safely commune with himself and make literal the symbolic distance between himself and the world.

During his worldly trials also the impulse to retreat is alive in him. When his difficulties managing with people seem insuperable, he has a "terrible longing . . . to leave everything here and to go back to the place from which he had come, to go away into the distance to some remote region, to go away at once without even saying good-bye to any one" (291).[4] Or: "Sometimes he longed to get away, to vanish from here altogether. He would have been positively glad to be in some gloomy, deserted place, only that he might be alone with his thoughts and no one might know where he was" (329). But at this stage of his career he must not take the way of Zossima. We are told, after the first of these passages, that he did not consider his "terrible longing" "for ten minutes; he decided at once that it would be 'impossible' to run away, that it would be almost cowardice, that he was faced with such difficulties that it was his duty now to solve them, or at least to do his utmost to solve them" (291). And after the second of these passages he turns back to the world to look into those taunting wild eyes of Aglaia. True to his Christ-like decision to mix with the affairs of the world, he must confess to Ippolit that he has "always been a materialist" (368) in a statement that Ippolit wisely considers significant. A very special sort of materialist, it goes without saying.

There is much else about Myshkin that is divided. Whatever duality we find in him is evidence of his humanity, his imperfection, his similarity to the lesser people about him. For

[4] From *The Idiot*, by Feodor Dostoevsky, trans. Constance Garnett (New York: Random House, Inc., 1935). Copyright by The Macmillan Company. All page references are to the Random House edition. Excerpts are reprinted with the permission of The Macmillan Company.

example, Keller, with Lebedyev the basest and most obviously "underground" creature in this story that is filled with them, has been confessing to Myshkin the confusion in him of the noble and the base, the undercutting of every noble intention by an insidiously base countermotive: he ashamedly admits that he had decided to make a full confession of sins to Myshkin and then, even while still feeling this need profoundly, had thought of turning it to profit by asking Myshkin for money. Indeed, he is even using this novel form of double confession as a new way of extorting money from Myshkin. And surely Myshkin knows this, although he cheerfully allows Keller to succeed. Myshkin tries to account to Keller for the following of the noble by the base, the impulse to confess by the impulse to extort:

> "But most likely that's not true; it's simply both things came at once. The two thoughts came together; that often happens. It's constantly so with me. I think it's not a good thing, though; and, do you know, Keller, I reproach myself most of all for it. You might have been telling me about myself just now. I have sometimes even fancied," Myshkin went on very earnestly, genuinely and profoundly interested, "that all people are like that; so that I was even beginning to excuse myself because it is awfully difficult to struggle against these *double* thoughts; I've tried. God knows how they arise and come into one's mind." (293)

In part, of course, this is God's humble man seeing in himself the weaknesses of others in order not to be the self-righteous judge. But Myshkin is indeed concerned about his own "double thoughts." Only a few pages earlier we were told, "of late he had blamed himself for two extremes, for his excessive 'senseless and impertinent' readiness to trust people and at the same time for his gloomy suspiciousness" (285).[5]

[5] One could point out, as evidence of Myshkin's less than angelic inconsistency, his bitter attack on Roman Catholicism (518) in that wild engagement party that culminates in the breaking of the vase and his

There is also Myshkin's conviction of the momentary ecstasy allowed by his epilepsy in the moment of pure light that preceded his fits. In phrases that sound like Mann in his more dangerously "*spirituel*" moments, Myshkin debates the ambiguities of disease and health with himself:

> . . . he often said to himself that all these gleams and flashes of the highest sensation of life and self-consciousness, and therefore also of the highest form of existence, were nothing but disease, the interruption of the normal condition; and if so, it was not at all the highest form of being, but on the contrary must be reckoned the lowest. And yet he came at last to an extremely paradoxical conclusion. "What if it is disease?" he decided at last. "What does it matter that it is an abnormal intensity, if the result, if the minute of sensation, remembered and analysed afterwards in health, turns out to be the acme of harmony and beauty, and gives a feeling, unknown and undivined till then, of completeness, of proportion, of reconciliation, and of ecstatic devotional merging in the highest synthesis of life?" (214)

We may be reminded of his earlier performance before the Epanchin women, his existential psychoanalysis of the executed criminal, which concluded with his speculation about the hear-

---

second fit. His fervent partisanship, his avid hatreds, might be looked upon as humanizing elements that bring him away from the world of love and closer to the world of principle and to Pierre. However, anxious as I am to make my case, this evidence seems unconvincing. For one thing, Myshkin, hopelessly out of place on this hopeless and even absurd occasion that is designed to domesticate him, is just talking and cannot stop—with an urgency and a compulsive panic that lead to the epileptic fit which may already have sent out its forerunners. For another, when Dostoevsky gets off on the problems of Roman Catholicism and of Russian-ness, he seems to lose all aesthetic presence and ventriloquizes freely. I cannot, then, take this passage seriously, as being more than an errant insertion in this book that is so full of them. Always uninhibited by formal considerations, Dostoevsky never lets himself go more recklessly than in *The Idiot.* Thus Myshkin's momentary invective is just one of many inconsistencies and excursions in this difficult, often confusing and imperfect novel.

ing of the clang of iron at the last moment or about that brief (and yet unending) all-significant moment in which the head may know it has been cut off. Alexandra's reaction to Myshkin's recital can serve for the later dialogue with himself as well, and perhaps for Myshkin's more than simple temperament generally: "That's nothing like quietism, certainly" (61).

I have claimed that it was Myshkin's ability to return to enough of a superficial similarity to his fellows that enabled him to return to society, but that his continuing difference from them got him and them into trouble. The examination of his divided temperament has revealed that much of him was capable of being truly similar to those around him, all too similar. Thus his difficulties may be traced primarily to his incompleteness in any direction, to his being only half-saint (or half-"idiot") and half-man, half out of the world but half committed to it. It is this double-ness that misleads Aglaia and results in both their falls. With this in mind we can trace the development of their relationship. We may note at the outset that Myshkin himself undergoes a significant development, a fact that argues for his all-too-human imperfections and complexities. Myshkin moves from saintly to human attitudes; and then, after Aglaia has been partly persuaded to trust his human emotions, he reverts to the saintliness that must desert her for a wider obligation of love.

Myshkin's initial championing of Nastasya is clearly presented to us in the framework of Quixotism. Aglaia puts his first note to her in a book which turns out to be *Don Quixote*, and in the poem she recites about the "poor kinight"—the title she both admiringly and scornfully applies to Myshkin—she inserts Nastasya's initials as those the knight, inspired by "an all-consuming fire" (238), inscribes in blood upon his shield to defend in battle. The perceptive Yevgeny, in that all-important dialogue with Myshkin at the end, corroborates the notion that Myshkin's chivalry in behalf of Nastasya was caused by "the first glow of eagerness to be of service" (553), which accompanied Myshkin's return to Russian society. Myshkin, "a virginal knight" "bewitched" by Nastasya's "demoniacal beauty," was "intoxicated with enthusiasm" (553), the word that returns us to the universe of *Pierre*. Yevgeny's claims remind us of Aglaia's definition of the poor knight as "a man who is capable of an ideal, and what's more, a man who having once set an ideal before him has faith in it, and having faith in it gives up his life blindly to it" (235). She leaves no doubt that she means the ideal to be a lady, the lady whose initials he carries. And she terms the poor knight the serious equivalent of Quixote.

Myshkin's feelings for Nastasya partly confirm the diagnosis. He urges Rogozhin not to consider him as a rival for Nastasya even though Myshkin repeatedly takes her away from him. Denying that he and Nastasya ever lived together, Myshkin says, "I explained to you before that I don't love her with love, but with pity. I believe I define it exactly" (196–7). But the kind of love Myshkin is capable of is to change. On the eve of his birthday, despite Rogozhin's account of Nastasya's most recent aberrations, Myshkin is able to claim cheerfully, "my new life has begun to-day" (348). Rogozhin himself acknowledges this fact by noting the remarkable change in Myshkin. The cheerful change is that he is able to believe in his personal and domestic future as this is related to his personal and normally human love for Algaia. So he can tell Aglaia of his feelings for Nastasya, ". . . I only pitied her, but . . . I . . . don't love her any more" (413). We cannot help noting that in his "new life" love and pity have become separate entities: he has dropped the saint's *Agape* to pick up the humanizing *Eros*. He can go on to tell Aglaia, "I can't love her now . . . I can't sacrifice myself like that, though I did want to at one time" (415).

It seems, then, that Myshkin is becoming Aglaia's knight rather than Nastasya's, the medieval knight-errant of the lady fair with amorous obligations rather than Spenser's allegorical, dehumanized knight in the arduous service of holiness. After all, we have only Aglaia's word for it that Myshkin was carrying Nastasya's initials. We may remember that in the poem, before hurling himself into battle, the knight shouted, "*Lumen coeli*"

(238). And we are told several times that it is Aglaia who represents the light-principle to Myshkin. Nastasya's ambiguous letters to Aglaia are full of Myshkin's assertions that Aglaia is a "ray of light" (432) to him; and Myshkin himself has told her, after denying his ability any longer to sacrifice himself for Nastasya, "In my darkness then I dreamed. . . . I had an illusion perhaps of a new dawn" (415). No wonder the vaguest prospect of a possible future with Aglaia prompted Myshkin to dream of beginning a "new life." So perhaps it is to be Aglaia's light rather than Nastasya's darkness that our poor knight must serve—which would mean that he would also be serving himself. For he would be lightening his own darkness instead of trying, however fleetingly, to bring the irrevocably lost Nastasya "to seeing light round her once more" (413).

Despite his continuing feelings of obligation to the spiritual burdens of Nastasya which he has helped to amass, Myshkin appears to have persuaded Aglaia that he has made a moderate return to humanity. Not a complete return to normality, since it is the "poor knight" in him that the fiercely romantic Aglaia loves. A childlike enthusiast herself, she must have something of quixotic dedication in Myshkin, but must have it sufficiently stripped of its most obvious idiocies to be undeserving of her bitterest contempt. And of course she must have it hers and not another's, despite any claim to misfortune that deserves a champion. But Myshkin has promised more than he can deliver at the due date. His partial saintliness that recalls him to duality will not allow him to sustain his "new life," and it leads him, as Yevgeny makes abundantly clear, to be false to obligations to Aglaia as sacred and at least as seriously undertaken as those earlier ones to a *caritas* that embraced Nastasya. When the mad Rogozhin, knowing Myshkin's weakness only too well, speaks of Nastasya's companion madness and of their doomed future together, he challenges Myshkin to say whether he can still be happy. " 'No, no, no!' cried Myshkin with unspeakable sadness" (436). Perhaps he already knows that he cannot keep his back turned and that his hopes for a new life were founded on self-deception. And when, as we know he must, he chooses Nastasya over Aglaia in that harrowing scene of mutual lacerations, we know he has returned to self-sacrificing enthusiasm. By the time of his final conversation with Yevgeny—during which the latter tells him that Aglaia loved him "like a woman, like a human being, not like an abstract spirit" (556)—he is able to assert once again that despite his fears he loves Nastasya "with all my heart" (556). When we are told that "in his love for her there was an element of the tenderness for some sick, unhappy child who could not be left to shift for itself" (562), we know that love and pity have become identified for him again and finally. We may wonder whether there may not be considerable truth in Yevgeny's accusation: ". . . didn't you deceive that adorable girl [Aglaia] when you told her that you loved her?" (554) As for Aglaia herself, Myshkin has destroyed her, has converted her childlike idealism into fraudulent and decadent romanticism, and has brought her incipient demonism into the open. When we learn that she marries a swindling Polish count and ends by converting to Catholicism, we should know Dostoevsky's prejudices well enough to be provided with incontestable evidence of the unhappy disposition he has made of her.

It is difficult to witness her fall and, seeing its relation to Myshkin's rejection of her, not to ask with Yevgeny, "And where was your heart then, your 'Christian' heart? Why, you saw her face at that moment: well, was she suffering less than *the other*, that other woman who has come between you? How could you have seen it and allowed it? How could you?" (554) But of course Myshkin is responsible for more than this. It seems that it was he who continually drove Nastasya into Rogozhin's murderous hands and who at the same time whipped Rogozhin into the frenzy needed to turn homicidal. And Myshkin is painfully aware of it. His analysis of Nastasya's madness, for example, is brilliant in its probing accuracy. He understands why again and again she has deserted Rogozhin after promising to marry him, in order to run off with Myshkin, only to be even more terrified of her feelings of guilt with the little saint whom she must in turn desert to seek her fated death once more at the hands of Rogozhin. Her final turn—and she knows it is to be the last one—is to Rogozhin. After the murder Rogozhin tells Myshkin, "it was you she was afraid of" (579). She feared death with Rogozhin less than life under Myshkin's all-discerning, all-forgiving eye. Myshkin's earlier analysis prepares us for all this:

> That unhappy woman is firmly convinced that she is the most fallen, the most vicious creature in the whole world. Oh, don't cry shame on her, don't throw stones at her! She has tortured herself too much from the consciousness of her undeserved shame! And, my God, she's not to blame! Oh, she's crying out every minute in her frenzy that she doesn't admit going wrong, that she was the victim of others, the victim of a depraved and wicked man. But whatever she may say to you, believe me, she's the first to disbelieve it, and to believe with her whole conscience that she is . . . to blame. When I tried to dispel that gloomy delusion, it threw her into such misery that my heart will always ache when I remember that awful time. It's as though my heart had been stabbed once for all. She ran away from me. Do you know what for? Simply to show me that she was a degraded creature. But the most awful thing is that perhaps she didn't even know herself that she only wanted to prove that to me, but ran away because she had an irresistible inner craving to do something shameful, so as to say to herself at once, "There, you've done something shameful again, so you're a degraded creature!" Oh, perhaps you won't understand this, Aglaia. Do you know that in that continual consciousness of shame there is perhaps a sort of awful, unnatural enjoyment for her, a sort of revenge on some one. Sometimes I did bring her to seeing light round her once more, as it were. But she would grow restive again at once, and even came to accusing me bitterly of setting myself up above her (though I had no thought of such a thing) and told me in so many words at last, when I offered her marriage, that she didn't want condescending sympathy or help from anyone, nor to be elevated to anyone's level. (412–413)

Yet Myshkin must persist, with what consequences we know, going on to condemn himself for the suspiciousness revealed by his acute perceptions. This leads him to insist with inner shame on his own unworthiness. Almost immediately before Rogozhin's assault upon him, Myshkin has been upbraiding himself for harboring dark thoughts about Rogozhin: "Ah, how unpardonably and dishonourably he had wronged Rogozhin! No, it was not that 'the Russian soul was a dark place,' but that in his own soul there was darkness, since he could imagine such horrors!" (218) Immediately before the young nihilistic invaders slander him mercilessly before his friends, Myshkin senses their ruthless intention but turns angrily upon himself:

> . . . he felt too sad at the thought of his "monstrous and wicked suspiciousness." He felt that he would have died if anyone had known he had such an idea in his head, and at the moment when his guests walked in, he was genuinely ready to believe that he was lower in a moral sense than the lowest around him. (244)

But of course his least generous thoughts about others are always his most accurate ones.

Myshkin is of course always ready to blame himself for the sins of others, a proper saintly attitude. But it seems to drive his more sinful fellows to ever more desperate crime. When Yevgeny concedes that he is willing to forgive Ippolit his behavior, Myshkin, unsatisfied, suggests this is not enough: "You ought to be ready to receive his forgiveness too" (324). He is answered rather skeptically by Prince S. (and wouldn't it be more appropriate if these lines were spoken by the shrewd Yevgeny himself?) that reaching paradise on earth poses more difficulties than Myshkin will face. His translation of this Zossima-like notion into action infuriates far more seriously those who have offended him. He very nearly treats Rogozhin as the wronged party when he meets him for the first time after the attempted knifing: "We were feeling just the same. If you had not made that attack (which God averted), what should I have been then? I did suspect you of it, our sin was the same, in fact" (346–347). Rogozhin's scornful laugh promises that he feels dared to do still worse. Myshkin's youthful tormentors are also frustrated by the impossibility of offending him, so that he drives them to exceed their viciousness moment by moment while he takes the blame for it. The ill and sensitive Ippolit softens momentarily and seems ready for conversion. Instead, there is reversion, and Myshkin, all-seeing once more, admits he has been expecting it, although he has done nothing to head it off.

> Suddenly Ippolit got up, horribly pale and with an expression of terrible, almost despairing, shame on his distorted face. . . . if I hate anyone here . . . it's you, Jesuitical, treacly soul, idiot, philanthropic millionaire; I hate you more than every one and everything in the world! I understood and hated you long ago, when first I heard of you; I hated you with all the hatred of my soul. . . . This has all been your contriving. You led me on to breaking down! You drove a dying man to shame! You, you, you are to blame for my abject cowardice! I would kill you if I were going to remain alive! I don't want your benevolence . . . (282–283)

We have seen, then, how through his Christian humility with Nastasya, Rogozhin, and Ippolit, Myshkin has refused to give his beloved humanity the human privilege of sinning, of being offensive and arousing moral indignation. Myshkin has the keenness to understand what he is driving them to do, and yet he cannot do otherwise himself. Instead of easing and consoling them in their raging "underground" ambivalences, he is making their way infinitely more difficult. His irrational Christlike transcendence of mere ethical judgment turns deadly. He knows it and persists, becoming dangerously offensive himself. By assuming himself worse than others, he gives them a greater moral burden than in their human weakness they can carry. They break under it and become worse than without Myshkin they would be—partly in order to spite him. But there is no stopping Myshkin, laboring as he is under the psychosis of humility, perhaps in its own way not much less blameworthy than Pierre's psychosis of pride.

This sprawling novel is made up of several long, climactic, and calamitous scenes well spaced and interspersed with digressions and minor movements. The calamities increase until the final catastrophe, and, as we have seen, much of the responsibility for all of them must be borne by Myshkin. What is so destructive in him is the sense others must get from his infinite meekness that they are being judged. Of course, Myshkin knows the sin of pride that is involved in judging and so carefully refrains, condemning himself instead. But this very inversion of the process constitutes a form of judgment too for the guilty, in many ways a more painful one than conventional judgment. Thus Aglaia can tell him, "I think it's very horrid on your part, for it's very brutal to look on and judge a man's soul, as you judge Ippolit. You have no tenderness, nothing but truth, and so you judge unjustly" (406). Myshkin charges her with being unfair to him, and perhaps she is. But there is some justice in her claim that Myshkin's unerring depth of moral perception makes it impossible for him to miss the slightest failing in others, however quick he may be to condemn his own suspiciousness and to ask forgiveness. The relentlessness of his moral candor makes any subsequent involutions all the more painful to bear.

Aglaia's judgment of his judgment seems more profoundly to the point than that of unworthies like Keller and Lebedyev. For these, Myshkin's refusal to play the judge, as in the case of Keller's "double thoughts" in the passage I have examined, seems most effective; for with their lackey baseness they find it useful, indeed profitable. Keller responds to Myshkin's confession of his own similar guilt rapturously: "Even the preacher, Bourdaloue, would not have spared a man; but you've spared one, and judged me humanely! To punish myself and to show that I am touched, I won't take a hundred and fifty roubles; give me only twenty-five, and it will be enough!" (294) Dostoevsky emphasizes the point by having Lebedyev walk in even before

Keller has left and begin the same routine, closing with another celebration of the prince's power to "judge humanely" (294). As these creatures shriek their abjectness throughout the novel, using their self-condemnation as their major weapon, we cannot help seeing in them a parody of Myshkin's own devout humility, a parody that perhaps strikes a resounding note in the monologue of that other buffoon, Clamence, in Camus' *The Fall.*

It is Myshkin's rational inversion in matters of moral judgment that Yevgeny appears to be referring to in speaking of his "lack of all feeling for proportion" (553), his power of "exaggeration that passes belief" (554) in their late dialogue to which I have referred several times. He must wonder "whether there was natural feeling or only intellectual enthusiasm" (554) in Myshkin's extraordinary actions in behalf of Nastasya. He indicates the nature of Myshkin's enthusiasm by adding, ". . . in the temple the woman was forgiven—just such a woman, but she wasn't told that she'd done well, that she was deserving of all respect and honour, was she?" (554) Compassion is admirable, but senseless inversion that inflicts pain on the more blameless is another matter. Contemplating the wreck of Aglaia, Yevgeny asks, "What will compassion lead you to next?" (554) Here as elsewhere in this conversation Myshkin miserably cries out that he is to blame. Yevgeny answers pointedly and "indignantly": "But is that enough? . . . Is it sufficient to cry out: 'Ach, I'm to blame?' [*sic*] You are to blame, but yet you persist!" (554) Precisely—he persists to the end. As we watch Myshkin preparing for his marriage with Nastasya, we are advised: "As for protests, conversations like the one with Yevgeny Pavlovitch, he was utterly unable to answer them, and felt himself absolutely incompetent, and so avoided all talk of the kind" (563).

The conversation with Yevgeny has furnished us with crucial commentary throughout. It is significant that Dostoevsky seeks to make certain that we take Yevgeny seriously, in part at least as his spokesman. For the book, like all of Dostoevsky's, is filled with the pompous prattle of fools, especially fools who try to be rational. But there seems to be no irony in the credentials our author gives Yevgeny, who in the key conversation speaks "clearly and reasonably" and "with great psychological insight" (552). The narrator admits strongly, "Altogether, we are in complete sympathy with some forcible and psychologically deep words of Yevgeny Pavlovitch's, spoken plainly and unceremoniously . . ." (550). Of course it is possible that our author is posing as a worldly, sensible narrator who cannot help but sympathize with Yevgeny—although Dostoevsky is hardly the sort of novelist who plays tricks with "point of view." It is true that some of Yevgeny's analysis reveals the limitations of the somewhat cold-blooded realist and skeptic that he is. He was the fellow introduced, ironically, into the midst of the recital and discussion of the "poor knight" and described there as having "a fine and intelligent face and a humorous and mocking look in his big shining black eyes" (237). Unlike Myshkin, he is often ironic and uncharitable, especially with Ippolit, but like Myshkin he is usually right. Although Dostoevsky is frequently cruel to his more rational characters—and Yevgeny betrays no "underground," no great internal life—he treats Yevgeny well at the close, even if Yevgeny knows "he is a superfluous man in Russia" (584). He becomes an influence on Kolya, takes charge of Myshkin's future, and is deeply moved by Myshkin's unlikely prospects. The author acknowledges that "he has a heart" and even gives him one of his most lovable and delicate creations, Vera Lebedyev. I think Yevgeny has won enough of Dostoevsky's approval for us to conclude that he is there to help us judge Myshkin rather than to be judged through Myshkin.

Yevgeny, neither a creature of the "underground" nor a proponent of a political or philosophical program, holds a unique position among the important figures in the novel. One of the major forces in it is what we might call a kind of Benthamite liberalism or, more simply, the "modern idea." Most forcefully —and brutally—represented by the group of young people surrounding "the son of Pavlishtchev," it receives in several places

Dostoevsky's usual and powerful attack that reduces it to the cannibalism that eliminates all moral questions. But the primary inadequacy we witness in this mechanical reduction of the human is that it fails to account for the very complexity of motive among those who hold it. Thus among several of Myshkin's assailants, notably Ippolit, we see the intrusion of the unpredictable "underground" elements that demoniacally counteract the push-button principle of self-interest. So the demoniacal is a second major force, most purely represented by Nastasya and Rogozhin. But as there are "underground" elements within the "liberal," so there are angelic elements within the demonic. In the portrait of Nastasya, after all, Myshkin saw "something confiding, something wonderfully simple-hearted" associated with the "look of unbounded pride and contempt, almost hatred" (74). The duality we see in Myshkin, that Myshkin sees in himself, he does indeed share with those around him, even down to Keller and Lebedyev. And, of course, the third major force would appear to be the purely angelic, with Myshkin its representative—except that we have had reason enough to worry about whether he really does not fall back into the second group. The final alternative is that of the withdrawn and unattached, the always uncommitted because skeptical, Yevgeny. It is from this position, the only one with which the narrator expresses any identification, that the third is made most persuasively to appear illusory, a self-deceived version of the second. One prefers not to be left with Yevgeny and suspects that Dostoevsky would have preferred someone more throbbing. But the alternatives come at a high price, and Yevgeny's presence as well as Myshkin's failure proves it.

Like so many others, *The Idiot* is a novel of the desperate struggle for personal human dignity in a world that finds endless ways of depriving man of it. In the major action, in the minor actions like Ippolit's "Explanation" and mock suicide or like General Ivolgin's pitiable end at the hands of the pitiless Lebedyev, in the countless minor tales that are related to us along the way, always it is the beseeching human cry that asks that one may really matter and may be cherished for mattering. The youthful, deluded "liberals" demand dignity with such ferocity and spite that we are assured of the savage sickness that speaks through them and their program. Our openly demoniacal creatures have a purity and an integrity of demand so intense that, given the alloyed nature of what we can be given at best in life, they can be satisfied only when their life itself has been refined away to the nothingness they have sought. Myshkin seeks only to give dignity to each, even—or rather especially—at the cost of his own. But the bizarre enthusiasm of his relentless efforts appears as an inversion that, perhaps more surely than any alternative, would deny dignity to others through its very magnanimity. Thus he too must be rejected. And Yevgeny, the retiring critical intelligence that knows the futility of the problem too well to bother confronting it, helps us reject Myshkin's kind of offer as the others do. Myshkin retires to his wretched safety, and we are sorry to see him go—as is Yevgeny who really "has a heart." For we are left with no further alternative possibilities—where can one go beyond Myshkin?—since Yevgeny's way is also the way of retirement.

Or is there not another possibility, however imperfect, after all? The last words in the novel are spoken to Yevgeny and not by him. They are spoken by one of Dostoevsky's most magnificent creations, Lizaveta Epanchin, the general's wife and Aglaia's mother. Totally Russian and totally winning, if perhaps not totally sane, she is complaining about the unreality of Europe: ". . . all this life abroad, and this Europe of yours is all a fantasy, and all of us abroad are only a fantasy" (586). She is always a vigorous force for life, however messily she runs it. Even the ruin of Aglaia cannot long deter her. She must return to pick up her reality at home and must speak to the expatriate Yevgeny "almost wrathfully" and in warning against withdrawal. For Myshkin has not spoken the last word, although he has spoken the most extreme word. Whatever word is spoken beyond this is not spoken out of the tragic vision.

CHAPTER EIGHT

Recent Criticism, "Thematics," and the Existential Dilemma

> [Dostoevski's] rejection of "reason,"—"the stone wall constituted of the laws of nature, of the deductions of learning, and of the science of mathematics,"—is clearly stated very early in his *Letters from the Underworld*. . . . At a time when the conflict between "life" and "reason"—the reason of the stone wall—was not yet resolved, Dostoevski, with full awareness of what he was doing, threw his lot on the side of life and against the stone wall. Old Karamazov is a depraved buffoon, shameless and corrupt; but there is a tremendous energy in him and love of life—the energy of the Karamazovs—and there is passion; there is something elemental in his sinfulness which flows whence all life, whether good or evil, flows, and which therefore draws our admiration since it is true, as Lise says, that in our secret hearts we all love evil. By contrast Rakitin is a thoroughly depraved and contemptible reptile with nothing to his favor. . . . What Dostoevski could not admit to himself is that the Bernards in the not too long run will win. One may sympathize with the writer of the *Letters from the Underworld* when he says, "I am not going to accept that wall merely because I have to run up against it, and have no means to knock it down." But one should not forget that the tragic alternative is ineluctable: either accept it or smash your head against it.
>
> Eliseo Vivas, *Creation and Discovery*

1. Recent Criticism: Formalism and Beyond

All I have done so far and the way in which I have done it seem to me to bear certain essential relations to the poetic theories being expounded these last decades in the purer domain of literary criticism. After all, this has been a criticism that has, like all criticisms, arisen to some extent in response to the demands of the literature that surrounded it and nourished it. The approach of these critics will be seen to have been largely influenced by what the phenomenological data of their moral world revealed to them, as the data was aesthetically grasped in the organized totality of literary creation. Thus the method may work in reverse too, so that studying the criticism may open the way to a new understanding of the data for which it seeks, consciously or unconsciously, to account. It should prove instructive to the thematic study upon which I have been launched to trace the reflection in recent criticism of the existential complexities that have been concerning me, to see the extent to which this criticism has been formed under these other than aesthetic—these thematic—pressures. In order to throw such new light upon our problems, I shall have to digress at some length to examine the theoretical basis of this criticism. It will be worth the effort required to collect the theoretical residuum of the critical revolution of this century if by means of it we can push on to the fresher areas of thematic problems that are more immediately relevant to those I have been grappling with until now.

Many of the critics I have previously called the new apologists for poetry,[1] while interesting themselves with endless

[1] In my book, *The New Apologists for Poetry* (Minneapolis: University of Minnesota Press, 1956). Most of the points I make in the early and summary portions of this chapter may be found more fully discussed and documented there. Here I want to accomplish the task of summary rather briskly so that I may shortly move on to my central concern. In my haste I may be forced at times to make my remarks too general and inclusive and to do less than justice to the all-important shadings that distinguish a

ingenuity in the complex operations of poetic language, have for the most part—or for the most important part—not done so out of a sterile Alexandrian dilettantism that runs after the verbally precious as a matter of self-congratulation: in order to reveal their powers of infinite division and multiplication. They clearly are not, as many would have them be, just so many deluded refugees from *The Dunciad*. Far from a barren formalism that in its ascetic purity scorns any interest in the teeming fullness of experience, such critics interest themselves in the poetic behavior of words out of a conviction that this behavior, with all its ambiguities, is reflective of the ambiguities of moral existence below the level of the finally inadequate abstractions which, through systematic discourse, we normally impose upon that existence. They want to restore the world in which the sensitive and fully human being has always found himself, a world never totally unambiguous which cries out for the illumination that the formally controlled literary work can alone bestow. And it can bestow it only through the very manipulations of poetic discourse and its complexities to which these critics must dedicate themselves with a meticulousness their detractors see as pedantic, as a critical ingenuity paraded merely for its own sake.

However, any attempt to reduce the utterances of these critics to pure formalism—that is, to an interest in the "how" rather than the "what" of poetry—must confront their continual and ubiquitous insistence on the indissolubility of form and content in the total poetic context, in our perception of it, and in the rationalization of our perception which we term criticism. The terms *form* and *content*, then, in their view mere

---

collection of critics who, after all, have not in any self-conscious way constituted themselves as a school. The variety which these sensitive literary minds have brought to a subject endlessly complex in its own right creates a multiplicity that defies even the most patient historian. It must deprive any such summary as this of much of its claim to accuracy and of most of its claim to adequacy. Hence my reference to the painstaking analysis of my earlier book for those who are troubled by these generalizations.

hangovers from a tradition of critical discourse that is invariably dualistic, are expressive of an obsolete critical strategy that these critics would discard. In answering a charge of formalism they would have to countercharge that their attackers are themselves so trapped by the form-content dichotomy that once they perceive that a critic does not talk about a separable subject matter—as so-called new critics certainly do not—there is no alternative but to label such a critic a pure formalist. To satisfy such attackers that he is not a formalist, a critic would be required to wrench from the poetic context, however distortedly, meanings which he wishes to relate directly to an extra-aesthetic interest, regardless of the way these are related organically to the other aesthetic elements which make up the poem.[2]

These critics, having leveled their countercharge, would leave their attackers desperately hugging one of the two poles left to them by their bifurcation of the poem: the untamed stuff of life to the neglect of the thin insignificance of mere design. Having denied the dichotomy, the apologists would address themselves to the more complex task of approaching the poem as aesthetic and yet insisting that, while remaining an aesthetic object, it has the capacity—and a unique capacity—to reveal life. But it can so reveal it only by revealing itself as self-sufficiently aesthetic. They see poetry as intimately related to life, more intimately than if it were related to life more directly—as directly, say, as more immediately referential discourse. Thus they distinguish between the autonomy of poetry in which they believe and poetry for poetry's sake in which they do not, between the enabling powers of poetic form organically conceived and the self-justified parading of poetic form that smacks

[2] I mean, of course, to use terms like "poem" or "poetry" or "poetic language" or "poetic context" in their broadest sense, Aristotle's sense, as including everything we normally think of as imaginative literature, prose fiction and prose drama as well as verse. If I have done my job at all well in the preceding chapters, I ought to have shown the language of prose fiction capable of developing contextual characteristics comparable to those of verse.

of the sporting aesthete. The autonomy of poetry they must assert since only as autonomous can its revelations be those which poetry can uniquely afford.

It is of course true that these critics seem to isolate poetry, as a unique and self-contained form of discourse, from life by insisting on the poem's independent existence as a world cut off from its author on the one hand and its audience on the other. They see this world as determined by the language context as it evolves partly, of course, under the author's guidance but partly also—and perhaps even more crucially—in response to the demands which the system itself, in developing its own *telos*, creates. Just as they must resist reducing the meaning of the poem to that intended by its author, so must they resist reducing the operation of the poem in the other direction: to its capacity to affect an audience. In these denials of what they see as reductions, we recognize two "fallacies" they speak of, the "intentional" and the "affective." They must see in such reductions the desecrating hand of positivism, one that would snatch from poetry its responsibility to reveal what can be revealed only through the unlimited sovereignty of a unique reality and would deprive the world of experience of depths which without the eye of poetry would be denied for being unapprehended.

In the organicism of their theoretical framework, these critics replace talk of form and content with talk of context, complexity, tension, texture. Eliot's original interest in the unity of sensibility and Richards' in a "poetry of inclusion" arising from the multivalence of a playful irony never at rest—both are consistent with, as they are derivative from, the all-embracing Coleridgean imagination that for the last century and a half has dominated organic theory as its prime symbol. And from these notions of Eliot and Richards has come most of what passes for the new criticism. And with it comes the notion of poetry as a special form of discourse—or, in its most extreme form, each poem as a unique system of discourse, obedient only to the laws immanently within itself, laws that evolve in accordance with the *telos* of the poem. If the context of the poem is to work upon us in the many simultaneous and even contradictory ways that Richards, advocating his poetry of inclusion, would insist upon, then clearly it must be inviolable. It must keep us inside, bouncing from opposition to opposition as we realize the fullness and the complexity of internal relations of the unique contextual system.

In his most distinctive work, Cleanth Brooks carries these notions out of Richards' psychologistic universe into our world of experience, so that he asks us to see in the inclusiveness of the self-complicating poetic context a reflection of the fullness of experience-as-lived. It is this fullness that Brooks would have poetry, as a unique mode of discourse and a unique mode of revelation, substitute for the abstractness, thinness, and incompleteness of experience-as-systematized in referential and propositional discourse, whether scientific or philosophic, and in poetic discourse wrongly pursued. John Crowe Ransom implies much the same thing in his famous metaphor about "the world's body," that which in its textural richness informs poetry even as in the interest of its skeleton it is ignored by other forms of discourse. When Allen Tate derives his term "tension" from the logical terms "extension" and "intension," he does so also to indicate the plenitude that transforms poetry into a special mode of discourse. These critics, then, see poetry as an alternative to the referential characteristic of other discourse in that poetry must multiply meanings within a closed context rather than, like other discourse, allow these meanings to escape one by one and point beyond. They see poetry also as an alternative to the propositional characteristic of other discourse in that poetry is governed, not by logical rules of systematic consistency, but by contextual operations that defy the systematic.

As one would imagine, these critics have little use for poetry of direct statement, for the poetic claim that does not carry its own contradiction within itself. We find Ransom speaking against "Platonic" poetry, that dualistic affair, perhaps sanctioned by an earlier criticism, in which meaning and poem are separate entities. At much the same time Tate was using the words of Yeats to decry that poetry which reveals "the will trying to do the work of the imagination." And when Brooks speaks about the "heresy of paraphrase," he joins the others in their essential claim: that the poem can mean only in the words that constitute it, that all else is a violation not merely of the poem's aesthetic wholeness but of its full cognitive powers. Even the somewhat unlikely ally, Yvor Winters, affirms that no paraphrase can yield a poem's meaning as he echoes Mallarmé in defining the proper poem as "a new word"—a word, presumably, whose definition can be provided only by its own closed system. Their distinction between a dualistic and a monistic poetry—that is, between a poetry whose meaning is transcendent and one whose meaning is immanent—is in effect a distinction between a poetry that could be exhaustively treated within the familiar confines of the form-content or message-embellishment dichotomy and a poetry that could be treated only in post-Ricardian terms. And yet of course it is a distinction that echoes the Coleridgean distinction between fancy and imagination and the Crocean distinction between allegory and symbol. The latter summarizes the argument in its extreme—if idealistic—form so succinctly that it is worth quoting here.

> . . . the *symbol* has sometimes been given as the essence of art. Now, if the symbol be conceived as inseparable from the artistic intuition, it is a synonym for the intuition itself, which always has an ideal character. There is no double bottom to art, but one only; in art all is symbolical, because all is ideal. But if the symbol be conceived as separable—if the symbol can be on one side, and on the other the thing symbolized, we fall back again into the intellectualist error: the so-called symbol is the exposition of an abstract concept, an *allegory*; it is science, or art aping science.[3]

But these critics, out of a classical pursuit of order, often retreat from so extreme an organic monism. Eliot and Richards

[3] From *Aesthetic*, by Benedetto Croce, trans. Douglas Ainslie (London: Macmillan & Company, Ltd., 1922), p. 34.

have much to say on the nature of belief in poetry that would seem to reconstitute the breach between meaning and poetic form. Ransom, in his insistence on logical structure; Tate, in his insistence on the denotative precision he terms "extension"; and Winters, in his insistence on rational motive—all manage to retract much of what makes their criticism distinctive. Apparently afraid of the reckless romanticism and misty idealism at the heart of a theoretical orientation mainly derived from romantic and idealistic sources, these critics as would-be neoclassicists wanted their new critical strategy without paying the theoretical price and at times seemed to be playing both sides of the street.

Only Brooks seemed for a long time to be holding out against any slightest surrender of the inviolable context to the demands of the referential or the propositional. He appeared rightly to understand that, like uniqueness, organicism is an all-or-nothing affair and that to qualify it was, theoretically, to yield completely. And so he held out even under attack by new-critical colleagues like Ransom who found him unmitigatedly romantic. But his recent association with William K. Wimsatt in their *Literary Criticism: A Short History* seems finally to have brought Brooks around as well. He now speaks of the need for "fixities and definities," of "the logical, the definite, and the unequivocal," as the antidote for "incoherence" and "symbolic fluidity."

These critics, then, have, each in his own way, made their imprint on the history of criticism by asserting the uniqueness and self-containedness of poetic systems of discourse (in the most extreme form a different one for each poem). The internal complications of a poem, while sealing it off and keeping us within it, also serve to reflect as no other discourse can the internal complications of the existential universe, those more things in heaven and earth than are dreamt of in anyone's philosophy. Then, having made these daring claims and having in their practical criticism made so much of them, these critics recognized the romantic implications of them: a self-complicating context with no outside check on the multiplication of complexity heading away from art toward the chaos of romantic obscurantism; an utterly closed contextual system that gives the reader no opening that will allow him to enter it. Further, in the attempt to reproduce those contradictions in experience that defy system, the poetry licensed by organicism, with no limits set upon the desirable extent of inclusiveness, seemed moving toward the self-destructive goal where the disciplined refinement of art is lost to the incomprehensible coarseness of pure experience. Only life itself can afford such infinite variety; and life is hardly poetry, which is probably a blessing for both. So Yvor Winters coined his "fallacy of imitative form" to describe the poet's surrender of formal control to the formless stuff of experience which he wants to capture but comes closer to reproducing. And the group generally reinstates, at least partially, the obligations of poetry to the restrictions of normal discourse—that is, the restrictions of reference and of propositional procedure.

The difficulty of their position arises not so much from their own indifference to theoretical consistency as it does from the very real nature of the dilemma they face. Some considerations demand that the poem be seen as a closed system, some considerations demand with equal persuasiveness that it be seen as opening outward to the world and to externally imposed laws of rational order. Yet it cannot be partly closed, partly open. If we want poetry to be more than a pleasing and pretty version of another form of discourse (one which, if less pretty and less pleasing, is more exacting) then it must have a different way of meaning. And since poetry is distinguished by its highly wrought internal relations and by its powers to do and say so many things at once, it would seem that whatever claims can be made for it as a special form of discourse that has a special way of meaning must be made in consequence of its special contextual characteristics. Organicism and inviolability of context being matters of kind and not of degree, poetry must be seen as a form of discourse in some sense nonreferential even as it must be in some sense referential to be a form of discourse at all. It must be seen as in some sense a closed world of meaning even as this many-faceted world is created largely to open onto and illuminate the facets we would miss in the outside world of every day.

This dilemma seems to me to represent the crucial point, if not the dead end, reached by modern criticism. We can sympathize with Brooks in his desire to broaden and ease his position by modifying its pure organicism and its unlimitedly romantic consequences. But alas, this is not the way to evade the dilemma; since, much as we would like to, we cannot take organicism by degrees, because this is the way only to an untenable, if seemingly unavoidable, eclecticism. Brooks merely joins his fellows who yielded earlier. With them he must confront the doubt that undermines his claims: however impossible an unqualified organicism may appear to be, a partial organicism is impossible, is in effect no organicism, and the alternative to organicism is destructive of all that recent theory has taught us about poetry.

Future theorists who will want to preserve the gains and the distinctive direction of these critics and who will not want to see them washed away into the common stream of Platonic theory, will have to find a way to keep poetry's contextual system closed; to have the common materials which enter poetry —conventions of word meaning, of propositional relations, and of literary form—so transmuted in the creative act with its organic demands that they come out utterly unique. The reader will somehow be seen to repeat the procedure: to find his way into the poem by its seeming use of ordinary reference, ordinary propositions, and conventional literary forms, only to find himself suddenly and wonderfully trapped by the transmutations that make these elements most extraordinary. And his explorations through this uniquely paradoxical world—at once so full existentially and so rarefied aesthetically—must be seen to show him what is unique about what before, in his blindness, passed as the ordinary world outside. These future theorists will have to find a way also to keep poetic form as a disciplining force while at the same time insisting that it is an inward form and that its disciplinary quality does not lead poetry to abstract from life as other discourse does. Instead of being ruled by general word meanings and by a ruthless, universally applied logic, each work is gently guided by contextual meanings and by a unique form which it helps to create. On the other hand, in seeing poetry as life that is *formed* (rather than as life that is logically systematized), they must still recognize that poetry, for all its inclusiveness, dare not be as inclusive as life without abdicating its form to surrender to experience in its unrelieved wholeness. Somehow the line which separates artful complexity from natural chaos must be finely drawn.

In the conclusion to their recent history of criticism, Wimsatt and Brooks try their hand at resolving this dilemma by suggesting how we may preserve the valuable conclusions recent critics have reached about the several opposed voices with which the poem can speak without encouraging aesthetic chaos and outlawing all moral commitment. While their suggestion is finally no more than a metaphorical one and is, I suppose, to that extent unsatisfactory, the metaphor is a most provocative one —one that will put us a long way toward drawing thematic implications from the aesthetic we have been examining. They are again contrasting the Platonic conception of poetry that sees a single transcendent meaning and the organic conception that sees an organized and complex opposition of immanent meanings. They again find both inadequate, the Platonic because it destroys the role of poetry by thinning it and thus trimming it down to other discourse, and the organic because it contains no final return to order, no final affirmation of a cosmic controlling principle. Indeed, by definition the ironic view can nothing affirm. Translating these alternatives into theological terminology, the authors believe

> that the kind of literary theory which seems . . . to emerge the most plausibly from the long history of the debates is far more difficult to orient within any of the Platonic or Gnostic

> ideal world views, or within the Manichaean full dualism and strife of principles, than precisely within the vision of suffering, the optimism, the mystery which are embraced in the religious dogma of the Incarnation.[4]

This soaring notion carries us in the direction of aesthetic order beyond the dramatistic theory of endless struggle, the dualistic or pluralistic—if not chaotic—theory of unresolvable tension most characteristically implied by many of the pronouncements of our critics. It may remind us of Ransom's earlier postulating of "miraculism"—the physical embodiment of the airily spiritual—as the alternative to the unworldly thinness of what he calls "Platonic Poetry" on the one hand and the unelevated density of what he calls "Physical Poetry" on the other. In Wimsatt and Brooks, too, the leap to the Incarnation represents their rejection of an all-exclusive intellectualism and an all-inclusive density as they embrace the final affirmation that can come as a miraculous, all-reconciling grace only after an *almost* total abandonment to conflict.

It is clear that in this kind of formulation the final reassertion of aesthetic order becomes a reflection of the reassertion of moral order. After all, we have seen not only that the tensional version of contextualism, in the extreme form that is its only consistent form, seems to forego any aesthetic order externally imposed upon its self-complicating dynamics; but also that this theory, in its ironic posing of counterclaim along with every claim, seems to forbid any final thematic resolution, any final moral commitment, in the name of experiential complexity, which readily supplies the skepticism that comes of a total awareness. Yvor Winters may have been more correct than many of his detractors, in their anti-didacticism, have credited him with being in his insistence that rational poetic form exerted upon recalcitrant materials is a reflection of the poet's moral control of his disturbing experience: to forego one is to forego the other.

[4] From *Literary Criticism: A Short History*, by W. K. Wimsatt, Jr., and Cleanth Brooks (New York: Alfred A. Knopf, Inc., 1957), p. 746.

Consequently, we begin to see how completely this aesthetic would seem to depend on a metaphysic or even a theodicy. In a recent essay [5] that pursues the implications of the concluding chapter of the history of criticism, Wimsatt turns more explicitly in the thematic direction himself. Again he at once attacks the Manichaean implications of unresolved thematic tensions and defends the dramatic need to give full due to the mixed and imperfect nature of the human condition. He ends by exhorting the Christian writer and the Christian critic to recognize the need for a clear moral commitment in literature, but only a commitment that has been earned through an *almost* total dramatic submission to the forces of opposition.

But can *anything* be withheld if the test is to be complete, if the ironic, self-contradictory nature of moral experience is to be allowed full sway? Is not even the slight rational, philosophic control of the stuff of drama infringement enough to ensure the stacking of the cards, the intrusion of an abstract order that pre-exists the poem upon thematic oppositions, even as we earlier saw the slight concessions by our critics to referential and propositional discourse to be enough to open the organic context irrevocably? For Wimsatt, and probably Brooks, the need in poetics to find an order that somehow does full justice to the internal complications of the context not only is analogous, but is intimately related, to the need in the realm of theme to find a moral order that somehow does full justice to the fearful paradoxes that inhere in experience. But can the pleasantly eclectic compromise satisfy in the one realm any more than it can in the other?

By shifting, then, from a merely metaphorical to a literal use of the drama which witnesses the Gnostic-Manichaean opposition and witnesses it yielding, through miracle, to the Incarnation, we can discover the unbroken realm that joins the aesthetic to the thematic—the moral-religious—dimension of poetry; and we can manage the tactical movement from one to

[5] "Poetic Tension: A Summary," by W. K. Wimsatt, Jr., *New Scholasticism,* XXXII (1958), 73–88.

the other. In making this movement we must observe an important peculiarity in the relation of the aesthetic to the thematic, a peculiarity that will force us to be careful with our terminology: What I earlier spoke of as the dualistic aesthetic—that Platonism, assailed by our critics, which splits poetry into form and content and sees it as the transparent vehicle of a prior, separable, indeed transcendent meaning—can obviously provide only for thematic singularity, for but one propositional system. On the other hand, the monistic aesthetic—the organicism which sees the poetic context as bearing immanently within itself a complex of opposed meanings—just as obviously provides for an equivocal thematic duality that Wimsatt calls Manichaean. A very different sort of duality indeed, this latter: one which can be produced only by a sealed and sovereign poetic context dedicated to the complexity of its internal relations.

2. "Thematics": A Manichaean Consequence

It is this sort of unresolvable opposition that leads to what I term the literary discipline of "thematics." I should like to pause here to say precisely what I mean by this coinage in hopes that this definition will help us along the road our explorations ought to follow. From all I have said, it should be at once clear that I cannot mean to use *thematics* in a way related to the usual and unsophisticated sense of the term *theme*. Obviously I cannot mean by it the so-called "philosophy" of a work, that series of propositions which we supposedly can derive—or, better yet, extrapolate—from the aesthetic totality that is presented to us. Since I am moving to the problems of meaning, of the "world" that is offered us, from a monistic, organic conception of that aesthetic totality, I can hardly think in terms of a separable philosophic theme that an author embodies in order to justify it literarily, to put it to the test of drama and its dialectic. (I might add that it was just this "putting to the test," but little that was more organic than this, that we saw Wimsatt recommending in his compromise between the "tensional" and

Christian approaches.) Rather, I must insist, on behalf of recent criticism in its consistently organic moments, that every self is to be confronted with the anti-self, every claim with its antithesis, with no possibility of an all-reconciling synthesis—unless it is one that is accompanied by a newly disruptive anti-synthesis. At least I must insist on all this in the good work, by which I must mean the work that demands the more delicate probings of the literary discipline of thematics since in its complexity it remains disdainfully inaccessible to the vain attempts to empty it by crudely tearing at it here and there to come up with some philosophical generalizations. And again, I suppose, I am allowing a single conception of the phenomenology of our moral life to support a single aesthetic methodology in that I acknowledge that, in support of this view of thematics, I must deny that the existential world—the world of felt human experience—can be anything less than a bewildering complex of seeming contradictions. Given this sort of world, how can any more systematic view of it—the kind of view we get in that dualistically conceived "Platonic" literature whose meaning really is exhausted by the extrapolation of its philosophical theme—how can such a view avoid, in its inadequacy, doing this world a grievous injustice?

Following the more organic aspects of the new-critical poetics, then, we can define *thematics* as the study of the experiential tensions which, dramatically entangled in the literary work, become an existential reflection of that work's aesthetic complexity. Thematics thus conceived is as much beyond "philosophy"—and in the same way beyond "philosophy"—as, in pure poetics, an organic, contextually responsible form is beyond a logically consistent system. There can be occasions on which the author means to be conceiving his work dualistically, as an embodiment and a demonstration of a "philosophy," except that he has been more faithful—dramatically and existentially faithful—than he knows; so that a fully thematic analysis would reveal that significant opposition is engendered when this philosophy enters the total poetic context, with the consequence that an objective hierarchy of values and the poet's full sympathies are not so easily identified or, thanks to the endless qualifications, perhaps not identifiable at all. I believe these occasions are more numerous than we may at first admit and the more numerous as the literature is more valuable—valuable, of course, in terms of this aesthetic and thus this conception of thematics. I can only hope that the preceding chapters furnish enough persuasive evidence to demonstrate this claim.

This way of conceiving thematics as a *literary* method, and as the only method capable of dealing with meanings in literature, would seem to predispose the moral-theological—indeed finally the metaphysical—issue toward the irresolution of Manichaeism. It would seem to argue against any cosmic resolution, however ultimate and however qualified, since this would reduce the complexities of theme (in my sense of the word) to the single-mindedness of "philosophy" and thus reduce poetry to its "Platonic" conception as a form of propositional discourse.

It may, of course, seem at best silly and at worst heretically presumptuous for a critic to argue for an intolerable world view just to satisfy the needs of an aesthetic and a literary method. But what is being insisted upon here as Manichaean is not the ultimate nature of metaphysical or noumenal reality so much as the existential nature of that reality which makes itself dramatically available to the poet whose only commitment as poet is to experience and to the dramatic exigencies of his art. Further, it must be admitted that there is an intimate relation between a man's view of existence and his view of art, that even so precious a fellow as the dedicated literary critic is first a man who has adopted an existential stance toward his reality and whose less basic activities—yes, even his beloved critical method—are finally derivative of this stance rather than in control of it. Of course it works the other way too: in the case of the sensitive literary man, the stance may be largely determined by what literature has revealed about the befuddling nature of existence. Surely this is what literature is for. Without it, with only the rival claims of neat philosophical systems on the one hand and totally undifferentiated experience on the other, such a man, resisting oversimplifications, may be unable to adopt any stance at all. If, then, this man believes what his experience with literature has revealed to him about his experience with life, he may very well adopt a stance toward moral reality which would lead to conceptions of aesthetics and thematics much as I have been outlining. All of which is perhaps to say only that a literary theory must be adequate to the literary experiences for which it is to account and that we trust our way of experiencing literature only as it is adequate to the life out there, which cries for a way of being organized literarily that will yet leave it preserved intact. And the stance implied by this critical method, the literary experience and the existential ontology that it seeks to account for, is manifestly Manichaean.

It is really a commonplace to say that every poet must, at least provisionally, be something of a Manichaean. This is but a way of our asking him not to stack the cards, but rather to give his drama full sway, always to allow his opposition its argument a fortiori. But if he does no more than this—if, that is, he submits his thesis to the hellfires of antithesis with no doubt of the issue and only to allow this thesis to be earned the hard way—he is no more in danger of heresy than is any profound version of Christianity that is willing to take into account all worldly imperfection without reducing the extent or the goodness of God's sway. Once more let me repeat that this is Wimsatt's position in the essay to which I have referred several times; and once more let me repeat also that this position, however mature and qualified, cannot finally make literature more than "Platonic," bearing its propositional thesis, any more than it can finally allow the dominion of God to be shared.

As we know from Augustine, the attractions of Manichaeism are disarming. For one struck by the ubiquity of evil it can be an assurance that he is not compromising with reality in order to appease an optmistic need for order, for cosmic meaning. A Christian as sensitive and mature as Wimsatt fights this temptation by distinguishing his view from the Pollyanna view that C. S. Lewis termed "Christianity-and-water" and by accepting the all-affirming grace only after a not quite total submission to the Manichaean face of reality (just as he is willing to have aesthetic reconciliation in literature only after a not quite total submission to contextual tension). It may indeed be more mature to be less rebellious, finally to resign from conflict and to acknowledge grace and the miracle. For this acknowledgment can come only in humility, the humility that calls upon one to accept a single, most crucially chosen paradox of the myriad of paradoxes that fill life, and having chosen, to embrace it to the rejection of all others which consequently must be seen as paradoxical no longer. But even this act of faith need not deny an existential Manichaeism since in it the metaphysical and existential realms do not touch, indeed, logically appear to deny each other. But the desire to have metaphysical order reflect itself on the existential level is more troublesome for being consoling and for limiting the drama of experience. For to him who has not merely tentatively—and in order to prove his faith —half submitted to an existential Manichaeism, but who has irrevocably submerged himself within it, the final affirmation that transforms all is not a humbling act of maturity but a mere yielding to creature comfort. And thus again the attractions of Manichaeism, that does not trust itself to move beyond the equilibrium, indeed the paralysis, induced by the existential absurdities it confronts.

In literature, with its delusions of a self-sufficient world in which the equilibrium of equivocal forces produces such profound aesthetic satisfaction, these attractions are multiplied and deepened; so much so that the sensitive and impressionable reader may return to life from literature newly dismayed by a vision of final cosmic disharmony. Which perhaps persuades us to conclude that Plato was not altogether ill-advised in expelling poetry from his Republic as a dangerously seductive mistress. The reader's awareness of the density of the literary work leads him to recognize the inadequacy of a single set of propositions to account for it and to recognize also the difference in kind between literature and propositional discourse. If he is persuaded by what he has read so that he believes its complexity to be a measure of the world it reflects and not a self-indulgent mystique of obscurity, then he will recognize finally the equal inadequacy of any set of propositions to account for that world. As he generalized in his aesthetic ramblings, moving from the extra-propositional nature of the work to the extra-propositional nature of literature, so he can generalize now about the extra-propositional nature of reality.

As I theorized in my first chapter and tried to demonstrate in those that followed, under the pressure and shock of an extreme situation, protagonists like those we have been observing are forced to reject forever the intellectual and human comforts of the "ethical," the deceptively rational life. For writers who deal in extremity, where characters are suddenly and utterly confronted by absurdity, the existential paradoxes are seen to be unresolvable as they point to the inadequacy of any systematically moral disposition. In viewing existential reality as extra-ethical in this sense, I am again reasserting in thematic terms the aesthetic claim that the poetic mode of discourse is extra-propositional. The propositional, then, becomes the discursive equivalent of that "ethical" substitute for existence, moral philosophy; and the poetic, contextually defined, becomes the discursive equivalent of that existential realization into which the extreme situation propels its victim. Where more than in literature can one meet so convincingly with the extreme situation and its existential consequences? Is it not, perhaps, in the very formulation of extremity, with the purification of the casual that extremity brings, that literature can manage formal control over experience even while managing to account for the entire extent of it? Literature in this way too may be seen as persuading its reader toward the Manichaean, the nakedly and unmitigatedly existential, in that the existential, as beyond (or rather prior to) the systematically ethical, sees the absurdity of unreconcilable opposition everywhere and ultimately. Indeed, with the existential so opposed to philosophy, literature becomes the only possible form of existential philosophy—or must I say existential thematics?—precisely because only within the liberal confines of literary casuistry can the existential be explored. Otherwise it is falsely reduced to just another philosophy, just as literature Platonically considered is reduced to just another mode of prose discourse.

It is, however, not really accurate to speak of the contextually poetic or of the existential as involving self-contradiction. Or rather it is not relevant. For in neither are we dealing with propositions. It has been suggested, for example, that new critics are inconsistent when they speak against the "heresy of paraphrase"; that they actually are not against all paraphrases as being inadequate to the poem but are only against over-simplified paraphrases that do not take into account the nuances and the paradoxes. In this case all one has to do is to elaborate and extend the paraphrase in order to satisfy them and exhaust the poem of its meaning. But I believe one discovers as he elaborates upon the paraphrase that, after a certain point, the work begins to slip through his over-solicitous fingers and to sound like capricious, self-contradictory foolishness. For what is likely is that just as the confining terms of any "ethical" system—the universals of the "ethical" stage itself—are inadequate to the raging existential world; so the world of propositions is simply inappropriate to it, although, viewed from the standpoint of propositional procedures, this existential world and the poetic discourse that reflects it may well *seem* to be filled with contradiction. This world is not, then, a propositional world with all coherence gone, with all the brakes removed—a self-contradictory propositional world that, through poetic economy, manages, with discursive waywardness, to state several incompatible propositions at once. It is rather an extra-propositional world, of another order, a pre- or post-propositional world—as you will—even if it seems to be contradictory when, using the only discourse at our disposal as critics, we try to talk logically about it, so that we come out with a confusing proliferation of would-be propositions.

But the dramatic and, as wholeheartedly dramatic, the unreconcilable polarities remain. And in their failure to find a higher peace, they reflect the intransigent dual principle that is Manichaean. Yet for the literary work there is still the need for aesthetic wholeness. Literature may deal with the experientially full in avoiding the single, thin line of system; but to the extent that it remains art it must claim to have some kind of aesthetic system all its own, a system still, though so different from a philosophical system. Can such a system be sustained if there is no final assertion, no single set of affirmations that resolves oppositions in the direction of order? Yet only by turning aside from the demand of aesthetic organicism and from the confrontation of existential absurdity can one so assert and so affirm. In my opening chapter I tried to find for the literature of the tragic vision (a term which, obviously, is closely related to the existential and the Manichaean as I use these terms) an ordering principle to replace the principle of catharsis that brought to a transcendent affirmation the old, full, more than Manichaean, aesthetic form of tragedy, now lost with the civilization that created it. There I said:

> . . . the balance of necessities between the tragic and the ethical must continue as the primary mode of dramatic conflict, with the inherent weaknesses of each—the moral failing of the one and the visionary failing of the other—poised against each other to create the unresolvable tension that must now replace tragedy's more sublime catharsis as the principle of aesthetic control.

Can we not, then, get at all beyond tension? If not, how are we to be assured that the tension, with its unyielding dualism, will hold the work together through the delicate poise it creates among its oppositions and not split it asunder through a tug of war among them?

We are in effect returned to the earlier and more purely aesthetic problem which asked how we were to assure ourselves of enough formal control to shun chaos and produce art when organic theory would allow us no form that was not contextually evolved. But now our thematic explorations should enable us to ask this question in a more useful way. If we grant the unreconcilable oppositions within the phenomenology of the moral life which prevent the literary work from achieving a finally positive thematic resolution, is there yet not some way in which at least an aesthetic resolution may be achieved? Or, to return to an earlier conviction, in part borrowed from Yvor Winters, that aesthetic and moral resolutions are two sides of a single coin—the work by its very aesthetic order attesting to an orderly universe—if we should manage even the merely aesthetic resolution, what transformations might be worked on the moral universe should the slightest touch of aesthetic harmony rub off upon it, as it must?

It is like asking not only whether the humanizing enlightenment cast by Ishmael organizes *Moby Dick* as a novel, but whether in so doing it also purges the novel of the demonism of Ahab. *Moby Dick* is ideal for my purposes because Ahab is so obviously, self-consciously, and even literally a Manichaean, while in Ishmael Ahab's oppositions are to be melted into the unity that joins in brotherhood a most imperfect and often ill-fated humanity. It is clear enough that Ahab, as Zoroastrian and as Puritan, has polarized his moral world, opposing good to evil irrevocably and refusing to see them alloyed in experience. He has worshiped fire so exclusively, rejecting any coarser element, that he has perverted the natural fire of God into the demoniacal hellfires that, consecrated by the black mass, drive the *Pequod* to her doom and even almost betray Ishmael to rudderless destruction by luring him from worldly duty to a contemplative wonder at them. But Ishmael finally resists, though, as always, in full recognition of the lure that has ensnared Ahab. The configuration is constant: Ishmael always makes the final acceptance of a natural order and a human order whose natures are fearfully ambiguous, in which the only order seems to be a disorderly confounding of good and evil. He seems able to bear this vision without denying an affirmative power to the universe and its Author, and without rebelling. Thus he understands the moral integrity that prompts Ahab to demand the purity of absolute separation between good and evil—although he understands also the immoral integrity into which this is perverted by the prideful refusal to accept the mixed universe.

There are other oppositions that Ishmael is able to see strangely united, accepting the *both-and* while the possessed Ahab will have only the *either-or*, demanding an unstained God-filled universe or worshiping it defiantly as exclusively the devil's. Not only was Ishmael, we must remember, saved from the *Pequod*, but the *Pequod*'s journey itself saved him, saved him from the "damp, drizzly November" in his soul. And his alien brother Queequeg was a principal agent of his salvation, both figuratively—in the "joint stock company of two" produced by their mutual human dependence as symbolized by "the monkey-rope"—and literally, in Queequeg's "coffin life-buoy" that allowed Ishmael alone to survive the wreck. Even Ahab, as Ishmael would, almost sees in the coffin now weirdly pressed into service as a life buoy, the ambiguous simultaneity, indeed, for the faithful, even the oneness of life and death:

> Oh! how immaterial are all materials! What things real are there, but imponderable thoughts? Here now's the very dreaded symbol of grim death, by a mere hap, made the expressive sign of the help and hope of most endangered life. A life-buoy of a coffin! Does it go further? Can it be that in some spiritual sense the coffin is, after all, but an immortality-preserver! I'll think of that. But no. So far gone am I in the dark side of earth, that its other side, the theoretic bright one, seems but uncertain twilight to me. (520–521) [6]

[6] From *Moby Dick*, by Herman Melville, ed. Luther S. Mansfield and Howard P. Vincent (New York: Hendricks House, Inc., 1952). All page references are to this edition.

He must return to the exclusiveness, to the fierce purity of his oppositions. All this Ishmael sees and even at times comes close to sharing, except that the grace of a final cosmic harmony, dearly bought, seems to save him from Ahab even as, after the wreck, it tosses him Queequeg's coffin and saves him from the sharks—and for the *Rachel.*

In his famous chapter on "The Whiteness of the Whale" Ishmael shows that he understands only too well Ahab's vision of Moby Dick as the challenging "pasteboard mask." He is not going the faithful, but visionless, way of Starbuck, who sees the whale only as natural "dumb brute." Ishmael too must cut a "little lower layer" and see how the whale can appear as ghostly symbol of the "leper"-universe, but unlike Ahab he must not accept this as his only vision. Instead, he must acknowledge the angelic as well as the demoniacal as being symbolized by whiteness,[7] and he must acknowledge the natural fact of the whale as well as its symbolic purposefulness. So while he comprehends the vision of the "leper"-universe—that blank colorlessness perceptible beneath the "cosmetic" secondary qualities to only "willful travellers"— he at last attributes this vision not to himself, but to "the wretched infidel," in effect, to Ahab. And in a most crucial passage much later—one that recalls the fullness rather than the emptiness, the glory rather than the mystic malevolence, of whiteness—Ishmael explicitly dissociates himself from the infidel:

> And how nobly it raises our conceit of the mighty, misty monster, to behold him solemnly sailing through a calm tropical sea; his vast, mild head overhung by a canopy of vapor, engendered by his incommunicable contemplations, and that vapor—as you will sometimes see it—glorified by a rainbow, as if Heaven itself had put its seal upon his thoughts. For, d'ye see, rainbows do not visit the clear air; they only irradiate

[7] Compare this more than tragic (and less than tragic?) envisioning of the snowy phantom with the more exclusively destructive use of snow we found in Gide, Lawrence, and Mann, or of the shimmering infinity in *Victory*.

> vapor. And so, through all the thick mists of the dim doubts in my mind, divine intuitions now and then shoot, enkindling my fog with a heavenly ray. And for this I thank God; for all have doubts; many deny; but doubts or denials, few along with them, have intuitions. Doubts of all things earthly, and intuitions of some things heavenly; this combination makes neither believer nor infidel, but makes a man who regards them both with equal eye. (371–372)

But this equivocation seems not absolutely noncommittal. Those heavenly intuitions can finally save him from Manichaeism despite his earthly doubts, because they allow him to accept the two, intuitions and doubts—and all oppositions—as coexisting within a sanctioned order. This is reconciliation much in the way recommended by Wimsatt: an almost total submission to Ahab in order that Ishmael may earn his faith and his salvation. Beyond the shallow ethical, mainly represented by Starbuck, Ishmael is yet seen as a force for ultimate affirmation, suggesting to many critics the profound Christian vision that transcends the tragic without superciliously denying it. Is this the way to abandon at last the discomforts of the existential for a return to a higher ethical and a less restricted propositional order?

All this, however, approaches overstatement. It threatens to make Ishmael our protagonist instead of Ahab, and that transfer of roles would obviously distort the novel. For Ishmael is not the actor but our narrator—"the reader's friend" rather than Ahab's, Henry James might say. And his thematic significance is determined—and limited—by his role. M. O. Percival, whose profound study of *Moby Dick* has influenced these comments extensively, puts the matter brilliantly:

> Character is fate, it has been said; and I hope that Ishmael's fate is implicit in his character. The essential thing about that character is its apparently limitless understanding and compassion. Ishmael lends his own identity to others, even to the point of having little or none himself. He pulls an oar in Queequeg's boat when boats are lowered, but he is seldom

> seen in this or any other physical activity. But spiritually he is everywhere and nowhere, observing and comprehending. In a dictator's way it is Ahab's crew; they jump when he commands. In a poet's way the crew is Ishmael's; they are his by assimilation.[8]

Precisely. They all, and Ahab too, are his by assimilation. Because they all are in him who as our narrator has created them. Let us take seriously the fiction that Ishmael is the author of the tale. On the very first page of his writing and at the outset of the events he is relating, we have already noted, he described the "damp, drizzly November" in his soul which had forced him to take to sea as his therapy. The journey of the *Pequod* cured him indeed, and it was the cure that saved him for the *Rachel*, that symbol of a chastened but still warmly responsive humanity. But the journey of the *Pequod* is also the writing of this book. So is it too much to say that Ishmael is saved also by this creating of Ahab and Ahab's vision, by seeing him through and purging the Ahab within himself through Ahab's necessary death?

Is this not really the way of every sound author? As we saw with Gide, he does not exhaust himself even in his most intensely created character but creates such a character as but one extreme of the dialogue the self conducts with the soul, an extreme that the very act of dialogue—so long as it is a disciplined act—manages partly to tame? The author is more than his creature—like Marlow with Kurtz—and proves it by the mere fact that he has created him, and has created him within a larger aesthetic whole that contains him as but a part of it. The very nature of Ahab's demonism, and, as we have seen, of Manichaeism at large, is destructive of unity through its insistence on irreparable division. Conducive to chaos, it is as inimical to aesthetic order as to cosmic. The author's tactic resembles that of Mann's Leverkühn, who in his final conversion

[8] *A Reading of Moby Dick*, by M. O. Percival (Chicago: University of Chicago Press, 1950), pp. 126–127.

transcends despair by giving it a voice. In the very act of creating his work the author is asserting his transcendence of the Manichaean, and Ishmael is asserting his transcendence of Ahab. But as author, still responsible for his character who is, as Percival says, "his by assimilation," it may be only through the painful necessity of aesthetic wholeness—and never through the simple need for outspoken moral judgment—that he does transcend his abandoned creature.

Or is this all, then, aesthetic delusion rather than final thematic salvation? Is Ishmael more a literary device than a final resolver? Speaking of Ishmael's "apparently limitless understanding and compassion," Percival, we saw, has significantly noted that in lending "his own identity to others," he has "little or none himself." He *is*, after all, narrator rather than protagonist. His final resolution stems from his need, as fictive author, to absorb all his characters and to transcend them all alike. But it comes at the high existential price of depriving him of an active role involving moral decision, indeed depriving him even of a unique moral identity. Instead, his is a consummate identity: surely wondrous and wondrously filled with the "humanities," as Peleg termed them, but perhaps in the end less human than even the wild inhumanity that Ahab chooses. As the only one who escaped, Ishmael is in one sense more alone than Ahab, as alone as his biblical namesake. His function is related to the technical device we call "point of view"; it leads us to an aesthetic wholeness rather than to a higher Christianity. As an observer in need of the comprehensive vision, in his final avoidance of extremity he can hardly represent an alternative to Ahab's way any more than he is a rival protagonist. For Ishmael has never been stricken himself and has only the vicarious experience of Ahab to challenge him; and that is a challenge not to him personally but to him only as consummate author through his creature Ahab, whom he must assimilate aesthetically, but whom he cannot replace existentially.

Some literal-minded commentators, and some merely disdainful ones, have suggested that Ishmael was saved from the catastrophe because there had to be someone left to relate the tale. They have to support them the words from *Job* that head the Epilogue ("And I only am escaped alone to tell thee"). Normally one does not want to take such a suggestion seriously enough to bother noting that with another point of view Melville could dispense with a narrator. But in a more profound sense this suggestion cannot be so lightly dismissed. We have seen that there is in *Moby Dick* an unending tension between the ethical and the tragic, what in the terms of the novel Percival has called the humanities and the inhumanities. Ishmael, as pseudo author on both sides of the oppositions, claims a fully human order in which they melt. But we discover that he is indeed the pseudo author and not a character; that, having assimilated his characters, he must create an orderly object out of them and must move beyond the tensions if he is to manage to control them and to avoid their divisive, Manichaean tendencies that threaten to rend the aesthetic quality of his story. So the salvation and the resurrection are uniquely his, but precisely because only he has no role to play, because he *is* "escaped alone to tell" us. Is it not, then, that the cosmic and moral affirmation we want to attribute to Ishmael is, finally considered, a kind of aesthetic delusion? that, for those who have been stricken and thus thrust into the boundlessness of the existential, the Manichaean opposition is not really dissolved by Ishmael's vision after all? that only the formal oppositions of the novel's poetic context are dissolved by it, and these aesthetically rather than thematically?

But the stricken necessarily finds an extremity that is unique, with none on the side who can compose the issue. So, viewed from beyond him, perhaps the illusion of reconciliation is more than merely persuasive, and aesthetic soundness *is* symbol of moral and cosmic soundness. After all, in art illusion —what aestheticians used to call *Schein*—is all. And we may have to rescue the thematic implications of Ishmael's affirmation through an all-restoring grace, even if we can never totally deny the terror and even the validity of Ahab's vision. All of this is of course not the same as the overt attempt at clean moral resolution that we find in *Billy Budd*, an attempt whose aesthetic honesty I would be forced to deny.

Is not this need to assert the reconciliation along with the unreconcilable precisely the thematic version of the aesthetic need to assert the restrictions of form along with the abandon of contextual tension? And does not the very notion of extremity bear the entire mystery? I have suggested that for the poet to formulate the extreme situation is indeed for him to play the casuist by purifying experience of the casual; that through the narrow intensity of a fortiori controls, the extreme situation can manage to account for the total breadth of experience, for all that is less committed and more compromising—and compromised. This is in effect what Henry James means in speaking of actual life that "persistently blunders and deviates, loses herself in the sand," in his complaints against the "stupid work" of "clumsy" raw experience which, unpurified, not merely militates against art but obfuscates its own meaning, leaving to art the role of mining this meaning anew. The extreme, then, is both more pure and more inclusive—pure in the adulterations it rejects and inclusive in the range of less complete experiences it illuminates even as it passes them by. Thus at once the rarity and the density, the order and the plenitude. But finally, in retreat as it were, there must be the observer, the more compromised and less committed, the resister of extremity who from his middle existence can place extremity for us.[9] Not fatally challenged, he has yet learned vicariously to see extremity as the necessary and most instructive vision, the illusion—*aesthesis*, *Schein*—that which creates reality for us by forcing us to see it as we never

[9] By now it is very likely superfluous to enumerate those who appear elsewhere in our novels in Ishmael's role of observer-narrator: Michel's "comforter," Adrian's Zeitblom, Kurtz's or Jim's Marlow. Where there is no such character combining this technical and thematic function, the novelist's task of striking his balance between the extreme and the compromised is made infinitely more complicated, as I hope my preceding chapters have shown.

dare to outside of art because in art we think it is appearance only. For secure in what we take to be mere aesthetic illusion, we plunge into the risk of art: we allow the comforting delusions we normally take for reality to trace their path to extremity, there to be given back utter reality, that which terrifies even as it returns us, newly sound and justified, to our middle (and muddled) existences chastened by extremity and taking up the order in our lives with tender hands that now know its delusiveness and its fragile, unsubstantial prospects.

3. A Pseudo-Christian Consequence and the Retreat from Extremity

Let me become more extreme before I become more moderate. Having shown the grounds on which Ishmael may be seen as pointing to a profound Christian affirmation that would take account of Ahab's darker vision even as it swept beyond it in the direction of divine grace, I introduced some formal questions about the conception and the shape of the novel, in order to indicate the grounds on which Ishmael's affirmation could be seen as more aesthetic than thematic in its significance. Thus the fallen and disharmonious world viewed by Ahab was brought to no final resurrection, so that on the thematic level I did not, after all, raise the Manichaean vision from its inconclusive dualism, whatever Melville's aesthetic persuasiveness.

But we can even make the case more negative. In considering Ishmael's role as the comprehensive narrator, we might say that he is fundamentally without a commitment. If we wished to play down the significance of his relations with Queequeg and of other suggestions of a transcendent grace which moves within him, we could travel even further from the direction of affirmation than I did earlier. We could argue that he is saved at the end, not through a grace that his faithfulness has earned, but through the insistence of a demanding God that the *Pequod*'s story be told. And Ishmael is chosen as the one to escape alone to tell us not because of his final affirmative commitment but because of his unique noncommitment, his powers of universal assimilation.

My earlier discussion implied that Ahab was the unmitigated Manichaean and Ishmael the near-Manichaean who stopped crucially short of Manichaeism or went crucially beyond it, as you please. But I said too that what in Ahab is expressive of a profoundly cleft moral universe perverts in action into the defiant worship, and thus imitation, of the single dark power. His satanic career may have taken rise out of dualism, out of the torments created by the maddening ambiguities of unyielding oppositions; but the word that most obviously describes Ahab's ailment—monomania—makes clear enough the singleness, and even certainty, that now claim exclusive dominion over his world. As with Ivan Karamazov, rebellion may begin out of the unrelenting purity of moral demand that, given this impure world, must lead to Manichaeism; but, again as with Ivan, the self-possessed rebel, once having assigned half of God's realm to the devil, ends by finding in the devil his only God. The Manichaean dualism that has denied the unity of God's world is in its turn transformed into an unequivocal demonism that denies one side of that dualism to assert only the other, the darker side. This is worse than Manichaeism: our hero is no longer a mere heretic but a "wretched infidel."

This view, then, leaves for Ishmael the true, still thriving Manichaeism and with it the noncommittal aesthetic play of counterpositions that recent contextual literary theory calls for. This is a rather different light for us to throw upon Ishmael's uncertainties about the angelic glory and the demoniacal terror of the whiteness of the whale, and under its influence his dissertation becomes quite a different bit of evidence. And so with his other moments of double vision that seem in part calculated to correct and to brighten Ahab's more exclusive vision. Even that all-important passage I quoted earlier—the passage in which Ishmael balances earthly doubts and heavenly intuitions—now reads somewhat differently. And I repeat its close: ". . . this combination makes neither believer nor infidel, but makes a man who regards them both with equal eye" (372). Just the description of the Ishmael who wrote "The Whiteness of the Whale" as the Manichaean's answer to supplement Ahab's demonic assertion of the "pasteboard masks." If I earlier emphasized the divine nature of the intuitions as an intimation of Ishmael's final acceptance of the world, the view I am suggesting now would emphasize the obviously noncommittal and Manichaean nature of the passage. It may be that against the unrelieved darkness of Ahab's vision Ishmael's balanced one appears deceptively bright so that the mere contrast has blinded our judgment of it.

Ishmael, then, may never reach beyond Manichaeism, although in his hands it is not a dangerous position; indeed, since he is inherently an observer and author, it is an aesthetically indispensable position. He can never be stricken but is able to assimilate and yet see around those who are. In this sense too he has escaped only because he alone can tell us; and his solitude may be seen as the inevitable solitude of the poet, inhuman in that he must stand apart from men in their tribulations in order most humanly to live through all of them vicariously—and more important, imaginatively. He has escaped to make his peace, but—perhaps not unlike the Ancient Mariner—he makes aesthetically, by telling, an illusory peace he cannot find by living.

According to this view, we are being even more deluded in our thematic interpretation of Ishmael by his aesthetic function within the novel than I earlier suggested. It is not merely, as I tentatively proposed, that his seeming Christianity may have no existential reality but may serve only to place Ahab's disorderly vision within a broadened aesthetic order; but it is that Ishmael, rather than resolving a Manichaean into a Christian vision, superimposes an inconclusive Manichaeism upon Ahab's exclusive demonism. In never rising beyond Manichaeism, Ishmael becomes a qualified author, with his universal human sympathy—an indispensable literary attitude—providing what, next to Ahab's darkly violent denials, shines like an all-restoring cosmic affirmation.

Moby Dick, then, which thanks to Ishmael at first seemed

so likely a case, does not finally seem to lead us beyond Manichaeism and to a thorough thematic reconciliation. I have spoken of it at this length and from these two views in order to show how delicate the manipulation must be by which an author can manage to transform his oppositions into an aesthetic whole that affirms order even while maintaining them as thematic oppositions that defy order. Just the final echo of ambiguity in the existence of the work itself.

It may be that in literature of the extreme situation there can be no unqualifiedly Christian vision without the author's superimposition of his theological resolution upon his drama. Of course, many authors have meant to embody this vision in their work, but fortunately the best of these have failed to be as exclusive as their more committed and less aesthetic selves may have wanted, so that a fully thematic study reveals they have strayed beyond their propositional intention. For example, since we are speaking of Melville, I have already indicated that I would dispute the successful Christian reconciliation many claim to find in *Billy Budd*, as they make this work the aged Melville's *Oedipus at Colonus*. That he attempts it I do not doubt: I would not go so far as to say with Lawrance Thompson (in his *Melville's Quarrel with God*) that Melville is being sacrilegiously ironic throughout. But the fact that one may even be tempted to say this is, I think, an indication that Melville has really failed to bring it off, to move to a Christian vision beyond the tragic which his best work revealed. He simply postulates a doctrine which I find unsubstantiated in the drama, since the pure dialectical play of claims and counterclaims is so obviously weakened by it. We are being imposed upon, and we may resent Melville for it almost as much as we resent Captain Vere and Billy. The austerity with which the one holds to code and the other yields to code in the story smacks more of a return to dull conformity, to a most untranscendent, shabbily pragmatic ethical, than a rare rising to any supernal order.

If it is conceded that our profoundest literature cannot reach beyond an existential conviction of dualism any more than it can reach to the propositional, what are the moral consequences of confronting and resigning oneself to the Manichaean face of reality? For the self-conscious demon, who from the outset defiantly strives to destroy all ethical ideality—a Michel, a Ch'en, a Leverkühn—this issue does not arise, of course. But —to move from my first to my second group of visionaries—for him who begins by being armed with nothing but good intentions and a fierce devotion to them, there is a most jarring consequence: action becomes impossible for him who would act only in the purity of moral integrity. And in literature that is existential in my sense, except in the case of the self-conscious demon the use of the extreme situation inevitably brings to the fore a protagonist who can act only in the purity of moral integrity—a Kurtz, a Pierre, an Ahab, in a qualified sense a Joseph K. The protagonist can decide on the justness of his action only insofar as it is consistent with his idea of righteousness. But his idea of righteousness is necessarily based on a system of ethical propositions. In acting and in assuring himself of the absolute integrity of his action (without which assurance he would not act), he is making two crucial—and fatal—assumptions: first, that his single ethical set of beliefs is necessarily adequate—that is, totally responsive—to the moral problem at hand in its full complexity and, secondly, that he personally is utterly disinterested and thus capable of utterly selfless action in the service of a universal ethical claim.

In identifying himself wholly with the single ethical set and acting in accordance with its dictates as if it were an unquestionable absolute (and it is impossible for him to undertake decisive moral action otherwise), the protagonist is necessarily insisting on its exclusive rightness, its right to dominate all other sets, to impose itself upon them and demand their capitulation. His ethical set, through its exclusive and absolute rightness, dares through his agency be just as tyrannical over all individuals. They now exist, not as persons, but as things, unindividuated particulars to be subsumed under this or that universal. Their full and dynamic existential reality is reduced to an operational function to be encouraged, tolerated, or obliterated as the rules of the ethical set dictate. Of course the protagonist has reduced himself as well to thinghood, losing his own individuality in his identification with his ethical universal. Where necessary—and he often enjoys this necessity—he can all too proudly sacrifice himself to his universal at least as easily as he can sacrifice others. In other words, it is no step at all in his beliefs to get from the rightness of the ethical set to his righteousness and then to self-righteousness. The Hegelian god, self-appointed by pride and in pride assuming clean hands, moves inflexibly forward directing the fortunes of his ethical set in the implacable war against absolute evil—as determined of course by his universal principles.

But the Manichaean face of reality stubbornly persists and will present itself. No ethical set is adequate to existential ambiguity, and any pretension to absolute sway—such pretension as is involved in any decisive moral act that claims purity of motive—is doomed to be confronted by its own arrogance, to see the willfulness, the self-aggrandizement, the absolute immorality of it all. Thus the existential takes its revenge by plunging the protagonist into the demonic, by asserting its own extra-ethical catholicity which shocks the ethical man by its seeming contradictions. But now demonic, he will be ethical man no more. Forced to look within himself, he sees his own evil which has been there from the start impurifying every motive and forcing him, through the pretension of disinterested ethical principle, to become the very hated thing he was fighting. And so he can hate himself—and can persevere in making himself worse and more hateful by the now conscious and purposeful pursuit of the evil principle. We have traced similar stages earlier in connection with Ahab. The simple belief in the moral order and action in accordance with it summon the shock that brings chaos and the fearful unveiling of the Manichaean face of reality, that most indestructible sphinx. Despair ensues and with it, in all likelihood, the spite directed at a seemingly spiteful universe and the madness that defiantly worships the immoral order (and only madness can see order in immorality).

But it is the Manichaean version of existential reality that dooms all action since, were there finally a moral order that was right absolutely, there would be *a* way, and the actor, in laying claim to being right, might actually be so. Of course, insofar as he is but human, the personal failing that impurifies motive would still be there; but his objective claim to principle would have to be examined as possibly being just. The Manichaean view dooms it sight unseen and absolutely, this negation being all that is absolute in this conception of Manichaeism. Even our final and last possible case, Myshkin, who commits the sin of excess on the side of humility rather than pride—this least daring and least arrogating of all well-intentioned actors—joins the others in their fate and in their destructive power over their fellows.

All action, then, is impossible—even as its impossible existence makes literature possible. To repeat the words of Axel Heyst again, ". . . all action is bound to be harmful. It is devilish. That is why this world is evil upon the whole." And Conrad's later comment in the Heystian spirit: "Action—the first thought, or perhaps the first impulse, on earth! The barbed hook, bated with the illusion of progress, to bring out of the lightless void the shoals of unnumbered generations!" Or there is the simple meditation of the Reverend Hightower, that Heyst-like figure in Faulkner's *Light in August*: "Man performs, engenders, so much more than he can or should have to bear. That's how he finds that he can bear anything." [10] As my brief glance at *Billy Budd* has indicated, I must deny—despite the moving insistence of R. W. B. Lewis [11]—that the transformation

[10] From *Light in August*, by William Faulkner (New York: New Directions, 1947), p. 283.

[11] In *The American Adam*, by R. W. B. Lewis (Chicago: University of Chicago Press, 1955), pp. 146–152, where he sees *Billy Budd* as the Christian resolution of the thematic indecisions of *Pierre*. As Nietzsche might put it, the resolution is really in the frigidity of the anti-tragic, rational Socratic mode rather than in the sublimity of the Apollonian, however it apes the latter. Mere utilitarian compromise is not enough.

of Adam into Jesus, the second Adam, can be rendered aesthetically believable. For it demands the kind of miracle that resists dramatic categories. As a result of the human and dialogistic limitations that bound existential reality, with or without the author's invitation parody is always present to subvert the intended parable: it mocks any pretension that "alone" would "save the world" [12] in a way that would leave it worth saving.

The extremity with which literature abounds produces the uncompromising hero who in turn produces an action falsely conceived in purity so that he is compromised utterly. Action presupposes adequacy of ethical belief and personal guiltlessness, while in its extremity it reveals the bankruptcy of system and the inherent vice as well as the folly of him who believed in the perfection of system and the purity of personal motive.

One can multiply fictional examples of these processes indefinitely—far beyond those I have treated in these chapters. Naturally, the procedure varies widely—and in this variation lies their crucial literary, or thematic, interest. But the similarities from stage to stage are striking—or should I say terrifying? If, then, existential ambiguity makes every act an act of self-damnation, what alternative is there? There is, of course, the purely Christian view—or the limited version I have presented as the purely Christian view—that is ethically paralyzed. And, strangely, it is a view that can be held while granting the validity of the Manichaean vision of existential reality. Recognizing the absurd in existence and recognizing the inhuman, anti-person-

---

Lewis sees that Billy is linked with Isaac. But Kierkegaard, we must remember, tells us that while all highest religionness attests to the absurd, the converse does not hold. More than an absurd requirement is needed, especially when this requirement happens to meet the most ruthless demands of official naval policy. In his more recent volume too (*The Picaresque Saint* [New York: J. B. Lippincott, 1959]), Lewis finds transcendent optimism where I find ethical inadequacy. For example, compare his essay on *Bread and Wine*, from which his book's title is taken (pp. 148–160), with mine in Chapter III, above.

[12] *The American Adam*, p. 152.

alistic cruelty as well as the untenability of any ethical system, one can embrace his irrational conclusions. He can insist upon his own and everyone's sacred uniqueness as person with the consequent fear that subjecting any person to the rationality that plays with universals—a rationality that destroys itself when it collides with intransigent reality—is to see him only in the common light of things and thus, in effect, to destroy him. Further, he may have seen the common human weakness in himself early—before a crisis would have forced it upon him all too late. Thus he may have learned the wisdom of self-distrust. Even were an adequate ethical system possible, and his irrationalism may have convinced him it is not; and were it possible to impose it without destroying persons, and he may know it cannot be universal without subsuming particulars; still he would never presume to represent this ethical system himself, since this would be a presumption of a purity of ethical disinterest that he cannot allow human pridefulness to make. For in asserting the person's uniqueness and in refusing to allow so much of him to be emptied in order to make him into a cog in the machine of reason, this Christian would be willing to admit that the person is worse as well as better than the cog: he is just different from it, and fuller. He would be anxious to preserve this worseness too, since personal uniqueness is all and morality is enigmatic; and so he can insist that the impurity of motive that would destroy any bearer of even the most promising ethical vision—were any ultimately promising—betrays the failing variously present in us all that is part of our unique being and that is damning only when, in ignorance or spite of it, we choose to act as if, inhuman and thus bloodlessly ethical, we were unexceptionally straightforward.

Thus acknowledging the inaccessible enigma of reality, this man may be ready to say through faith that behind the Manichaean face there is a deeper reality in God, in Whose eyes all absurdities are miraculously resolved. But this "leap"—the embracing of the one absurdity that explains the rest, or rather that justifies the rest as inexplicable—does not concern us here since it cannot be communicated or subjected to dramatic portrayal. What does concern us is his attempt to escape the demonic by fleeing to an extra-ethical, subjective, existential Christianity. By definition, however, this rare and saintlike attitude must reject action, decision, even moral judgment; and, viewed from the ethical sphere, it is paralyzed, useless, and, as subversive, actually dangerous. It was in order to look at this kind of alternative that I examined Conrad's *Lord Jim* and found how totally and fatally inaction there served as a most committed form of action, thus discovering the existential trap closing about itself—the same trap that victimized the more overt forms of action that it strangled in horror.

Of course man will—must and even ought to—act, as literary protagonists continually show us—even the most reticent ones like Heyst and Hightower who, despite all that experience has taught them, find their only glory (a destructive glory inevitably) in a final, futile attachment to life and action. And if the extremity encroaches upon him, then so will the Manichaean realization and with it the tragic. For the rest, we can with our Marlows and our Ishmaels turn to the example and the hope of Lena Grove and Byron Bunch in *Light in August:* the hope of common mankind for a retreat from extremity, from the demands of purity and integrity, to the homely sanctity of the commonplace, where there can be an acceptance of the imperfection of all things, human action chief among them. It is what the Melville of *Pierre* would term the cultivation of the catnip to the neglect of the amaranth. This is not to deny the Manichaean face of reality so much as to deny the need to confront it. Much in the manner of Wordsworth in his "Elegiac Stanzas," with "welcome fortitude, and patient cheer" Byron Bunch will bear "what is to be borne." He bears the truth in Hightower's ruthless analysis that reveals a questionable morality in his new commitment to action in behalf of Lena, as he bears the biological and moral facts that surround the birth of Lena's child, and as he will bear much more.

> It seems like a man can just about bear anything. He can even bear what he never done. He can even bear the thinking how some things is just more than he can bear. He can even bear it that if he could just give down and cry, he wouldn't do it. He can even bear it to not look back, even when he knows that looking back or not looking back wont do him any good. (New Directions, 1947, p. 401)

A moment later, seeing that looking back upon what he is losing is the more painful alternative, he adds, ". . . I reckon I might as well have the pleasure of not being able to bear looking back too" (402). And in forcing himself to bear looking back, through what he sees Byron is rewarded by being allowed a final return—after a ritual defeat in battle—to his resolute counterpart, Lena. Neither Byron nor Lena has the vision or even the searching intelligence, but they neither need nor want it. As Hightower sees in the brief regeneration that precedes his death, they are the makers of the race, their energies, unsapped by the past, relentlessly crawling to the future. They can bear any "burden," unlike Joanna of that name, without resorting to extremity because they must bear those who carry the future of the race; they endure woe so that humanity may endure. They evade, with their continual willingness to relent, the unrelenting and demonic divisiveness of a puritanism that echoes Ahab's, just as their Christ child, doomed to a mild hopefulness, will evade the lot of Joe Christmas, destroyed by the puritan—the morally overearnest—world of extremity. The child of common humanity, it will, like them, be freed from the perverse burden of an exhausted history that, in imposing fanaticism, has smothered Joanna Burden and Hightower as well as Joe Christmas.

If they persist, Lena and Byron and the fresh Christ, if they are not stricken beyond endurance (and Joseph K. has assured us that only those prepared to recognize trial are tried), they may be able to cultivate a life blessed in the way of what, with Eliot, Lionel Trilling calls "the common routine," the way of Melville's homely catnip. For those amaranthine strivers who must at all costs look—and these are perhaps the most rewarding characters in our literature—the Manichaean will still be there, unresolvable. These are the cultivators of extremity, that which destroys itself and all it touches. Even Faulkner must dwell upon these too, though he can—with friendly and pleasantly supercilious irony—end with a common human alternative that does not answer them but affirms the simple grace of life in disregard of them or in retreat from them.

We have come a long way—"a fur piece," the indomitable Lena Grove would say—and I hope over not too disorderly a route, from the purely aesthetic considerations with which I began. But it has been worth it if in the byways we have found, perhaps to our surprise, a rich yield of the illuminating powers of literature and its recent criticism: their powers to illuminate the high existential cost of living and our endless ability to pay, thanks to our not inglorious obligation to vision and our persistence in the common human enterprise that reveals a faith that endures despite all.

INDEX

Aeschylus, 3
Aesthetic (Croce), 234
American Adam, The (Lewis), 263–264
Amoretti (Spenser), 199
And He Hid Himself (Silone), 76–85
Aristotle, 2, 3–5, 6
Arnold, Matthew, 23

Bartleby the Scrivener (Melville), 144
Beethoven, Ludwig van, 89, 91, 97, 99
Benito Cereno (Melville), 171
Berdyaev, Nicolas, 50, 203
Billy Budd (Melville), 256, 260, 263–264
Birth of Tragedy, The (Nietzsche), 9–10, 198
Blake, William, 197
Bleak House (Dickens), 138–140
Bradley, A. C., 5, 6
Bread and Wine (Silone), 72–85, 264
Brod, Max, 127
Brooks, Cleanth, 233, 234, 235, 237, 238–240
Brothers Karamazov, The (Dostoevsky), 61, 108, 139–140, 141, 142, 144, 152, 211–212, 221, 228, 258

Camus, Albert, 130, 144–153, 224
Coleridge, Samuel Taylor, 232, 234
Conrad, Joseph, 13, 14, 19, 123, 129, 154–194, 251, 263, 266
Creation and Discovery (Vivas), 212, 228
Croce, Benedetto, 234

Dante, 122, 199–200
Days of Wrath (Malraux), 53–54, 71
Death in Venice (Mann), 43, 95, 104
Dewey, John, 14
Dickens, Charles, 138–140
Doctor Faustus (Mann), 87–102, 103–104, 110–113, 143, 253, 256, 261
Don Quixote (Cervantes), 216–217
Dostoevsky, Feodor, 15, 61, 108, 139–140, 141, 152, 209–227, 228
Dunciad, The (Pope), 230

Elegiac Stanzas (Wordsworth), 266
Eliot, T. S., 85, 232, 234, 235, 267
Emerson, Ralph Waldo, 197, 199, 203, 207
Eumenides (Aeschylus), 3
Euripides, 10

Fall, The (Camus), 145–146, 224
Faulkner, William, 90, 263, 266–268

Faust (Goethe), 88–90, 104
Faustbook, 88–90
Fear and Trembling (Kierkegaard), 1, 7–8, 11, 16, 117
Flaubert, Gustave, 53
Frank, Joseph, 87, 100
Freud, Sigmund, 9

Gide, André, 19, 22–37, 38, 39, 40, 42–46, 89, 90, 117, 135, 196, 251, 253
Goethe, Johann Wolfgang von, 30, 88–90, 99, 104, 197, 206, 207

Heart of Darkness (Conrad), 13, 15, 19, 123, 129, 154–165, 167, 171, 178, 253, 256, 261, 266
Hegel, Georg Wilhelm Friedrich, 5–7, 12, 13, 63, 203, 262
Heidegger, Martin, 14
Heller, Erich, 87
Homer, 110, 143
Howe, Irving, 50

Idiot, The (Dostoevsky), 209–227, 263
Immoralist, The (Gide), 19, 22–37, 38, 39, 42–46, 89, 135, 196, 256, 261
Ironic German, The: A Study of Thomas Mann (Heller), 87

James, Henry, 252, 256
Job, Book of, 37, 128, 255
Journals (Gide), 22
Jung, Carl G., 9

Kafka, Franz, 12, 114–144, 146, 147, 153, 167, 267
Kierkegaard, Soren, 1, 7–8, 11–21 *passim.*, 115, 117, 130, 146, 191, 264
King Lear (Shakespeare), 4, 206
Krieger, Murray, 168, 229–230

Lawrence, D. H., 37–49, 68, 105, 135, 185, 251
Letters from the Underworld (Dostoevsky), 228
Lewis, C. S., 245
Lewis, R. W. B., 263–264
Light in August (Faulkner), 263, 266–268
Literary Criticism: A Short History (Wimsatt and Brooks), 235, 238–239
Lord Jim (Conrad), 13, 165–179, 182, 187, 189, 195, 256, 266
Luther, Martin, 94, 101

Madeleine (Et nunc manet in te) (Gide), 32
Magic Mountain, The (Mann), 27, 43, 92, 95, 96, 101, 102–110, 112–113, 143, 190
Mallarmé, Stéphane, 234
Malraux, André, 50–72, 73, 74, 77, 85, 112, 123
Mann, Thomas, 27, 30, 43, 86–113, 143, 185, 190, 196, 197, 215, 251, 253
Man's Fate (Malraux), 50–72, 73, 77, 85, 112, 123, 178, 261
Marx, Karl, 52–54, 60, 62, 63, 71, 75
Melville, Herman, 12–13, 43, 90, 114, 115, 141, 144, 153, 171, 195–209, 210, 211, 249–255, 256, 257–260, 266, 268
Melville's Quarrel with God (Thompson), 260
Moby Dick (Melville), 12–13, 43, 114, 115, 141, 142, 153, 171, 196, 202, 204, 208, 249–255, 256, 257–260, 261, 262, 266, 267

Murder in the Cathedral (Eliot), 85

New Apologists for Poetry, The (Krieger), 229–230
New Testament, 36–37, 75–77, 83, 151
Nietzsche, Friedrich, 8–10, 14, 53, 61, 62, 63, 198, 263

O'Brien, Justin, 31–32
Oedipus at Colonus (Sophocles), 4, 110, 260
Oresteia (Aeschylus), 3
Oxford Lectures on Poetry (Bradley), 5

Percival, M. O., 252–253, 254, 255
Philosophy of Fine Art, The (Hegel), 5
Picaresque Saint, The (Lewis), 264
Pierre (Melville), 13, 195–209, 210, 211, 215, 217, 261, 263, 266
Plato, 206, 207, 245
Poetics (Aristotle), 3–5

Rainbow, The (Lawrence), 47
Ransom, John Crowe, 233, 235, 239
Reading of Moby Dick, A (Percival), 252–253, 254, 255
Rice, Philip Blair, 100
Richards, I. A., 232, 233, 234, 235
Rime of the Ancient Mariner, The (Coleridge), 259

St. Augustine, 244
Sartre, Jean-Paul, 41, 132
Schiller, Friedrich, 197
Secret Sharer, The (Conrad), 177
Shakespeare, William, 7, 171
Sickness unto Death, The (Kierkegaard), 191
Silone, Ignazio, 72–85, 264
Slavery and Freedom (Berdyaev), 50
Sophocles, 4, 110, 143, 260
Spenser, Edmund, 199, 217
Spinoza, Baruch, 206, 207
Stranger, The (Camus), 144, 146–153

Tate, Allen, 233, 234, 235
Thompson, Lawrance, 260
Thus Spake Zarathustra (Nietzsche), 14, 61
Trial, The (Kafka), 12, 114–144, 146, 147, 153, 261, 267
Trilling, Lionel, 20, 267

Victory (Conrad), 179–194, 251, 263, 266
Vivas, Eliseo, 212, 228

Wimsatt, W. K., 235, 238–240, 241–242, 244, 252
Winters, Yvor, 234, 235, 236, 239, 249
Women in Love (Lawrence), 37–49, 68, 135
Wordsworth, William, 6, 26, 266

Yeats, William Butler, 158, 234

Zabel, Morton Dauwen, 182